ughton Mifflin Company   Boston

ork   Atlanta   Geneva, Illinois   Dallas   Palo Alto

Ho

New Y

Developmental Counseling and Therapy

Bill L. Kell

Josephine Morse Burow

Michigan State University

Editor's Introduction

Some of the most troublesome questions in counseling have been with us for the past twenty years or more, and it seems clear that they are to be with us for some time to come. For example, the war cry of the 1940's was that "counseling and psychotherapy are indistinguishable." This is true only if one defines counseling as dealing primarily with the client's feelings and attitudes and psychotherapy as dealing with problems of personal development rather than pathology. This interpretation is accepted by many counselors now but is still a call to battle for some. Yet for the many, perhaps the majority, a client's feelings about himself and others, be he child, adolescent, or adult, enter into all decisions that he must make. They enter also into the meaning of all information provided him about himself and others. For an even greater number of counselors today, what was formerly maladjustment or *pathology* is now maladaptive, *learned patterns* of behavior and of attitude. Correcting them is a relearning process involving both rationality and reinforcement.

Another troublesome question concerns the involvement of the counselor as a "professional" in the counseling process. Clients are ambivalent about being helped: they seek help but resent having to do so. Perhaps the counselor's attempt to be an objective, "professional" person increases the client's feeling of resentment. One of the most worrisome and persistent problems of both the initiate and the experienced counselor is the extent to which he should allow himself to engage in a relationship that may change him as well as the client. If he plays "himself" in the relationship rather than a "role," he may well be affected. Dare he risk this—risk being himself to the other person? Is this necessary? Is it desirable?

v

A third crucial issue is the manner in which the counselor deals with his own feelings and needs. How does he recognize these? Is he justified in responding to them in the counseling relationship?

This volume deals with these and related issues in a clear, direct fashion. A creative and helpful book, it presents ideas that have genuine depth, concisely stating most of the basic concepts in the first two chapters. Therapy is seen as "having to do with the repair of some failure in the developmental process." Antecedent, interpersonal relationships—sometimes those in early childhood—are seen as the primary factor in the developmental failure. The provision of a new interpersonal relationship in the counseling process is regarded as the primary factor in the "repair." The counselor again must recognize the subjectivity of the client's experience (that the meaning of an experience is unique to him) and the need for the client to understand the relation of his subjective world to the objective world (as others see it). The authors firmly believe that the counselor must early find something to respect or like in the client so that he, the counselor, can contribute to the client's confidence in his ability to handle his world.

To these authors, therapy means change—change in feelings about self and others, change in interpersonal relationships, change in understanding past experiences, change in habitual ways of thinking and learning. Counseling is never complete, always partial. Timing is important, for to prolong the counseling relationship beyond the point where the client himself can assume responsibility for trying out new behaviors may be worse than no counseling at all.

A major strength of *Developmental Counseling and Therapy* is the breadth of its theory. Most authors say that counseling should be either phenomenological or interpersonal or rational. Kell and Burow suggest that all three points of view are relevant and then proceed to integrate them theoretically and practically. However, it is true that the author's *main* approach is phenomenological, *modified* phenomenological—an approach in which *past* experiences as well as *present* feelings are to be taken into account. The authors stress also that the client must learn to *behave* differently in the new relationship as well as to *perceive* himself with greater rationality. The theme of how to improve counseling effectiveness is greater sensitivity both to client and to self.

A chapter on the training and supervising of student counselors will be especially useful to students and their supervisors in the practicum stage of counselor preparation. Little has been written on this subject, which makes the chapter a valuable addition to the field.

One distinctive feature of this book is the personalized writing style. The authors share their own confusions and their efforts to clarify for themselves the meaning of what they experience in relating to the client. The reader is not *told*, as subject to object, but *shares* with the authors in a mutual process of understanding. In fact, the writers treat the reader as they treat clients, not "treating" them at all but sharing an experience with them. They state, "Our goal is to engage the reader as fully as possible while we write about conceptions and how they have evolved. The degree of our success will be measured not by the amount of agreement he has with us but rather by the extent to which he has become involved."

Three-fourths of the book is devoted to a careful exposition of the client-counselor relationship and of the counseling process that leads to change. Almost one-fourth, however, concerns *multiple therapy*. This is a topic of considerable interest in the field of professional psychotherapy, as evidenced by a bibliography of 120 items, some of which were published twenty or more years ago but two-thirds of which appeared in the 1960's. Multiple therapy has had little play, however, in the literature of counseling and of psychotherapy viewed as counseling. Yet it is a powerful tool that needs careful examination. Multiple therapy is not the "multiple counseling" of Froelich nor group counseling in any sense of the term but *two counselors* working with one client, each interacting with the other and with the client. In this section the authors tell how they chanced to develop this new counseling method. They take the reader through their own intensely personal experiences as they continuously work out their concepts and their relationships. This section is a "bit of icing on the cake," deeply engrossing and designed to open up a significant new dimension for the counselor's consideration.

This book is a human document. The reader is not likely to forget that two flesh-and-blood people wrote it, sharing their thoughts and lives with him. Counseling is with *people*, not ideas, and it is refreshing to have a book in which people as well as ideas appear on every page.

C. *Gilbert* W*renn*

Preface

We were enabled to write this book by years of working, learning, and sharing together. We were encouraged in our experimenting and theorizing by some of our colleagues. More particularly, a number of graduate students helped us to believe in ourselves, in our thinking; they helped us to believe that what we were thinking about was worth writing down for others to read. Drs. Pat Patterson, Clyde Crego, and Jerry Casey were especially persuasive in convincing us that we knew enough to write a book. While we were writing, Drs. Ted Hill, Gladys Strahl, Tony Jabury, Joyce Moore, Roberta Vogel, and Carole Dilling met with us for a year in a case conference about multiple therapy. Their help to us and ours to them clarified many ideas. Drs. Ken Nunnelly and Jerry Treppa compiled the bibliography on multiple therapy. They also devoted their doctoral dissertations to some of the phenomena of multiple therapy.

We owe another debt to our own teachers and to other theorists and practitioners whom we have known and read. This debt is acknowledged by the General Bibliography at the end of the book. This bibliography is not comprehensive but instead includes some of the writings of those persons who have most influenced us. The Multiple Therapy Bibliography which follows is quite complete and should be an instructive guide to the reading material available about this less-known therapeutic approach.

We have tried to write in a way that would draw the reader into our struggle to clarify and express our ideas. We will have accomplished our purpose if our readers are stimulated to think and feel about themselves and their own ways of doing therapy. Feelings and thoughts of likeness to us and difference from us should occur.

Who may find this book of interest? Psychologists, psychiatrists, social workers, counselors, anyone who struggles to help others with their problems may find our ideas interesting and possibly useful. Research workers should find some testable propositions. Trainers or supervisors of mental health workers may read us and, hopefully, recommend us to those they train.

B.L.K.

J.M.B.

Contents

Chapter 4   44

Phenomenology:
Living in the
Internal
World

Chapter 5   88

Interpersonality: Vehicle for Human Development and Therapy

Part Two

Multiple Therapy: Therapists in Collaboration

Developmental Counseling and Therapy

Part One

Developmental Therapy:

Multiple Processes

Chapter 1

Who Are We?

This book is a personal document. It is an expression of the beliefs and attitudes of us, the authors, beliefs growing out of years of experience as persons who share a world of excitement, pleasure, disappointment, and sometimes tragedy with our clients. These experiences have pushed us to think and to feel about ourselves, and perhaps to better be ourselves. We have learned about our clients and from our clients and thus have developed a practice and theory about them.

Growth comes from knowing that sometimes we have helped, that other times we have failed. We tend to be pragmatic in the sense that we believe in what has made us and our clients be more fulfilled, more fully human. We are empiricists in the sense that we tend to observe and discover the meaning of what we do as we do it.

Our Beliefs Are: We have beliefs about the nature of human beings and of the world which affect our practice and theory. We have these beliefs in an evolving system of practice and theory so that they may be modified and changed. Thus we have something to believe in and something to change; something stable and something fluid. To us, this describes the essence of human development.

One belief we hold about ourselves is that we are optimistic. We look for and expect to find in ourselves and in our clients changing aspects, changes that we seek to enhance and facilitate. We know that because we look for growth and change we find it. But we strongly believe that this set is facilitating. What we attend to about ourselves and others in a large part determines what we are. That we can experience disappointments with ourselves and with our clients is also true. But we experience these disappointments with hope.

We Choose Our Clients. Because we look for potential, we choose to work in a population where we expect to find it. We work with people who are functioning, even though they are troubled. Thus our expectation is supported, and we are enabled to develop further our positive, optimistic psychological set toward our clients. We are convinced that this is an important variable in our practice.

While it is true that the functioning population is important to us for personal reasons, there is also an evident need for the psychological study of such persons. A good deal of generally accepted personality theory is based on the study of the smaller group of troublesome, nonfunctioning people who fill our mental institutions. We question the efficiency of the undifferentiated application of this kind of theory to the larger population.

When, for example, we try to apply to our clients the commonly understood theory of defenses developed from a study of a sick population, we find ourselves dissatisfied. To think of functioning people as pathologically defended seems to us to distort reality. Often the defenses our clients have are useful and enhancing. The concept of defensive rationalization offers a convenient example. A psychotic person rationalizes and remains psychotic; a functioning person rationalizes and so gains mastery and an ability to cope with a problem in his life.

Actually the term "defense" has additional meaning for us. We use it to talk about the very human quality of resistance to change. We also use it to describe the mechanisms which a person has developed to help him live in a less than ideal environment. A defense can be either adaptive and facilitative or maladaptive and interfering.

How We Are Helpers. The psychological set which we have described leads us quite naturally to see strengths rather than weaknesses, developmental problems rather than disease, somewhat impaired methods of functioning rather than lack of capacity to cope. As a consequence we expect to treat our clients as persons who need us to stimulate their own efforts rather than to excise their disorders or to control their behavior.

To us, therapy is a matter of assisting people to change the effects of developmental hurts or failures and to expand their awareness of choices and alternatives. We view psychologically distressed people not as sick but as unhappy, unfulfilled, un-being, and ineffective. They are people who are impaired functionally but still very human and capable of being more fully human. Thus our approach in working with people emphasizes potential rather than deficit. In this respect we are demanding of ourselves and our clients, and we expect our help to be fruitful.

Problems Arise. Human psychological problems are the consequence of developmental tasks undone, incomplete, or poorly accomplished. We have used the term "developmental tasks" to denote the orderly sequence of change and growth which makes up the experience of every human being from birth to old age. An infant discovers his separateness from his mother, a boy learns he is different from his sister, a child learns to make friends with other children, a young person leaves home. All these tasks and many others make up the panorama of developmental process.

Human accomplishments have both an objective and a subjective side. The meaning of the successful completion of developmental tasks is found in one's experience of both these sides. Accomplishment can be observed by others or by the one who accomplishes. However, accomplishment has subjective meaning to the individual which may or may not coincide with objective observations. We believe the ideal developmental goal is that subjective experiences parallel approximately the objective and observable. To be able to know ourselves both subjectively and objectively is so primary an accomplishment of being human that discrepancies are painful. We find ourselves, then, attending to discrepancy.

In our population the developmental tasks necessary to functioning have been for the most part objectively accomplished. It is the subjective experience of accomplishment which is discrepant and so becomes the focus of our attention. We all know the A student who worries that he is not doing well enough. He is curiously resistant when we emphasize the reality of his A's, the objective fact. Instead, we must attend to his internal sense of inadequacy and distress. No matter how irrational his attitude may seem, there are reasons in his developmental history for the disparity. Thus we understand that his problem is the discrepancy between subjective and objective experience, and that is the focus of our concern.

We find the origin of such discrepancies in meaning, in developmental history when we consider interpersonal experiences. So as we work with the A student, we will look for interpersonal reasons for his feeling that A's are not good enough. Who demanded more? Or who said, "That's good, but. . . ." Who was critical? Who was so hard to satisfy that the internal experience of accomplishment could not be real?

Rationality Is Important to Our Population. People in a functioning population view coping with the world as a reasonable experience. They are distressed and disrupted to a greater or lesser degree when their world is not rational, when they cannot make sense of their feelings or their behavior. It is a way of life to look for reasons and to experience mastery of a situation or of oneself. We, too, accept the importance of rationality in the on-going pattern of life. As a developmental task, the process of learning about relatedness, of learning the tools of thinking, of learning the patterns of relationship between experiences, is always an interpersonal experience. It is learned within the family first, then from peers and other outsiders, and it is the central purpose of the formal educational program.

Rationality and Emotions: Both Real and Discrepant. If we compare subjective reality with objective reality, both of which are cognized through an observation process, we can readily think of discrepancies between them as having their origin in interpersonal experience. For example, parents who express anger toward their child by passive rejection but who explicitly deny their anger if asked, present the child with an interpersonal experience of learning in which his subjective observation differs from the objective information they are providing for him. This objective information is what his parents want him to believe, and coming from them it has the force of consensus. We believe that most discrepancies between subjective observation and objective reality have their origin in such interpersonal interaction.

We have thought of the rational process in human beings, with its first step the making of accurate, acceptable observations, as serving a most important need in human beings. This is the need to master themselves and their environment. The subsequent steps by which a person learns to use his rationality effectively are also interpersonal, and failure can occur at many points along the way. Teachers and fellow students as well as parents and siblings have their influence.

In describing how we see the people with whom we work and how we conceptualize the sources of their problems, we have mentioned three concepts: subjectivity, or the phenomenological experience; rationality; and, finally the interpersonal process. The last is both a process in its own right and, as we have suggested, one which facilitates interactive effects among all three.

Thus our theory of the origin of the difficulties which people discover in themselves is that they began in interpersonal failures, and our theory for alleviating these difficulties is that interpersonal means must be used.

We Depend and So Do Others. It is worth while at this point to say something about our own interpersonal relationships. Our students have let us know that they rather freely depend on us. As we think and talk with them about the nature of their dependency, we realize that it has a quality reminiscent of the validation of subjective experience we discussed earlier. Thus they frequently check with us to see whether something they are feeling is appropriate to the circumstances. Or they ask us whether something which seems to them incongruent or discrepant really is. In our function as trainers we see our students as capable of having valid, useful, understandings of themselves and those with whom they work, and we seek to implement and to maximize their confidence in their own observations and thus to enhance their effectiveness. In accord with our developmental theory we may help them to be children again, and to recapture and believe in observational powers that socialization has impaired.

Incidentally, we serve this kind of function for each other. Such phrases as "I see it this way; how do you see it?" and "It seems like this to me; does it make sense to you?" frequently are prefaces to exploration and understanding. This kind of interaction led us, the authors, to work together experimentally at first; then as we gained a growing sense of the added effectiveness of our joint effort, it led us to work as multiple therapists with single clients and married couples. Our experience as multiple therapists gave us added opportunity for exploration and validation and finally conceptualization.

This book will present a theory of interpersonal therapeutic process based on a theory of personality development. We will describe the implementation of the three process constructs in multiple therapy as well as in traditional dyadic therapy. We will discuss the way in which our students learn to be therapists, a process which is within the same conceptual framework.

This chapter has been a brief overview of many ideas that we will discuss in more detail as we go on. Greater explicitness should make our ideas more understandable. But we would also like to suggest a way of relating to what we are going to say. We believe that there is a pattern which is repeated in all our professional relationships; that the pattern occurs between us and our students, between us and our clients, between us, the authors, as we think together to form ideas. The pattern develops out of a common problem which is somewhat clear to the participants. Interaction begins around this topic, and when being involved in thinking about the problem is mutually agreeable, the interaction flows back and forth. Ideas evolve, feelings become clearer. The next thing which commonly happens is that we stop and think about the process that has been taking place. This "looking at" frequently reveals that the on-going process was the living out of the problem and that the key to approaching it is our active efforts to deal with it.

Then there is a kind of discovery experience: "Oh, I see what I've been doing" or "Maybe that's the way for us to handle it." If this does not happen, we find ourselves puzzled and then try a different approach. We may begin to explore what we left unsaid. What does the experience of blankness mean? Why did we pursue one particular idea? If we are able to free ourselves of inhibitions on free interpersonal interchange, we may then find communication flowing and can carry the process to a meaningful point.

In this fashion we wrestled with the problem of how we wanted to offer the ideas which make up this book. We finally concluded that we would like to provide the reader with an experience of understanding or learning through an interaction with us. Since the reader is a participant in his own way but one who cannot communicate his participation, he will also have the individual experience of looking at the process. Our goal is to engage the reader as fully as possible while we write about our conceptions and how they have evolved. The degree of our success will be measured not by the amount of agreement he has with us but rather by the extent to which he himself becomes involved.

Chapter 2

Forming Therapeutic Interpersonal Relationships

How shall we write about the way we believe therapeutic interpersonal relationships are formed? How can we talk about the processes and intents involved? What are the sources of our present conceptions?

The last question suggests a way to begin. We have learned much, of course, from observing and understanding our own lives. We were professionally trained, too, and have retained much of what we learned. But we have also lived and practiced since this basic education. Many of our original conceptions from our training have been changed, reformulated, or discarded. We are not now as we were trained to be, although we still utilize some aspects of our training.

Each client we have seen has undoubtedly contributed something to our understandings of the processes of therapy as well as to our understandings of ourselves. Our many colleagues and students have learned from us, and we have learned from them. Finally, we, the authors, have learned much from our professional and personal relationship with each other. We have thought together, felt together, and sometimes disagreed with each other. In particular, working together as multiple therapists with one client, with a pair of clients such as a married couple, and with groups has changed very significantly both our practice and our conceptions of the nature of personality development.

INITIAL SET
AND ATTITUDES

From all the above sources, we have evolved some propositions about how therapeutic, interpersonal relationships are formed. We think now, quite naturally, of the fundamental set which we hold as we approach the subject of therapeutic relationships with our clients.

The first aspect of our set, not so simple as it may sound, is the conviction that an interpersonal relationship must be formed. The nature of the relationship is, of course, determined considerably by how the personalities of the therapist and the client or clients interact. But neither we nor our clients are mindless automatons who come together and aimlessly form a totally unpredictable relationship. We make certain choices about what we do or say, and so do our clients. We have found, for instance, that certain definable ways of behaving and responding, verbally and otherwise, are effective in getting underway interpersonal relationships which may prove to be therapeutic.

Basically, the first set we hold is that as human beings we need to be understood phenomenologically, or subjectively. We find this need not only in ourselves and in our clients but in our colleagues, our friends. The need to be understood in this way is heightened in the person seeking help with his emotional problems. At such times he has frightening feelings of apartness, which stem from past and present conflict with significant others. Fears of abandonment and isolation are common.

Under such conditions it is likely that he sees meaningful bridges to other human beings as difficult to accomplish, if not impossible. Careful listening and sensitive responses by us to these thoughts and feelings of the client help him to feel that there is someone who can know and share with him something of how he feels within himself. Thus if our initial efforts as therapists realize our intent, or set, our client will find, at least temporarily, that he can be understood, that his overwhelming anxiety is lessened, that belonging rather than isolation may be possible.

Thus our initial intention, or set, is simple: Human distress is real and must be understood and accepted as such, but it need not be devastating. Our ability to understand and perhaps to verbalize accurately the feelings of another person does not solve the problem or totally take away the distress, but it does help to rouse in him subjective feelings of hopefulness, tentative coping and thoughts of possible mastery rather than irrational despair.

As therapists carrying out the initial set we are describing, our gestures and verbal responses represent a constant search for precision in understanding and reflecting the feelings the client is experiencing. We have accurately understood when the client is able to move on to a new feeling or content. If he keeps repeating the same content or feelings, or if he becomes silent or withdraws, we must assume that we have not yet empathically understood and reflected what is present in his subjective experience.

Simply repeating his words to him does not convey understanding. Some phrase, some theme, must be found which shows we understand and which at the same time strikes another chord enabling him to move on and begin to enlarge himself. It is in this accurate, precise, and yet different understanding and reflecting that a client begins to feel genuine support and reassurance. Further, this is the beginning of the therapeutic, interpersonal relationship.

There is another meaningful aspect of our set. We think of this most easily as finding something to like or respect in the client. What do we mean? We are referring here to some of the reciprocal effects which clients and therapists have upon each other. These effects begin immediately when client and therapist sit down together, and they take forms congruent with the particular interpersonal interactions which occur.

An aspect of the reciprocity is that therapists, too, have a phenomenal, subjective world. Part of the makeup of the therapist is a need to feel or be helpful. How do we as therapists know that it may be possible for us to help? How can we feel assured that our need to help may be realized? We think that the therapist feels such potential when the client is able to "take" and to use, however minimally, the therapist's understanding of the client's world. Such taking by the client gives pleasure and reassurance to the therapist. He is able to think and feel that he is effective. His pleasure, in turn, translates into liking the client because the client may be able to allow him to be what he needs to be.

We believe that training and experience are most helpful to us in seeing and feeling the oftentimes "minimal takes" by a client. Thus our own needs though felt, can be controlled so that we do not grow overly impatient or feel deprived ourselves. Deprived or frustrated feelings in the therapist often lead to punishment or rejection of the client before a viable relationship is formed.

Depersonalization and the Subjective Discrepancy. Reassurance and support, one person to another, are then important aspects of the reciprocal interaction which leads to meaningful, helpful relationships. But we need to say more, because what is reassuring, supporting, and tentatively enlarging is often dynamically complex and quite different from what objective, observable facts about a person may suggest.

The A student, for instance, is not necessarily reassured nor does he feel understood when we point out to him, as others probably have done, the objective, observable facts about his past and present high level of academic performance. We believe that he is more likely to feel supported and to feel that our relationship is off to a good start if we are able to understand, to accept, that he is genuinely distressed and unfulfilled in spite of his good performance. Why and how can such a strange, discrepant experience come to be? We have found the concept of depersonalization to be very useful as an explanation.

A person's developmental history in regard to depersonalization is not available to us in first or early interviews, but the subjective feelings of distress, of not being a person in some significant ways, are available to us. We respond to these facts of subjective, internal life without necessarily understanding their origins. That our A student does feel depersonalized we do understand as best we can, even though neither he nor we can yet explain or understand in any historically meaningful way why or how he is depersonalized. We do assume, however, that the origin of the failure and of the sense of depersonalization can be discovered and the latter dynamically "undone" because our interpersonal, therapeutic relationship will be significantly different from the prior, conflictive relationships.

With such a client as our dissatisfied A student, we often find that as a child he felt valued and cared for by his parents and others because he could do well in school. He was, and is yet, fearful that he will not be accepted or cared about if he does not do well. Thus the present conflict was created. On the one hand, he feels that love and approval are conditional upon his performing well. Yet the love and approval are directed toward an attribute rather than toward a human being who is loved and cared about simply because he lives and is human. Being loved for an attribute is often powerfully depersonalizing, and this is what our A student may be feeling.

Further, we find that the feelings of distress and depersonalization could not be expressed to and talked about with the parents or significant others. After all, what could be said or felt which would not threaten loss of love or acceptance? The parents may even be sure that they love their child, and it is even probable that they do. Their behavior and what they attend to may powerfully suggest to the child, however, that what is loved is his brain, his performance, an attribute, but not so surely himself, his being.

Thus in subtle and yet clear, describable ways can depersonalization occur. Put another way, the developmental task of accomplishing, of doing well, is demonstrated and known; yet the internal, phenomenological experience is discrepant and distressing.

Our basic point about the developmental importance of the subjective-objective discrepancy in the accomplishment of developmental tasks can be illustrated by another kind of example.

Further, through this example the importance of responding accurately and with understanding to the discrepancy and distress may be better understood.

In our functioning, yet often troubled, population, it is quite common for an attractive, charming young woman to seek help from a therapist. If she happens to see a male therapist, it is even likely that she will be especially charming, even seductive possibly. Yet while she is being purposefully engaging, and thus very probably attracting her therapist's attention to some of her obvious attributes, she may at the same time complain bitterly that she is dissatisfied with her relationships with men. How can such a state of affairs be?

What our male therapist may or may not realize is that her conflict is real for her and that his own attraction to her attributes constitutes or symbolizes her problem with men. She has felt and still feels disvalued and depersonalized by her own attractiveness to men. That she has a part in creating her own conflict is either not obvious or not known to her. Moreover, efforts to reassure her about her attractiveness may be felt by her as a further depersonalization, even though some of her behavior may have urgently elicited such reassurance. Again, as with our A student, one way to understand and respond to her is in terms of her present distress and the discrepancy she presently feels. Too, although the content and nature of our attractive young woman's problem are different from the A student's, the interpersonal, interactional genesis of the problem may not be so different.

LEARNING ABOUT
PAST RELATIONSHIPS

We approach early meetings with our clients with a second set, one which has evolved out of our cumulated experiences of working with and thinking about clients in a functioning population. This is the intent to formulate hypotheses about what the client needs from us and how we can go about helping him. We believe, for instance, the clients present most of their problems in a compacted, cryptic form in the first interview. It is ordinarily not possible to deal with or resolve the problems in the first interview, but it is possible to make inferences which can help to direct the course of therapy.

Experience Helps. We have learned that the hypotheses we make have their origins in our background of therapy experiences. We have come to realize this as we have observed our students. We find that our expectation to make this kind of assessment is different from our students' intent. They may make some judgments, but they seem less willing to express them or to depend upon them. Even those with fine diagnostic skills do not see clients in the terms we are talking about. Other students are apparently unaware that in the first interview they might begin to formulate ideas about the course of therapy. They do learn to make more such judgments as their training progresses, and we are able to be helpful to them in their learning. Yet such learning cannot be completely telescoped into the few years of a training program. We can offer the reader some guidelines which we find useful to us and our students.

What are these judgments that we make? Actually, they start with educated guesses about the nature of our client's developmental history. The nature of the problem is a clue, and in order to validate a specific hunch, we may say something like, "You know, I've noticed that people with your kind of problem have had such and such an experience. Do you have any feel for that?" Or perhaps in another instance, "In order to feel so worthless, it seems to me you must have felt criticized rather often. Do you know about that?" The answers to these kinds of questions lead to further exploration and tend to set the direction of the client's thinking, remembering, and expression and to generate further data for making hypotheses.

A second kind of clue to the client's developmental history is found in the way in which he relates to us. Our multiple therapy experience has taught us much about how differently clients relate to different people. We have noted often, for instance, that a client may talk freely and affectively to one of us while his communications to the other therapist may be fluent, yet obviously controlled. In such instances we often find that these different ways of relating mirror his ways of relating to his parents and perhaps to significant others. From our multiple therapy experience we have learned that in the dyadic therapy the way the client relates to the one therapist is only part of his relating repertoire. However, we have learned in dyadic therapy to take note of the quality of the client's relating and to use it for further exploration. If he talks readily about one parent and not the other, then we may ask about the parent who is not talked about. Further, we may note that the quality of the communication may change to become more like his communication with the other parent. In such ways we can tentatively learn a great deal about the probable nature of past relationships with important people.

We also learn something about how a client wants to be perceived. Almost without exception in a functioning population, a client presents himself in a way which his experience has taught him is effective in gaining what he wants. For example, suppose a young man telling a woman therapist about some very real hurt begins to cry. Common, pathologically oriented theory would say that he is regressed and does not have very adequate defenses, and the therapist would probably have a set of impressions which would be diagnostically accurate.

On the other hand, suppose the therapist assumes that the client's crying means that he would like to have his mother comfort him. A different set of inferences about him and what further needs to be known becomes apparent. For instance, is this an extremely deprived youngster? If he is, how can the therapist help him in a way which will not repeat the experience with his mother which turned out to be so unfulfilling? A question or two about his relationship to his mother may be needed to confirm the hypotheses and give the therapist a direction for further therapeutic interaction.

To think of the young man's crying as expressing something he wants, perhaps from his mother, gives the therapist a set from which to predict, and offers her a range of choices about how she may be helpful to him. The set is to focus on the need, rather than the pathology of regression.

Let us return to our statement that the way a client presents himself reflects his experience in getting what he wants. In our example, and in all clients who we decide need help, we must assume that the client's way of gaining what he wants is now somehow not effective. If it were effective, he would not now be asking for help.

Suppose a young woman when talking to a young male therapist presents her most charming self. He frequently asks himself, and perhaps asks her, what kind of problem can this doll have? When he becomes aware of how her charm immobilizes him and keeps him from understanding her or knowing anything about her, he can also know what an empty billboard her charming facade is. Then he can perhaps help her to learn what she may safely want so that she can get more out of her interpersonal experiences than she has in the past.

And We Note Some Directions for Therapy.   When a client belongs to the functioning population, both he and the therapist expect him to continue to function during the therapy. With this kind of set the first encounter will include some type of assessment of his strengths and weaknesses. In addition, there will be some minimal decision-making about the course of therapy and the rate at which necessary regression should be permitted and/or facilitated.

Thinking about the developmental process and clients' partial success or failure to accomplish developmental tasks is for us a primary way of conceptualizing our understanding of clients and what they need. In this context we view regression as a psychological experience related to the tasks unfinished rather than as a pathological state. In a later chapter we will discuss more fully the function of regression and the purposes of primary process reactions in therapy. Since we think of therapy as having to do with repair of some failure in the developmental process, there will of necessity be some regression to the point of the failure with the risks attendant on this. The intent in regressing is to note the client's strength or weakness—or, in developmental terms, to see the degree to which the developmental task has been completed or impaired and to consider the risks involved in doing something about it.

Our concept of risk involves assessing the degree to which re-entering the developmental sequence will impair the capacity of the client to function. This assessment of strengths and weaknesses has two components. One component has to do with the degree of impairment and the other with the probable age or task level at which development was incomplete. For instance, in the earlier example of the woman therapist with the tearful young man, if the therapist feels his deprivation occurred in infancy, the decision about how to work with him and how much regression is appropriate will be different from what it would be if she believes it is a later developmental problem.

Here, the test mentioned earlier of ascertaining whether the client can take something from the therapist and let it be meaningful to him is useful to the therapist in deciding whether the regression will facilitate growth or not. It lets the therapist know whether interpersonal interaction has meaning for the client and whether the possibility of helping him is real. If the client is unable to find some meaning for himself out of his first interaction with his therapist, he, too, will face the decision of whether to continue. The therapist, in some instances, may decide to refer the client to someone else; or he may inquire about the meaning of help or even simply suggest that an interpersonal, therapeutic experience is not what the client needs.

Our last statement says something about our expectations regarding the speed and length and nature of therapy, our third set. We wish to be explicit about these expectations. First, we expect to involve the client in his own therapy from the beginning so that this will be an information-gathering time not only for the therapist but also for the client. Second, we do not believe that therapy must be prolonged to be effective. When we offer a client a chance to have a new interpersonal experience around the developmental tasks which were unsatisfactorily accomplished, we are not offering to "make up" to him for the past failures. An impaired client is, in part at least, impaired by his assumption that he must have whatever it was he missed before he can be happy, feel good, or work well. This belief is present whether he is consciously aware of it or not. We think that for the therapist to make this same assumption not only perpetuates the problem but may exacerbate it. And we relate this assumption to the length of therapy. Thus if we are able to make clear the interpersonal meaning of the client's problem, make it have emotional and rational meaning for him in a rather energetic way, then we avoid being caught up in the client's belief that he cannot change because he has this deficit, whatever it is. We have come to believe that, at least with some clients, long therapy has made them worse.

Thus our third intent in this first interview includes establishing for both ourselves and the client some expectation of the length and nature of the therapy. In this way we intend to begin to develop the meaning of the helping relationship to both persons. We hope to let the client know something about what he may expect from having a relationship with the therapist. For this reason we try to present ourselves as real people, interested in understanding him, having ideas about how we can be helpful to him. We are willing to change within the relationship as we expect him to change; and we recognize that the relationship will perhaps be "parentlike" but that we are not parents.

It is important to clarify how we carry out this last intent. Implementation is largely through our set. Thus we do not usually state what we expect of the client and what he can expect of us— although we do so if it seems appropriate.

The interaction between the therapist's set and the client's needs usually enables the client to form some idea of the nature of the therapeutic relationship. One of us recalls, as an example, a particularly lonely, tortured client who had painfully described his problems. At the end of a discussion of therapy he said, "Then you can be a friend to me, and I can learn something about how to get along." Neither friendship nor interpersonal relationships had been the focus of discussion in structuring therapy. Yet the ongoing interaction with the therapist, plus the client's interpersonal needs, allowed him to conceptualize the prospective relationship in a way which seemed to the therapist to be appropriate.

WHAT ACCEPTING HELP
MEANS TO PEOPLE

Functioning people are sometimes reluctant to accept help when they feel that they must turn over to another person the prerogative of thinking about and understanding themselves. To give another person the right to know more about themselves than they do, particularly when they feel that they have failed in this regard, can be a very threatening thing to them. If our hypothesis that understanding is a way to mastery is true, the threat is clear. Sometimes a client solves this dilemma by letting us know that his distress is so great that we may do or say almost anything but must make it quick. It may appear that the client does not want to commit himself to the relationship and to change. While this may be true, his fear of losing his autonomy may be a more relevant motivation. Thus we have found it is important to let the client understand early that he will be an active participant in the process and that his part will be of primary importance. His understanding and his thoughts about himself will be respected.

But the therapist is a person, too, and he has needs and feelings about his interaction with the client. He needs to feel that he is helpful and even that the client perceives him as helpful. Furthermore, his training, experience, and personal value of himself are invested in his being a person who understands others. He wants to feel that his knowledge is not only acceptable and unthreatening but also helpful. Sometimes he may even feel a stronger need to be a knowing person than to be helpful. And there may be many different reasons for this, some stemming from the interaction and some from his own dynamics.

We have, then, two people with a mutual concern: understanding one of them. They have almost conflicting needs in this respect. Thus the problem is a complex one; and although a solution may not be worked out in the first interview, some of its complexities will almost certainly become apparent.

To help preserve the client's sense of autonomy, we have found it useful to engage the client in working on his problems from the beginning and to help him work on them. Almost all functioning people who seek help have been trying very hard to solve whatever is bothering them, and they have come for help only because they have been unable to work things out for themselves. They may fear that there is no solution and they may resent the fact that the therapist is doing nothing but listening. On the other hand, they may also be resentful if the therapist offers suggestions and interpretations, because in a very real way these offerings may imply that the client's efforts have been ineffectual. The therapist, then, must be more than a sounding board and usually do more than give the client a chance to hear himself. He must be understanding in a way which shares the client's understanding, and he must work actively with the client without taking over from him the task of thinking and understanding himself.

We do not believe that there are necessarily specific techniques by which a therapist can accomplish this task of shared, purposeful interaction. We can describe the set, the attitude toward oneself as a therapist which will facilitate this accomplishment. To the therapist's need to listen, to learn about this other person, and to be helpful to him without taking over, should be added the need to be willing to let the impact of the other meaningfully affect him. What does it mean to let oneself be affected by the client? Willingly being surprised by the client, willingly reacting to him personally, willingly being a person ourselves rather than simply a professional.

To forego being our professional selves in the ways in which being professional functions as a protective cloak in our first encounter with another person may be a risky experience. It is, however, one which can be most fruitful because it communicates to the client from the very beginning that here is a person who will be a human being and who will let him be a human being in turn, with all the attendant pleasures and risks. Hopefully, the therapist's sensitivity to the client's feelings will help control the demand on the client that he respond in a given way. Such expectations for reciprocal responsiveness come much later. In a real way we avoid many of the pitfalls of therapy as an interpersonal experience when we are willing to be persons rather than just professionals in this first encounter because we do not let ourselves be trapped by our client's expectations of what we should be.

OUR RELATIONSHIP TO
THE READER

What have we tried to say in this chapter? Each reader will, of course, have his own reactions, thoughts, and feelings. We can neither control nor predict what these reactions will be. We can confidently predict, however, that there will be some reactions even though we can only guess at their nature.

Let us tell some of our own thoughts and feelings as we prepared to write this chapter, as we were writing it, and as we now look it over. We were concerned with presenting certain conceptions, and intents or sets, that we find useful in our work with clients and in facilitating the training of other therapists. We wrote about these intents as clearly as we could. Yet we have avoided, we hope, prescriptions or a cookbook on how to do therapy.

We have hoped to stimulate and to involve. Perhaps we shall provoke shock or disagreement. Whatever reactions we engender will be pleasing to us if we know about them. Perhaps for persons as interpersonal as we are, being ignored is the only thing that would distress us!

Chapter 3

Building Our Theory: An Introduction to the Process Constructs

We have been discussing how a therapist goes about forming a relationship with his client. The relationship changes, grows deeper, sometimes breaks down, is tested, is repaired, and is a dynamic, purposeful process throughout the course of therapy. However, the relationship, or interpersonal process, is not the whole of therapy. Some persons may think that all that is necessary is a good relationship or a comfortable relationship and that the client by some magic process makes the changes he needs to make. In writing this book we have wanted to understand and give observable meaning to some of these psychological phenomena which have an aura of magic. We have tried to conceptualize an expanding, theoretical system within which a wide range of therapeutic experiences can be looked at and studied. That there will continue to be therapeutic surprises and mysterious, unexplained therapeutic instances, we acknowledge, but, on the other hand, we also welcome them. They are part of the continuing excitement of working with people. We believe that our theoretical system has in it the capacity for change and growth, which we think is the essence of human behavior and experience.

What About Change?   Let us consider, then, something of the nature of change in human beings. What do we know about change? What constitutes change? We see change rather broadly. We believe that learning changes one, forgetting too; but more explicitly change is a subjective experience. We believe also that its effects may be objectively evidenced. When objective change is reacted to by another person, then further change occurs, and the subjective experience of change is enhanced. Thus a college student who has understood some of his feelings about his parents decides to go home and talk to them, and finds that they react to him differently. If he also finds that both he and they can feel and express themselves differently, then he has an experience of the expanding reciprocal effects of his original change.

Change has dimensions other than the reciprocal. Learning is change, and learning seems to occur in at least two ways. First is learning by adding to, accretion. Numerous kinds of change seem to be of this adding on nature—gaining weight, for instance. Second is learning that involves disruption, emotional stress, anxiety perhaps, exhilaration sometimes; but in any case there is a breakup of ongoing emotional tranquility. Frequently the disruption is what is felt as change and seems more real subjectively than the first-mentioned, added-on type of change. The person who has gained twenty pounds with no attention to the fact other than noticing that his clothes seem tight has changed objectively without the disruptive subjective experience. Similarly, one can add one hundred words to one's vocabulary in a foreign language without feeling disrupted by doing so. But anxiety and stress or exhilaration may occur when one begins to use those one hundred new words to talk to another person. In a similar way, when one recognizes the twenty pounds of added weight, a more or less disruptive experience of the change takes place.

Perhaps the rate of change has something to do with its disruptive character. Certainly, the subjective experience of change which occurs gradually is quite different from that which happens suddenly. The subjective experience of twenty pounds gained over a year is much less anxiety-producing than breaking a leg, for instance. The disruptive sense of change may be experienced as fear, anger, anxiety, irritation, or in some cases as surprise, pleasure, excitement, even exhilaration. We believe that anxiety is a usual accompaniment of subjective change. It may, in fact, be a clue to its occurrence. In short, we don't believe that meaningful change often occurs without an accompanying disturbance of the ongoing emotional homeostasis.

Therapy Means Change. People tend to protect themselves from anxiety or from being disrupted too greatly, and these kinds of psychic protection have been called defenses. We believe that psychic defenses are needed. They are important and useful to the person in several ways, preventing change that is too disruptive being only one.

However, the goal of psychotherapy is change. If change is to occur, the need for psychic defenses must be lessened, and accomplishing this is a part of the psychotherapeutic endeavor. Here we believe that the relationship between the client and therapist plays an important part, acting as an agent in reducing psychic defenses. The degree of trust between the two persons and the capacity of the client to accept his dependency on the therapist facilitate change. The relationship somehow reduces the risk, perhaps because it promises that the therapist will share the client's anxiety. In fact, we believe that unless we can share the anxiety with our client, subjective change may be limited or may not occur. Other ways in which the defenses against change are lowered or circumvented will be discussed in later chapters as they pertain to the therapeutic processes.

If the rate of change is a factor in the disruptive, anxiety-producing aspects of change, then it is clear that psychotherapy with its expectation of relatively rapid change would require measures for reducing the subjective sense of risk and the defenses erected. What we have said about therapy thus far carries a clear implication that change and the direction of change could then become an issue. Certainly, the client suffering with the pain and discomfort which motivated him to seek us out wants desperately to get rid of his distress. Frequently the thought of any other kind of change is threatening, and often it is not even something he thinks he wants. As therapists we want our clients to obtain relief, but we also want them to desire more than that. At the same time we want to facilitate their efforts in making the particular changes they may need to make.

What changes occur in psychotherapy? The answer is that many things change. We may name a few and qualify these by saying that in whatever way a person changes, it is highly individualized. As already mentioned, subjective reality comes to approach objective reality. Feelings about self and others change. Behavior changes. Feeling states become more differentiated and are replaced by feelings. Interpersonal relationships change. There are changes in ongoing present experiences and in understanding and attitudes about past experiences. There are changes in habitual ways of thinking and in methods of learning. Sometimes physical changes such as facial expressions and body posture take place; energy level may rise, and symptoms may be alleviated. In addition, change once under way in one area frequently seems to produce changes in other aspects of experience.

That changes occur is often evident to us and to many other therapists as well. But explanations of why and how changes occur seem to us to be too simple, reductionistic, and certainly insufficiently individualized. Thus ascribing change to overly simple cause-and-effect models seems essentially fallacious.

Since we do not understand psychotherapeutic change to be a simple cause-and-effect process, how can we conceptualize it? Let us begin by describing our experience as we conceptualize the ideas in this book. In a real sense we subject ourselves to and participate in the processes involved in psychodynamic change even though the motivating factor of psychic distress is not as acute as that of clients seeking psychotherapeutic help. The outcome is change in feelings, change in attitudes, change in cognition, and finally change in behavior. The processes involved are strikingly similar to those occurring in therapy as we know and practice it. A description of how we think together about the processes in psychotherapy as we develop and set down the ideas for this volume will both present our theory and offer incidence of change in ourselves.

We Experience Change Through Feeling, Thinking, and Interacting. As we feel, think, and observe the processes we believe to be so characteristic of both therapy and human development, we feel competing needs. On the one hand, we find it necessary to think and write about the processes as separate and dissimilar in their nature and functions. Yet at the same time we are aware that the phenomena characteristic of the processes may occur at the same time and are intimately interrelated. For example, as we sit in our chairs thinking, feeling, and interacting with each other as we write this book, we become acutely aware that all three processes occur in us, usually in sequence but sometimes almost simultaneously. What is the sequence we refer to? Let us see if we can describe it meaningfully.

First of all, we often find that as we labor to clarify an idea, we seem to be merely laboring and going nowhere. Often, then, we stop laboring and retire within ourselves; we sit quietly saying little for as much as half an hour. Fortunately we usually find that one of us is eventually stirred by inner feelings of excitement. The excitement is usually quickly associated with the discovery of some new facet or way of conceptualizing the problem, but there is also an internal sense of enlargement, phenomenological growth, if you will. As the new way of thinking and feeling grows, the urge to communicate with the other grows and becomes irresistible. The initial communication is often unclear, fumbling, and in many ways is a plea for help. If the other is alert and interpersonally sensitive, he hears the cry for help, and the process of interpersonal facilitation begins. He, too, becomes excited and involved, and together we explore, polish, and add to our new discovery, which has became mutual and interpersonal. The excitement and thinking, which are now interpersonal as well as phenomenological for both of us, may go on for some time, hours perhaps.

Finally, as we enlarge our discovery, we become more and more satisfied, and the sense of excitement in the immediate, personal sense grows less and less. Then finally, interestingly enough, we become observers of our own creation. We begin checking to see how our new conception relates to other concepts we have developed. We ask: "How does it fit? What else is needed? Is it really meaningful?" We become more purely thinkers who are integrative, yet critical. We sit in judgment on our creation—but afterward, not before we have gone through the experience of the other processes.

There are many variants on the series of experiences we have just described. Sometimes the whole sequence occurs in a few minutes. Occasionally it seems that we experience all three processes at once. At other times the whole sequence takes a week. On another occasion the sequence truncates, and we return to the more phenomenological, interpersonally separate, kind of experience. Yet generally we find we must go through the entire sequence before we can accept our effort as complete.

How and why is the sequence of experiences or processes aborted on some occasions? We have noted, for example, that if the one appealed to for help in regard to a partly formed conception is not appropriately sensitive or facilitative, then the sequence usually is interrupted. What seems to be called for is a real willingness, even an eagerness, to enter into the half-known, even the unknown, with the other. Criticalness coming too soon from either of us, but particularly from the less involved one, seems to be especially disruptive and destructive. We think that "too soon criticalness" may be the essence of punitiveness in interpersonal relationships. Dynamically what happens, we think, is that the effort of the less involved one to be sensitive and facilitative may fail or seem to fail, which may lead, in turn, to unacceptable feelings of inadequacy on his part. He may then resort to criticalness of the idea and even of the other person in order to restore his sense of adequacy. The consequences are that although he may succeed in this, the creative effort is damaged or aborted, and the original needer of help may feel hurt or punished by the interpersonal exchange. Put another way, the interpersonal support of sharing the anxiety of the unknown has been lost and the consequent normal sequence of processes broken.

As it is with the two of us, so it often is with us and our clients. Now on to a discussion of further aspects of change as we know them in our relationships with clients.

SOME THERAPIST UNDERSTANDINGS:
FACILITATIVE OF CHANGE AND OTHERWISE

The preceding description of our own interactions as we write this book can be applied directly to describing and understanding how we may help our clients as the therapeutic relationship develops. How can we help? What can we say? It is very difficult, isn't it? The effort is great. Will the return be commensurate with the risks we, therapists and clients alike, may feel we are taking? Ah! But the clue to what to do may reside in the feelings and thoughts of effort and risk. Will we, therapist and client, help each other to help the client with his problems, conflicts, and concerns by working harder? Not necessarily so. Greater efforts may only intensify the sense of risk and consequently produce failure in our mutual effort.

An error is committed only if the effort continues without eventually breaking the ever tightening effort cycle in some way. Fortunately, either client or therapist or both may contribute productively to changing the interaction so that we may move on. The client may contribute by complaining that nothing helpful is happening. He may be right and should be listened to! Or the client may observe, in the inimitably perceptive way that clients often have, that the therapist is working very hard and may or may not be a good fellow for doing so. The therapist may feel that such client observations are hostile, and so they may be, but the client may well have a constructive reason for his hostility. He is not being helped! The relationship is not moving along.

In such ways we may learn that our effort is not necessarily useful. But most often we find that it is through our feelings of efforts, constriction, and anxiety that we come to know that something different needs to occur. The first step in doing something different often involves the conscious recognition of our own feelings. Once we become aware of possibly fruitless effort and strain, choices become possible. What are they? Continued effort in the same vein is certainly one possibility, but it is not likely to be useful. For then the repeating cycle remains unbroken, and fears of inadequacy and despair are likely to continue to increase for both participants.

As the therapist becomes aware of effort, he may also become aware of the probable concomitant feelings of fear and despair he, and his client as well, may be experiencing. With such further awareness, the choices for the therapist can become more dynamically and therapeutically meaningful. What the therapist may realize, while the client may not, is that the two of them have recreated, reenacted even, what has probably occurred often in the client's own past life. If and when the therapist can arrive at such an awareness, then his own sense of threat to his adequacy frequently diminishes and the way of doing something different emerges.

Different therapists may do different things at such a time, and we are not prepared to claim that one alternative is better than all others. We often find in our own practice, however, that we report our own awareness and its possible past and present interpersonal meaning. We may say to the client, for instance: "We've been working awfully hard, haven't we? Our hard work doesn't seem very productive, but could it be that this has often happened with you and others like your mother or father? Does this mean anything to you?" If we are able to strike the right note, whatever we may say, then both therapist and client are enabled to move on and to talk and feel in meaningful fashion again. Memories may come to the client, sometimes in a flood, sometimes slowly, but nearly always with different affective and/or cognitive meaning. The client's impassed relationships from the past can be explored, felt, even changed within the context of a present relationship which is no longer unproductive and despairing.

Let us recapitulate in another way what we have just been saying. The sequence of events which occurs is often astonishingly similar to the one we described in regard to ourselves as we write this book. We are finally enabled to make the appropriate observations of ourselves and to state clearly the nature of the frustration in our present relationship. Further, we suggest the possible meaning in terms of past relationships. Most usually, the freeing observations and suggestions are made by the therapist, and in this sense the process here is more likely to be one-way than in our collaborative, authoring relationship. If the freeing observations and suggestions strike the right note, then there is often a period of silence, thought, feeling, and a sense of separateness while we both enlarge ourselves.

Usually—although this is not always so—the client eventually breaks the silence and our separateness by beginning to speak of his own developing awareness, his feelings and thoughts. At such a time the client may need help in expressing himself because he is anxious—but in a different way than formerly. He is likely to be stumbling and only partially articulate. There is an implicit cry for help. He may need assistance in shaping and giving meaning to his evolving feelings and thoughts.

Ordinarily we hope we are interpersonally sensitive enough to provide only the help that is needed. If we say too much, we run the risk of enlarging ourselves at the client's expense. The discovery is then ours rather than the client's. But we can share with and assist our client as he goes about the exciting and rewarding experience of knowing himself and his relationships with others in some new ways. The client ventures into exploration, shaping, changing, his feelings, thoughts, and perceptions; and this may go on for minutes, hours, or even weeks. Much goes on between interviews, too. Eventually, sometimes within the same hour, sometimes in the next interview or even in a later one there comes to him the sense of completeness, of deeper understanding, of integration. Finally, there comes the examination, the criticalness, the judging and evaluating, which seem to consolidate the gains.

Terminations typically occur at the point of integration and completeness, when the client feels that sufficient changes have occurred so that he is able to go on by himself. He is optimistic about his future and yet knows that all his problems are not and never will be solved. In his own way the client learns about the sequence we have described, comes to know that it need not be devastating and that he has within himself the resources to work through it. Also, he has usually learned that others besides the therapist can help him if he still needs help on occasion.

Timing: A Facilitator of Change. In the immediately preceding section we have described a cycle which is often characteristic of human interpersonal relationships. Further, we have suggested that such a cycle is found in therapeutic relationships particularly often and that the affective concomitants are experienced intensely. Redoubled effort is not necessarily the most therapeutically effective behavior, and we have described a way in which an impassed interaction can become useful, changing, and productive. Yet we have suggested that the cycle, including the sense of impasse, is often inevitable, even necessary. We think that one of the most rewarding human experiences is the relief and sense of growth which occur when such an impasse in a therapist-client relationship is experienced and resolved. In one sense, then, we think of the feeling of impasse as a necessary concomitant of the generation and resolution of conflict. Consequently, one important belief, or set, of an effective therapist is that deeply felt conflict, even impasse, is a necessary prelude to human change and growth.

Timing of certain kinds of therapist behaviors and responses then becomes an important variable in the interaction between therapist and client. What do we mean by timing? Is it mechanical? Is it easy? Can it be learned? We think of timing, in the sense in which we use the concept, as neither mechanical nor easy to do well. We do believe, however, that it is possible to learn to time better. We have learned most from observing ourselves and each other and from paying attention to our own thoughts and feelings as we work with clients in both dyadic and multiple therapy. We suggested earlier that timing is an important factor in dealing effectively with phenomena associated with conflict, impasse, and effort. It is when these psychological experiences become real, even threatening, that it is time to act or behave differently. We have indicated something of how it is possible either to allow the experiences to continue or to act differently and how the new and different behavior may be facilitating and therapeutic.

Ambivalence Resolved Through Timing. The concept of timing can be used in other ways to help resolve conflict phenomena characteristic of human relationships. We think of ambivalence, for instance, as being a usual part of human relationships. Particularly, we think of ambivalence as an experience common to therapists and clients and their relationships. Ambivalence, as a human experience, is especially distressing when the need to solve a problem or reduce a conflict is urgent. Frustration, anger, and other feelings, too, may be concomitant. Yet the "why" of such feelings often cannot be easily understood. This is because of the human necessity to express ambivalence through a time dimension. According to our understanding of ambivalence, psychologically opposite or opposed feelings, thoughts, or experiences are involved. The very oppositeness of the feelings or experiences means that it is difficult, if not impossible, to experience them at the same moment in time.

For many persons—and this seems to be especially true in the case of emotionally distressed individuals—the time span between the expression of the two kinds of incompatible experience is considerable: hours, days, or even weeks. In a way we think of the length of the time span as indicating the degree of incompatibility of the experiences for the person. Further, usually only as a human relationship develops do the opposite feelings come to be expressed in whatever order they occur.

How can we make this clear? Let's use an example. A young man comes in seeking help for his problems with girls. Let us suppose, further, that he sees a woman therapist. In the first interview he speaks of his fears, frustrations, his anger, or whatever feelings he has about girls and his relationships to them. In that same interview he expresses very positive feelings about his mother. He even includes the therapist as a woman he likes. The woman therapist may or may not infer that the negative feelings expressed about girls may also be the other side of an ambivalence about his mother. In any case, whatever she infers, we think that the therapist, since she wishes to build a relationship with the young man, will respond phenomenologically to the feelings as they are expressed. As the relationship develops and intensifies, the therapist may become aware that the client expresses both negative and positive feelings about her, about girls, and even about his sainted mother. Yet the opposite feelings may still be expressed with a considerable time span between them. Further, the time span may vary according to whether he speaks of girls in general, a particular girl, the therapist, or his mother.

When we perceive the ambivalence generating, it is tempting to try to point it out to our young man and even to generalize about it in regard to mothers and possibly even the person of the therapist. The success of the effort may be limited, however, by the client's inability to accept and use the observation except in regard to girls in general. If our therapist is wise and experienced, we think she is likely to accept the limited effect of her effort. As the therapist-client relationship grows, the client's opposite feelings about a particular girl ordinarily will come closer together in time. Perhaps with the help of the therapist he can accept and integrate them as they are. Finally, the opposed feelings about his mother and those about the therapist will come close enough together in time for him to perceive that they belong together. Thus he can accept, integrate, even "resolve," and live with them as feelings which are real, different, and yet not devastating.

Incidentally, the therapist's ability to "time" her observations and suggestions and also to "take," or accept, both positive and negative feelings about her is likely to be very important for the young man. We think that in the case of such a client the mother has usually wanted and accepted love from her son but has been less able to accept his angry, critical feelings.

Another aspect of the client-therapist relationship which is related to timing is the client's ability to take help from the therapist. The client's contradictory feelings ordinarily need to come close together in time before the client is able to accept the therapist's observations of and responses to these feelings. Need we mention that taking help is a very ambivalent undertaking? Additionally, the manner in which the help is offered may affect the client's ability to take and use it.

The Matter of Therapeutic Errors and Timing. Ordinarily we think that clients can better accept or take help when observations are offered rather than insisted upon. Nuances of language and attitudes in the therapist can make a vast difference. Let us return to our prior example in regard to ambivalence. If the therapist says to the client, "You are ambivalent," the statement may not be acceptable for several reasons. First, the client may not understand very well the meaning of the word "ambivalent." If he does not, of course it is possible that he is simply being defensive, but is he? Why does the therapist use a word he doesn't understand? Could it be the therapist's impatience, or could it be his lack of wisdom? In any case, if any considerable explanation of the term is necessary, then we must conclude that what has been said may not have been very useful.

Second, the client may regard the statement quoted as a flat assertion, even authoritarian or judgmental. While clients may need to feel that their therapists are knowledgeable or authoritative, yet flat, assertive statements by therapists can adversely affect a client's sense of participation and control in his own emotional affairs. Further, he may be unnecessarily reminded of past others who have told him how he felt or thought instead of inquiring whether he felt or thought in some particular way. We add, incidentally, that while certain kinds of therapist responses may be more immediately useful to clients than others, the less immediately useful responses can lead to dynamically important matters.

In such an instance the therapist's ability to recognize the consequence of his error may be crucial. In the case of our young man seeing the woman therapist, it is likely that he often feels criticized by women. It is further likely that he has quite a capacity for being self-critical, too. Our young man, then, may feel criticized by the flat, assertive statement, and he may soon, if not immediately, begin to speak critically of himself. Our woman therapist may then be able to turn her "error" to good use. She may say, "Seems like you may be feeling that I was critical of you a bit ago when I said you were ambivalent. Could that be?" Thus, although some therapist responses may be technically better at a given time than "erroneous" responses, the latter may prove productive provided that the therapist recognizes the consequences of what he has said or done and responds appropriately at that time.

Another point. Therapists may "need to help" before the client can accept and use such help. A characteristic dynamic consequence of the therapist's too early need to help, which may be felt as a demand by the client, is that the client feels his separateness has become threatened. He may feel that he is in danger of being swallowed or engulfed, that his autonomy is in danger. Such a consequence may be evidenced if a client begins to talk either of his own insatiable feelings or the insatiable feelings and demands of others. Again, if the therapist is able to recognize and respond appropriately, an "error" in timing may lead to good timing later.

Perhaps we have begun to make our conception of the nature of timing clear. We think of the concept not as absolute but as relative. Certain consequences flow from the interaction if the therapist's behavior is timed optimally, that is, therapeutically "good." But behavioral consequences also flow from less than optimal timing, and in turn provide new opportunities for good timing. Thus we think that a deteriorating therapeutic relationship may often be saved by therapist behavior which is appropriately timed even though a good deal of inappropriately timed behavior went before.

We have been describing our experience of the processes involved in therapy first as we have known them in the creative effort of writing this book and then in the interaction between therapists and clients. We need now to say something more specific about these processes as theoretical constructs. We need also to think of them as they are interrelated and as they interact on each other.

TO BE SPECIFIC ABOUT
OUR PROCESS CONSTRUCTS

We begin our discussion by describing how we first thought of and then gradually became convinced about the nature of the processes which go on in therapy.

In our own professional development the first process construct we knew about was the phenomenological. We have given much thought to the phrase "phenomenological process." We have wondered if it has the same meaning for other professional people. For us it now has a meaning that is more generic than specific. We have added nuances and connotations not originally associated with the term "phenomenological." We have even considered not using the word at all. We need, then, to describe the meaning which "phenomenological process" has for us, and we will do so both in this chapter and in a later one.

The second process which became to us an acceptable process construct has been long recognized. For many able therapists it has been a source of problems. In some of the earlier theories it was a process which had to be suppressed, negated in some way, and if not totally done away with by some technique, then it was certainly to be ignored. We are referring to the "interpersonal relationship process" construct. Probably the most sensible thing to do when a fact of human interaction won't go away is to face it squarely and find its meaning and usefulness. This we have tried to do.

The third process construct is one which we tried to avoid for a long time. We were at first unwilling to recognize more than a part of it. We didn't want to admit to ourselves, let alone to our professional colleagues, that this was an important part of our therapy. Here our multiple therapy experience played a part. We could not avoid knowing that at times in multiple therapy one therapist was observing what was going on between the other two persons.

For some time we puzzled over the meaning of what we then called the observer process. We could not make clear to ourselves how simply making observations could help another person.

Isn't it strange that we are so reluctant to say that we thought about those observations and arrived at some conclusions, even shared our thinking—in short, that we had an entirely cognitive, intellectual experience? Perhaps it is the admission that we are intellectual in therapy that is so threatening. But finally having admitted that much to ourselves, it seemed rather silly to insist that the therapist must not think. After that we were free to go on and expand the meaning to the therapeutic interaction of the observer process, which we now call the "rational process." The rational process, which begins with observing and goes on to include all the capacities of an intelligent human being to think, to fantasy, and to abstract, now becomes for us a viable dynamic form intertwined with the other two in the total process of helping a person to help himself.

Processes Separate Yet Intertwined: An Example. Talking about each of the three separate processes as though they were really separate is similar to assuming that one understands how a human being functions from knowing the organs and systems of the body. Let us try to understand the interaction among the three within a specific unit of communication before we look at and spell out the dimensions of any one of them. We can take as an example an experience of trying to tell another person how one looks at or observes one's own thought processes. At the same time there is involvement in that the other person has the same experience or at least says in what way his experiences are the same or different. One may begin by saying:

(1) "I am thinking about so and so" (rational), (2) "and as I think about it I remember the time that" (rational). (3) "I have a picture of" (rational/phenomenological), (4) "and I can almost smell the smells and hear the sounds" (phenomenological/rational). (5) "I can even feel the excitement" (phenomenological). (6) "I am telling you so you can know" (interpersonal). (7) "Where did I lose you?" (phenomenological/interpersonal); (8) "I thought you would understand that" (rational). (9) "I can sense that

you feel it too" (interpersonal/phenomenological), (10) "and that makes me feel good" (interpersonal/phenomenological).

The above sample of communication will be more meaningful if we specify why we have used the process labels in the way we have. We do not pretend to offer clear definitions of the processes because they may mean different things to different people. However, we think that it is important to separate thought from feelings and to be able to recognize when an experience of thinking is associated with feelings. Our earlier discussion of change provides a reason since from it we understand that change occurs when feelings are associated with the thought process and does not necessarily occur when thinking alone is involved.

A therapist's sensitivity to the presence of feelings with a thought then becomes of great importance. Thus we separate the rational process from the phenomenological rather generally on the basis of whether feelings are involved. In (1) there is a clear statement of thinking as there also is in (2), the statement about remembering. On the other hand, in (3), where fantasy is introduced, some feelings may be associated with the picture so that both the rational and phenomenological processes may be involved. We understand fantasy as a kind of linking experience between the purely rational and the feeling experience of the phenomenological process. The same is true of the more clearly sensed experience of smells and sounds in (4), which we have also labeled rational and phenomenological. In (5) a feeling is expressed, while in (6) the intent is to involve the other person. In (7) the involvement with the other person includes an awareness of his feelings and thus exemplifies another aspect of the phenomenological process. As an expressed thought (8) is a rational statement; under some conditions it could also be phenomenological. In (9) both the interpersonal and phenomenological are evident, and this is similar to (7), where the phenomenological is related to the other's feelings. Finally, (10) is an expression of the phenomenological experience of pleasure resulting from the impact of the other person, illustrating another dimension of the interpersonal process, i.e., the reciprocal effect.

In this unit of ten simple, short statements are intermingled all three processes and variants of each of them. We find the rational as thinking and remembering along with indulgence in fantasy; the interpersonal with its impact flowing from the speaker to the listener and back to the speaker; and the phenomenological process of the speaker, experienced both with respect to himself and to the listener. Even in such a contentless unit we see all three intertwined, reacting on each other and yet having separateness because, we believe, each serves a different purpose. The uniqueness of the function of each is more apparent in therapy than in other human interactions; at the same time it is true that all the separate functions are present in any meaningful human relationship.

To Go Back to Facilitation in Therapy Again. From the prior theoretical examples of the process constructs, let us move on to therapeutic examples of them. Let us consider again, for instance, impasses and their meaning. An impasse in terms of the process constructs is an interpersonal event which is resolved when it is recognized phenomenologically by the therapist, the client, or both. Before the feeling becomes clear, considerable interpersonal pushing and pulling, work, if you will, may take place in the course of the interpersonal-process effort to break the impasse. But nothing good happens until one or both persons have a phenomenological experience of recognizing the feeling involved, "We're trying too hard." Then it becomes possible to observe and think about the excessive effort, even to remember and relate back to a past experience and its meaning. As this occurs, the therapy is moving again.

Timing is another concept in which the process constructs can be identified. In timing there is an intent to have an interpersonal impact of a certain type. Also involved is what we have called therapist "sensitivity." Can we be more specific about how one is sensitive? Usually it has to do with paying attention to one's inner self, one's feelings about the client or the interaction with him, or one's fleeting fantasies. These we have identified with the phenomenological process. When a choice is involved (and timing clearly implies making a choice), then thought, reason, cognition, integration—all aspects of the rational process—come into play.

FROM HERE TO HUMAN DEVELOPMENT

The problem of ambivalence and its resolution offers an opportunity to illustrate how the processes interact with each other in therapy. In the example of the young man and the woman therapist, if his ambivalent feelings toward women are expressed and understood in relationship to the therapist, the client has a good chance of being able to confront his feelings in a real life situation. Further, a process of resolution, of change, is permitted because the emotional components are present. The interpersonal process generates the conflict and also permits it to be dealt with. The phenomenological process assures that ambivalent feelings will be experienced and accepted. And, finally, looking at and understanding the meaning of the experience both in the present and the past give the client a sense of understanding and mastery. This use of the rational process differs from interpretation in that resolution does not come out of intellectual understanding, according to our theory. Resolution comes from the interaction between the interpersonal and phenomenological processes, and the intellectual experiences come afterward.

We have been describing therapy in terms of some of the common therapeutic issues and showing how the processes which we have conceptualized can be identified and recognized. But still we must ask, "Why are these processes therapeutic?" Why should an interpersonal interaction, generously interlarded with a phenomenological experience and carefully kept thoughtful and rational, help a person who is disturbed? With these questions we became objective psychologists and removed ourselves from our subjective, intuitive approach to psychological problems as much as we are ever able to do. We looked at our empirical, working hypotheses about how people become disturbed and why others do not, and recognized that again we had been making assumptions about the developmental history of the people with whom we worked. We asked ourselves, then, what is the relationship between these three therapy processes and human development? It is not difficult to recognize these processes in adult interpersonal relationships, particularly if they seem to be relatively satisfying ones. But they must also be a part of the growing up experiences of children and must play an important part in whether they achieve psychological maturity and satisfaction as they develop into adults.

Certainly, the interpersonal process is clearly evident. Other personality theories have recognized and advanced the interpersonal aspects of development and impairment. What about the phenomenological process? Is it possible to think of growth and change in terms of phenomenological experiences and communication about them? It seemed to us that here we were further afield. We were dealing with interpersonal impact on phenomenological development. Then we turned our attention to the rational process. How do people, adults, come to use and depend on rationality, as obviously they do? This has been of large concern to educators, but we are less sure that a personality theory has been developed around a rationality theory.

In subsequent chapters we will present our efforts to formulate a partial theory of personality development oriented around the three therapy process constructs. We will also discuss the parallels we have seen between therapy as it progresses and the usual ongoing development of personality. While, as we have noted, in practice the processes are not separate, for the purpose of clarity of understanding it is appropriate at this point to treat them as though they were. We will begin, then, with phenomenology.

Chapter 4

Phenomenology: Living in the Internal World

By tracing single processes we can more clearly demonstrate our basic thesis that therapy recapitulates development—or more accurately, that it enters the development sequence to make repairs. Let us begin, then, to explore the phenomenological process and to explicate its meaning to us as therapists and to our clients as people in trouble.

We are phenomenologists in the sense that we believe the reality which matters most for us and for others is subjective and internal. When subjective reality is inconsistent with objective reality, the distress is also internal and subjective. We believe that change can occur and will occur phenomenologically, that is, in the subjective experience. Thus while a result of the subjective change may be a different kind of objective, interpersonal relationship, this added external environmental change is also known subjectively. The young man who had recognized some of his ambivalent feelings about his parents and went home to find that he could have a better relationship with them exemplifies this notion. What is the effect of our phenomenological view? It means, in large part, that we understand the behavior of others in terms of what they must be internally feeling and experiencing.

In contrast, a nonphenomenological approach would utilize more discrete, perhaps well-defined, constructs as a means of explaining behavior. As an example, the directions of thinking which can derive from the phenomenologist's observation that a person has "good access to his feelings" are quite different from those derived from a test score which indicates that the person is introspective or an introvert. Thus our initial bias is phenomenological, and we invite the reader to take a look at us and our clients from this point of view.

Phenomenology: Feelings and Change. As a therapy process, phenomenology needs a clear explanation of its scope and limits. Phenomenology involves knowledge and understanding of one's self and others from an inner frame of reference, whether it be emotional, cognitive, behavioral, or attitudinal. Primarily, however, the phenomenological therapist will be most interested in making clear for himself and his client the inner experience of feelings.

Our earlier discussion of the meaning of change suggests why feelings are of primary importance in therapy. Let us recall the example in which a person gains twenty pounds in a year. His phenomenal self may be unchanged although objectively he has become rather pudgy. He may even say he feels that his clothes are tight. But this is not the kind of feelings we are concerned about. We do not consider that his phenomenal experience has changed until he feels heavier and also experiences whatever other feelings about himself this recognition produces. If he feels different from what he was last year, whether he has a sense of being enhanced or of being less attractive, he is having a changed phenomenal experience of himself. He is changed with respect to his feelings about himself. Change, then, is associated with feelings about self.

Thus for the purpose of therapeutic change, the client's understanding of his inner experience generally needs to be directed to feelings rather than thoughts. We are particularly emphatic about this because we believe countless hours have been and continue to be spent recounting intellectual understandings about feelings; and this has no therapeutic impact because there is not a feeling in the entire process, only thoughts about feelings. Phenomenological this may be, but it is not therapeutic.

When Talking About Feelings Doesn't Result in Change. Yet another distinction needs to be made concerning the therapeutic phenomenological process. A help to us in understanding why talking about and mutually recognizing feelings does not always result in change has been our realization that feelings about an individual or event sometimes occur in more than one form. We have learned to recognize ambivalence because we have heard our clients talking at different times about two quite different feelings concerning the same person or experience; and we have learned to wait, to recognize and call attention to, the opposing nature of these feelings until our client could express them almost simultaneously. So feelings which somehow do not become resolved even though they are apparently understood and accepted may be ambivalent.

Feelings Are Different from Feeling States. Another distinction is of help. We have found it useful to think of feelings as different from what we have called feeling states. There *is* a difference. Naive people and clients talk about the two experiences as different; they recognize that being angry for a reason is different from being a hostile person, for example. In the same way, sadness at the death of a friend can be distinguished from depression. And although the phenomenal experience is sometimes confused, we frequently hear our clients struggle to distinguish their feeling states from feelings. Because of our own and our clients' struggles, we have tried to develop and clarify our understanding of the differences between the two and what the origins of feeling states may be. We add that talking about and re-experiencing a feeling state is usually a nonproductive experience.

Feelings Have Integrity. What can we say, then, about feelings to help us discern their distinctiveness? Feelings, we believe, have their own kind of fundamental accountability, or integrity; and because they do, they seem acceptable. We can say, "I am sad because . . ." and the simplicity of the relationship affords its own integrity. But feelings don't always occur in a simple way. As we have seen, feelings can be mixed—both good and bad—and can surprise us by their complexity. Feelings follow each other in a succession, being sometimes puzzling and often delightful. Their complexity contributes in an unmeasured degree to one's humaness as a person.

Yet all this complexity, even when the person does not understand it or is incapable of verbalizing it, can and often does include an experience which is integrating and therefore honest. When we have a feeling of which we are ashamed and which we want to deny, for us to be able to understand why we feel thus is somehow reassuring. For instance, if upon hearing of an accident to a friend one feels sorry and then glad, this can disrupt one's feeling of worthwhileness. It can, in fact, make one feel very guilty. But if the thought also occurs, "I've always been a little jealous," then the momentary feeling of gladness about the accident seems more human and acceptable, and the sense of guilt is lessened. So the possibility of assigning reasonableness to feelings may be one difference between them and feeling states.

Feeling States Control and Defend. The immediate origin of feeling states is much less clear than that of feelings, and the former frequently are accompanied by some discomfort, which suggests that all is not as clear and real as the person doing the alleged feeling has wanted to believe. In this respect feeling states lack the integrating quality of feelings and, we have thought, make a person feel somehow not quite honest.

We must try, then, to understand the source of this dishonesty. At times it stems from the fact that one set of feelings has been substituted for another. It is not uncommon to find that a very hostile, destructive person is one who is terribly frightened or deeply hurt; he behaves angrily so as not to experience the fear or hurt. Even euphoria by its very exaggeration suggests an under-lying tension that belies the reality of great happiness. And de-pression is recognized even by the depressed person as somehow not sadness but some little understood mixture of feelings which are not being clearly experienced or expressed.

A second aspect of feeling states which is a clue to their fundamental untrustworthiness is the fact that they interfere with interpersonal relationships. Perhaps they exist to disguise feelings between people. Sometimes they serve to control a re-lationship. That feeling states serve some purpose, certainly not well understood, is attested to by their perseverative quality. Both feelings and feeling states have interpersonal impact but in differ-ent ways. When one understands one's feelings, it is possible to do something; but a feeling state frustrates any but circular kinds of expression and often creates its own continuity. Feeling states serve to maintain a status quo, while feelings can effect change.

We understand the phenomenological process in therapy to be important in clarifying and differentiating between feelings and feeling states. In the case of feeling states, frequently the victims must understand their origins in order to free themselves enough to experience feelings.

"Owning": A Phenomenological Outcome. We have de-scribed the phenomenological process in therapy when it is an effective agent of change as a process dealing with feelings, but this is not the whole of it. There is also a phenomenological outcome or resolution called "owning." Phenomenological therapists have long talked to each other with very real understanding about this concept. It is an important one in that it denotes a feeling, atti-tude, or some kind of phenomenological entity which presents no conflict, thus distinguishing between this type of psychological event and that which is conflictive. It represents comfort as op-posed to discomfort, acceptance of self as opposed to defensiveness about some characteristic of self. In our earlier example the A student concerned about his grades could not be said to own his achievement. Resolution for him would include some kind of simple

acceptance that he is a good student and that he is satisfied with his accomplishment.

Something which is owned phenomenologically can be talked about but usually isn't because it isn't important enough in awareness. And we are implying here that entities in the phenomenological self are usually talked about, thought about, or worried about only if they are a source of conflict or discomfort.

Clear Identification Is Related to Owning and Integrity. We come, then, to another concept which we have placed in the phenomenological realm—that of identity. We recognize that working adults commonly identify themselves occupationally. We all have heard college students with problems in choosing a major say, "I don't know what I want to be" with an emphasis on the "be," which is a tip-off to a probable identity problem.

However, we believe that clear identification has most to do with an acceptance of self and a sense of integration phenomenologically. This may have some of its origins in job satisfaction, but it also may result in job satisfaction. And in the case of the college student it may lead to the ability to choose a compatible major. The person who says, "I have a great deal of trouble making decisions" or "I can't commit myself to anything" is usually not identifying himself as indecisive in useful, integrative ways. He does not own his indecision even though he sounds as though he has reconciled himself to it.

We emphasize that comfort or lack of distress does not necessarily indicate phenomenological integrity. However, self-acceptance or internal comfort arrived at after a period of stress or pain is quite convincing evidence that appropriate change and differentiation have occurred. For example, when one of a married couple changes in therapy, frequently the other seeks therapy too. The immediate cause of distress in this case is apt to be that he/she is no longer a satisfactory mate. The hurt is in the relationship rather than in the self. Some time may pass and some behavior change may occur before the person can experience the pain of the phenomenal self. Sometimes such a person will say,

"You know I don't think I've ever known how unhappy I was," clearly demonstrating that the previous comfort did not mean phenomenological integrity.

In speaking of phenomenological integrity and of "owning" one's feelings, attitudes, capabilities, and deficiencies, we are talking about the internal experience or awareness of one's true identity. Interestingly, we speak of a person as "knowing who he is" and, conversely, of another as "having identity problems."

With respect to a problem of sexual identification, we understand it phenomenologically as a state of being unsure about whether feelings and attitudes are appropriately masculine or feminine. Once such a person becomes clear about the nature and origin of his feelings, he no longer worries about whether they are masculine or feminine. We think that the pain comes from conflict over feelings which are unowned or undifferentiated or even unexpressed. We frequently see a young man who has a sense of conflict about his strength—and we mean here psychological strength—because he has perceived his father as a weakling and his mother as strong. He perpetuates his conflict by finding other men whom he sees as weak and relating himself to their weakness. He doubts his own masculinity because for him strength is always found in women.

It sometimes happens that the warmth, understanding of people, and affectionate feelings that a girl experiences she has found in her father. Her mother is constricted and preoccupied with controlling her own anxiety so that the girl feels close to and likes her father and may dislike women. She may express her conflict about being a woman to the point of wanting to have her father's profession and yet discover that she does not really want to be as totally committed as the profession requires.

If the young man learns from another man that men feel strong and if the young woman learns from another woman that women as well as men have these cherished feelings of warmth, understanding, and affection, each has clarified his phenomenological experience of himself as male or female with valued personal attributes. We believe that to say either the young man or young woman has mistakenly modeled after the wrong parent is to exacerbate the young person's doubts about whether he is masculine or feminine. Phenomenologically the experience may be, "I am a woman, but women I know don't feel the way I do. I wonder if I really am a woman." For the therapist to say, "You copied the wrong parent," will produce a lingering doubt about whether the self can ever have integrity and wholeness as a man or a woman. Or, to put it phenomenologically, masculinity and femininity are feelings about oneself, not attributes.

DIFFERENTIATION: A MAJOR
PHENOMENOLOGICAL CONCEPT

Differentiation of feelings has become an increasingly important therapeutic objective to us. For instance, feeling masculine can be differentiated from feeling strong or weak. Such phenomenological differentiation is a desirable, anxiety-reducing experience and, we repeat, a goal in therapy for some clients. What is the initial step in accomplishing such differentiation when a feeling state is controlling a client? The tangled, unclear, unspecified controlling experience of the feeling state is made manageable and meaningful when the feeling state is replaced by feelings in the present, which, as we have seen, are readily differentiated.

Differentiation Is for Therapists, Too. The therapist as well as the client must be internally differentiated. How can this differentiation occur? We begin by determining to allow the client to have as total and clear an impact on us as possible and by recognizing that this requires us to be internally differentiated ourselves. Or, to put it another way, we want to be able to give our full intellectual and affective attention to the client. However, sometimes feelings about some personal matter occupy our attention. Can we force ourselves to ignore the feelings and attend to the client? Probably not; it may take too much of an effort. The best way to remain intrapersonally differentiated is to attend for a time to our own feelings, whatever they are. As we do, let us say we discover that we feel rather anxious. The soliloquy goes like this:

Wonder what that's about? Well, guess I don't know, but let's see if it persists. The client seems anxious; ask about it. No, the client is feeling pretty good—guess it must be me. I'd like to hear about what is making the client happy; maybe that will help my anxiety. "Your feeling good is infectious. I can feel it, too. Isn't it nice that you had such a good time! It makes me feel good. I notice you're getting anxious. Am I making you anxious? Oh, I see you're thinking of terminating. I am anxious again, excited, sad, all at once. Perhaps my anxiety at first was because I sensed that this was coming."

We need go no further with the sequence except to point out that two kinds of differentiation are illustrated. The therapist's feelings are differentiated from the client's, and the intrapersonal feelings of each one are also differentiated. As a result of this separation by therapist and client, the feelings of each are modified by the feelings of the other.

Let us now pursue the sequence when differentiation is less clear.

I'm feeling anxious. The client seems anxious, too. Wonder what is wrong. "You say nothing? That seems strange because you seem very anxious to me. Let me see if I can't help you with it. Well, O.K., I guess if you don't feel it, you just don't *feel* it. Oh, you have been thinking of terminating? I wonder if you could be running."

Whether the anxiety is the client's or the therapist's and whether the client is, in fact, running by terminating are unanswerable questions. As therapists we generally behave in terms of the belief that if we attend to and own our feelings, then we have the experience described in the first sequence. We emerge differentiated and enlarged in contrast to the second sequence, in which we are more critical and are perhaps trying to wrest control.

Phenomenology Becomes Interpersonal. The two sequences above illustrate another concept which we, along with other therapists, find useful—the concept of interpersonal phenomenology. By speaking of interpersonal phenomenology we are merging two therapeutic processes which we have named as separate. Perhaps this is contradictory, but, on the other hand, we need to have some way of describing how the processes interact on each other.

In essence, we are talking about how people understand each other and, more than that, how they make that understanding have impact on each other. Suppose a client recounts to two therapists a particularly bitter, hurtful experience, as often happens in multiple therapy. The one therapist feels hurt and cries; the other feels angry. Both these feelings are equally appropriate even though different. We judge that the client had both feelings. Why did the first therapist experience one feeling and the second therapist the other? Our answer is that each therapist experienced his own feeling, the one most characteristic of him, and that each also felt what the other did but not so clearly or actively. If we are correct in our hypothesis that the client had the two feelings, hurt and anger, then it can be said that both therapists are empathic.

If the therapists change their feelings in some way—for instance, if the hurt one begins to feel helpful or the angry one becomes sympathetic—then the client may get help and sympathy. But he may feel very much alone with his feelings, since nobody else seems to feel as he does. He may feel that the therapists are sorry for him, which is degrading in a subtle kind of way.

We believe, then, that the therapist has to be able to be touched affectively and that the feeling which he understands in the client is the one like his own. Sensitive understanding of another person's feelings, we believe, is always essentially an awareness of one's own feelings which have been activated by the client.

We further believe that one gains this understanding of another by permitting oneself to be affected by, to respond with feeling to, all the clues which the client gives in expressing what he feels. And this can happen whether the client is aware of his feelings or not. Note we are not at this point saying anything specific about how the therapist should react in his own feelings to his client; we are simply saying that he should permit himself to have these feelings, if possible, and not to distort them. What he does with them we will be talking about in a later section of this chapter.

DIFFERENTIATION AND
DEVELOPMENTAL TASKS

So far in this book we have given considerable thought to how people learn about their feelings and discover that some may not be tolerated while others are acceptable. We have also considered how feelings become differentiated and why at times some are not well defined, tending to become confused with others.

In addition, we have observed that our theoretical, therapeutic processes occur in some form in human development. Furthermore, we have found ourselves making assumptions and inferences about human beings that rightly could be assigned to a personality theory. At this point, then, let us recount our thinking about how a person learns about his feelings in the usual developmental process.

Some Early Differentiations. In the developing human infant, inner experiences and the baby's reactions to them are the earliest manifest activity of the child. The baby cries and the mother responds with a bottle and/or a myriad of efforts to relieve some possible discomfort. Gradually the mother learns —and she may be the only person who knows—the difference between crying due to hunger, pain, desire for attention, etc. The infant teaches the mother and the mother in turn teaches the infant—in a clearly interactive process—the meaning of the infant's inner experience. Thus what begins as a global, undifferentiated feeling experience begins to be expressed differentially and responded to differentially. As the child grows and additional sensory and motor systems develop, discrimination between sensory and emotional experience becomes possible but may not occur unless the child and mother develop an interactive recognition of these differences. A young child can learn to say whether he is hungry or has a stomach ache.

Then with maturity and development of a wider range of emotional experiences these, too, become differentiated and named. For example, a crying child may be asked, "Are you hurt, or are you mad?" Since the mother is often interested in treating the hurt and therefore insistent that the child point out the injury, the child struggles to clarify his own feeling so that he can tell her and get what he needs. We also see how distortion and lack of clarity can occur in the differentiation. If the crying child is found to have no injury and the mother ignores or rejects the anger, soon he may develop pain where no injury is evident and learn to accept pain as the appropriate substitute for his angry crying. Or if the mother always assumes that crying in a young child means hunger, then it can be hypothesized that the overeating of the child at a later age and the accompanying obesity are evidence of an early failure of mother and child to differentiate sensory hunger pains from emotional feeling with the result that the two needs are permanently confused.

We can carry this train of thought a step further and speculate about some possible sex differences. Women and girls have been called intuitive and have appeared to have a range of differentiated, inner experience greater than or unlike that of men and boys. If we consider this phenomenon from the point of view that differentiation, therefore variability with respect to inner experience, is enhanced by an interactive recognition of shared inner experience, we may find an answer.

We are proposing that mothers are able to help their daughters understand their feelings more easily and completely than their sons. A mother interacting with her son to help him learn about his inner experience usually has only two alternatives. She may think that his inner experience as a male is exactly like hers and so is recognizable and understandable in the same way as hers. This attitude will leave him, if not confused, certainly doubtful. Or—and this approach probably occurs more often—she may say, "You are a boy and different, and I can't understand you too well." In view of the fact that most small boys have no other long-sustained or close, same-sexed source for helping them differentiate and understand their feelings, the relatively little aid they get from their mothers could account for the apparently smaller range of differentiated feelings they have as compared to their sisters.

It is interesting, too, that the names we give to feelings are finite. However, girls and women seem to have some kind of contact with or knowledge of their feelings which is not clearly verbal; yet it is understood and accepted among them as no great mystery, just not something they can communicate to males.

How Other Problems Develop. We have been hypothesizing about the development of differentiation of feelings and what is usual and "normal." There is an important dimension other than differentiation versus nondifferentiation, and this has to do with control of feelings—more exactly, control of expression of feelings.

The psychotic or the near psychotic experiences a fear of being overwhelmed by his feelings and appears to need help in controlling them. Somehow he seems not to have learned adequate ways of perceiving the limits of a feeling experience and fears that the limit will be reached only in self-destruction. And certainly some psychotics do carry their feeling expressions to this extreme.

But in the more usual developmental pattern the individual learns to control expression of feelings and discovers the limits of a feeling experience. This happens in a number of ways, some of which are more adaptive than others for an individual. There is the direct interference which says, "Don't be afraid," or "Don't be angry." On the other hand, there is the statement, "Boys don't cry; only babies cry," which does not say anything about whether boys have feelings. Such injunctions serve only to limit the way the individual can express his feelings. When we hear a young man say, "I am only mad when it's justified, and, well, I'm seldom mad," we begin to wonder whether this clear a limit on his feelings is as adaptive as he seems to think it is. It is as though anger is truncated by lack of a way to explain it.

In some families it is inappropriate to express affection. Perhaps the only talk of love has to do with an abstract love of God. Almost by default, the children grow up not knowing about their own experiences of giving and getting affection. Because little positive attention—perhaps even some negative attention—is given to feelings and their expression, the children "learn" that feelings and their expression are somehow bad.

A similar kind of failure to learn seems to account for some of the problems in sexual development. Here, as a result of a person's failure to recognize a sensory experience, the relationship between that experience and emotional concomitants can become hopelessly confused for him. How confused is evident when a young person who has begun to sort them out says, "You know I've been mixed up about sex. I thought all strong feelings were sexual."

If infants and young children learn to differentiate their feeling experiences through intimacy with their mothers or some other important older person, it is not too surprising that the experiences of sexuality are more frequently a source of trouble than the others. In our culture as a child grows older, intimacy with parents is replaced by activities in which the sharing usually has little to do with explanation of feelings. The interaction is no longer about how one feels but is more likely about how one did something. By the time a child begins to experience his developing sexuality, no cultural milieu exists within which he can explore and sort out his sexual feelings with another person. There is, in fact, a vast umbrella of silence and secrecy, which every child knows better than to break. Frequently, behavioral exploration with the peers takes place, but this is so taboo insofar as it relates to adults that its meaning—as comprehended through verbal understanding—often remains confused and guilt-ridden. We are not implying that we know how our society should go about teaching its children the meaning of their sexual development. We know much more about society's failures in this area than about how such learning can be successfully accomplished.

The failure of a child to differentiate because the adult with whom the child is most intimate is ambivalent and confused about his/her feelings is most striking. Suppose an eight-year-old rushes into the house saying, "Mom, Mom, I'm the best reader in the class!" His mother hugs him warmly and then says with anxiety in her voice, "You're feverish." Whether he is actually ill or not, his triumph and the expected pleasure from his mother's sharing are lessened by her anxiety. She has also communicated to him that he has, or should have, two feelings at once: pleasure in his accomplishment and anxiety over his physical state. This child may grow up to believe that he can never have a clear personal experience of success without having it spoiled in some way. The mother may not know the source of her anxiety, or her anxiety may be so great that it affects all her relationships so that she cannot have a clear feeling reaction to any single experience herself.

If the ambivalent experience is repeated often enough, the child may become anxious about telling his mother when he feels good about anything. He may even become anxious about feeling good. If emotional exuberance has some sexual origins, as has often been assumed, it is easy to see how confusion about sexually derived experiences, especially youthful primitive ones, can develop.

The "Acting-Out" Phenomenon.   In addition to those people who fail to differentiate clearly between specific feelings, we quite commonly find persons who not only do not differentiate but also do not seem to feel at all in the phenomenological sense which we have been discussing. We think first of the group of young adults whose behavior has been called "acting out." They are often promiscuous sexually, both heterosexually and homosexually. They may be the experimenters with drugs, freedom marchers, demonstrators, the highly rational, intellectual demanders of change who notwithstanding are unable to say what changes they want. We, along with others, have hypothesized that they are in some way the product of an era of so-called permissive child-rearing.

In understanding them, the most important thing to keep in mind may be that they do not clearly experience or differentiate their feelings. This is important because their behavior appears affectively motivated to a high degree. They seem to be caught up in carrying out an emotional experience, which indeed they are, but largely without experiencing the feelings. How can this be? If we go back to our notions of the way that infants learn to differentiate their feelings and think of what permissiveness might mean in the process, we find a way to think about the problem. The word "permissiveness" as used by mothers usually means permissiveness to express oneself. Expressing oneself is, among other things, a behavioral experience. It is not necessarily a feeling experience alone; in fact, it is seldom such.

One small child when asked, "Why do you cry so loud?" answered with complete honesty, "Because it gets me what I want." Yet the cry was anguished and sounded as though it expressed a clearly understood feeling experience. The adults who responded apparently misinterpreted the meaning, that is, they responded to the seeming anguish rather than simply to the wanting. Apparently to some parents, permissiveness with regard to feelings means permissiveness with regard to behavior. When such is the case, the child with no other cues to his feelings and their meaning then learns to identify his feelings through his behavior without experiencing and recognizing feelings and behavior as potentially separate and different.

Let us see if we can work out how this may happen. One common idea in permissive child-rearing is that babies should eat and sleep on demand and that time schedules for baby care should largely be abandoned. No doubt there is a great deal of sense in this notion, but it does not take into account the infant's interaction with the rest of the family. He may be alert and stimulated by the older members so that his need for sleep, for example, may seem unimportant to him. If he becomes fussy and is put to bed by his mother, he may create such a disturbance that he is able to convince someone that he is lonely and not sleepy. Families, especially those with only one child, find themselves tyrannized by an infant's unwillingness to be put to bed before everyone else retires. The child experiences an undifferentiated misery since no meaningful, consistent limits are set. Thus permissiveness, which should enhance differentiation, can lead instead to confusion and distress.

Young adults who act out are characteristically rather unanxious and insist that they do not feel guilty. If the therapist says to the client, "In order for us to understand what is troubling you, you will have to stop [whatever the client is doing], the client will experience anxiety and need help in dealing with it. On the other hand, if he breaks the prohibition, he is apt to feel quite guilty in his relationship to the therapist. This lends support to the theory that in such cases the parents have not set meaningful behavioral limits, and it negates the notion that these clients are incapable of interpersonal concerns. The first step in working with these young people is to give them an experience of their own personal feelings and to help them to know the feelings as their own. They are frequently surprised to find that the feelings involved in the sexual acting out are much less real than the feelings they have about promises made and broken by their parents, for example.

Because acting-out clients do not have feelings that they readily connect with their acting out, they frequently do not seek help voluntarily, or they seek it for some other reason. Working with them presents the special problem of acquainting them with their phenomenological experience.

Clients who act out pathologically are not the only ones who do not know about their feeling experiences. There is some evidence that large numbers of people carry on their daily living with a minimum of attention to what they feel. That they sometimes need and seek help because they don't understand themselves adequately is also true. We have hypothesized that they are well aware of their behavior and generally exercise appropriate controls; and when they seek help, they seem to be somewhat bewildered to find that they have problems. The confusion appears to be related to their unawareness of feelings. Their behavior, in contrast to that of the acting-out client, has been appropriate, and they are dismayed to learn that they have emotional difficulties.

DEVELOPMENT: RATIONAL
AND IRRATIONAL

Irrationality is generally assumed to be a significant aspect of the human experience of impulses and feelings. Further, it is usually assumed that in the very young, impulses and feelings are without limits or controls. Learning rationality and limits and controls with respect to feelings is one of the basic tasks of socialization and is largely accomplished within the family, although institutions such as the school play a significant part. Some of the common familial, institutional, social, and cultural means of attempting to help the person to be rational and appropriately controlled in self-expression seem often to go awry. In fact, we are much inclined to believe that many human interactions result in increased irrationality, feeling states rather than feelings, heightened maladaptive anxiety, and less control rather than more as the young person grows up. How can it be that good intentions can turn out so badly?

For some possible insights we turn again to consider the child as he develops through his interactions with his parents, siblings, and others. For example, many human problems apparently arise from inappropriate adult assumptions about the nature and function of impulses, feelings, rationality, irrationality, and limits or controls. The inappropriate or inaccurate assumption of adults, of course, stem from the forces, influences, and interactions which have shaped the adult's personality and knowledge of his own impulses, feelings, and behavior controls. Thus the links are formed for passing on personality characteristics and behavior patterns from generation to generation.

Some Distortions Occur. More concretely, what can happen with feelings and impulses? The feeling of anger provides an instructive example. Let us assume that a man has learned that the direct expression of anger is destructive and therefore should not be indulged. Or it may even be that the feeling is so terrible or potentially destructive that he must deny its reality, the fact that it can be experienced, let alone expressed. What will such a man do when confronted by the fact that his son can be angry? It seems highly unlikely to us that this father can permit, or perhaps even recognize, the reality of the son's anger. He may insist on and succeed in mislabeling, distorting, or even substituting another feeling—guilt, for instance. At what price? The price, we think, is often the distortion of reality for both son and father with consequent internal confusion and feelings of inadequacy in knowing what is real about themselves and others.

Let us use another example of anger to illustrate how reality can be distorted. If a father is angry with his son over the son's misbehavior and if the father, for reasons of his own, must deny or too firmly control his anger, then the son must necessarily have a perception whose reality he doubts. The son originally knows that his father is angry, but since denial or distortion by the father occurs, the son may in turn be impelled to deny or distort his own perfectly good, original perception of the fact that father is angry.

Children are, we believe, astonishingly good observers of feelings in others, in large part, perhaps, because they originally have excellent contact with their own feelings. Children do not often misperceive their own feelings or impulses or the feelings of others until they have been "helped" to misperceive, mislabel, or distort by others. Expressions such as "Out of the mouths of babes" reflect our uneasy adult awareness that the child is perceptive and that his contact with the world of feelings may often be better than our own. What mother, for instance, has not been deeply concerned over the possibility that her child would burst out the truth about some fraudulent or distorted interaction between adults, perhaps even interactions between father and mother? Such threat to adults can lead to determined, and often successful, efforts to change the child's perceptiveness about himself and others so that he feels, thinks, perceives, and speaks not as he is but as adults wish him to.

We accept the fact that to some extent such efforts to change the child are necessary in order to "socialize" him so that he will be able to live in the world we all live in. However, we believe that much can go awry, that some human problems are increased rather than decreased, and that some valuable human attributes are lost or diminished by some of the methods of socialization. It is our belief that perceptiveness, the ability to observe (if that is different from perceptiveness), fantasy life and imagery, access to emotional life, rationality, and personal and interpersonal adequacy are changed by what we do with and to each other as we grow up. Many of the efforts undoubtedly enable us to function better as human beings. Yet many others are adverse.

Feeling States and Affection. Let us illustrate further some of the subtleties we refer to by examining a few of the means by which we give and get affection from others. Ordinarily we may think, for example, that an emotionally "deprived" child is simply not loved by others. That may be true, but such an explanation is often inadequate to encompass the more complex and subtle meanings. The assumption, for instance, implies that the deprivation lies wholly in not being sufficiently loved and ignores the possibility that not being able to give affection is also depriving. In our view, both are equally valid. To put it simply and concretely, a child may enjoy and be deeply satisfied by a hug from mother, and he may equally enjoy and be satisfied by the reciprocal experience of hugging mother.

Affection giving and taking can be distorted and impaired in many ways. In fact, it is in connection with impairment of affection giving and taking that, we believe, feeling states often occur and tend to become fixed in the human personality. It is interesting to note, for instance, how an individual who is subject to depression as his characteristic feeling state will quickly become manifestly depressed when confronted by painful, anxiety-producing stimuli. Thus he may more or less successfully defend himself against the experience of pain and anxiety, and need we say how maladaptive depression ordinarily is?

How are the development of feeling states related to interference in the processes of affectional give-and-take? We turn again to mother and child interactions as sources for gaining some understanding here. It is rather common, for instance, for mothers to be overburdened and to need support and affection from those around them, including their children, and a child is well capable of knowing mother's need.

Let us suppose, however, that mother is threatened by the power of her own need. She may then respond to her child in ways which deprive her of the support and affection needed. At

the same time her behavior may have a destructive effect on the
child's feelings about himself as someone who can be supportive
and loving. In the same way the child's affection-taking capacity
is likely to be damaged since a deprived and needy mother is
seldom able to give affection and support freely and consistently
—if at all. Thus a damaged affection-taking and affection-giving
capacity can be passed on from parent to child. The common
concomitant feeling states engendered in the child are inferiority
or inadequacy, particularly in regard to affection giving and taking; guilt; and/or depression; or buried and continued feelings of
hostility.

It is often true that the feeling state or states which become
characteristic of the child are still present or readily available in
the adult as a primary means of self-expression and defense. But
how is our adult likely to appear to others in more particular ways?
There are many possibilities, of course, but we will mention those
which seem especially salient.

If the maintained feeling state is inferiority or inadequacy, then
our adult may be harassed by a deeply felt need to help and care
for others, and an equally strong doubt about his ability to help
and care effectively. (Remember how much in need mother was
and also how she couldn't or wouldn't be helped?) Further, our
adult is likely to have serious questions about his capacity to
love, to marry, or may even wonder whether he is sexually potent.
Along with his doubts about himself as a carer or a lover, he is
likely also to question whether he is someone who can be loved or
cared about. Thus the woman or women, if any, in his life may
find themselves puzzled, even bewildered, by his anxious, tentative approaches, which are so often followed by equally anxious,
disorganized retreats.

Both the approaches and retreats seem rather irrational. Yet
the irrationality appears to us to be most related not to the impulses to love, to care, or to be close, but rather to the self-criticalness and inhibitions learned so long ago in relationship to mother
who could neither take nor give. Stated another way, mother's
irrationality is passed on to the child and is, in our view, more

closely related to inhibition of feelings and impulses than to their expression.

If the retained characteristic feeling state of the adult is guilt or depression, what may he be like to himself and to others? His internal phenomenological experience of himself is likely to be that of impairment or defectiveness. He may achieve, and yet he remains prone to feeling impaired. Accomplishments are "added on" rather than incorporated as part of himself. Whatever he achieves, he minimizes, instead of feeling pleased and accepting of himself and his accomplishment. He is likely to be compulsively active, and yet he may be continually undoing himself, thus maintaining his defectiveness. Further, the approach of success may be quickly reversed by sudden, self-induced guilt and depression. In such ways does our guilty, depression-ridden adult maintain himself. And how does this same adult affect others? What is likely to be his interpersonal effect? We are constantly struck by the likelihood that he affects others much as he affects himself. They are diminished rather than enhanced by knowing him. The guilt and depression seem almost infectious; they appear to rub off on his associates. Guilt in him seems to produce guilt in others.

How does it happen that guilt as an emotional experience can become a relatively fixed, basic facet of a human personality? Further, how is it that as an interpersonal phenomenon guilt is often shared between persons or at least transferred back and forth between persons? The richness of language—in this instance our own English language—suggests both a way to explain this and a way to draw an important distinction. Most of the time words and language serve people well to express their meanings and themselves. Yet at times, it seems to us, important distinctions in the meanings of words that express internal experience are lost or distorted. Further, the distortion occurs very often in the emotional realm, or "feeling" aspects, of human experience. Interestingly enough, the distortion seems also to be highly related to interpersonal—"between persons"—interactions. How can this be and how can we make what we wish to say more clear?

Let us begin with the proposition that the words "guilty" and "guilt" do not have and should not have the same meaning and, further, that a distinction between the emotional, or feeling, concomitants of the two words should be made. "Guilty" means a feeling which can and should be experienced, which serves to tell us something we should know, and yet which passes, for it is a feeling and not a feeling state.

"Guilt," on the other hand, to us denotes more clearly a feeling state and as such is more fixed, enduring; and paradoxically the person is likely to feel it as the "way he is" and yet at the same time feel that the experience of guilt is both irrational and intolerable. It is in connection with efforts to lift the near intolerable burden of being guilt-ridden that much can go awry interpersonally and phenomenologically. Mislabeling can occur, for instance. Or since such a feeling state as guilt is strong, the substitution of another way of feeling and expressing may only relieve and not change the guilt. It is not uncommon for the guilt-ridden person to do something for which he now is and should feel guilty. Thus the feeling state becomes temporarily a feeling and understandable because there is now a reason for feeling guilty. Yet the underlying feeling state remains and recurs to be dealt with again and again.

The substituted way of expression may deceive both the person himself and those who relate to him incidentally. Anger, for instance, is a commonly substituted expression for the guilt-ridden person and may be his way of attempting to alleviate the intolerable burden while the anger serves also, paradoxically, to maintain the feeling state of guilt, which is the "way he is."

Friends, and therapists as well, have often been confused by the powerful pull for help they feel from the guilt-ridden, accompanied by even more powerful angry defenses of the feeling state. While guilt may be intolerable, it is also familiar to the person, known, regarded as "the way I am," and in this sense it has its own peculiar "coping" qualities. Dynamically, we propose that with guilt, as with other feeling states, the approach of helpful friend or therapist precipitates a concern that guilt, hostility, or some other feeling state will be even more sharply and intolerably experienced. That this is plausible psychologically is explained by the probability that the feeling state has become known to the person, fixed, and well incorporated during earlier significant interpersonal relationships.

Thus the approach by another, be he friend or therapist, stimulates defense of the near intolerable, yet precariously balanced, system of "adjusted maladjustment" so characteristic of feeling states. It is as though help is asked for, sometimes desperately sought, and then the approaching helper is powerfully attacked, even rejected. The person seems to say, "You won't help me. You'll hurt me just like those others did. Better just keep things the way they are for I've been hurt enough." In a way our help-seeking person is right in his surmise that help may hurt, for it is true that as he becomes more sharply aware of himself as he is and perceives something of how he has become so, he may well come to feel deeply deprived, terribly hurt, frighteningly angry, and so on.

Yet if the therapeutic venture is successful, the sharp, clear, heightened feelings, fantasies, and imagery seem to break up and dissolve the frozen, truncated, near intolerable yet tolerable state of being that is a feeling state. In a way rationality is restored, for feelings, fantasy, and imagery can be more fully felt and known, and yet at the same time the "stability" of flow and change can be known and felt with pleasure and with manageable, appropriate anxiousness. A recent client so well said: "I can feel guilty, but it passes, for it tells me what to do rather than what to avoid. I get angry, but I don't feel hostile. I can hurt, but it passes. People can be close to me and I to them. I even feel lovable rather than having to justify my unlovableness. My feelings change, but they're reasonable. I'm not going to overwhelm or be overwhelmed by anyone. I manage rather than being managed. I can choose rather than feel only obligated—that I should or that I must."

Feelings Can Be Rational. We have yet to make clear how feelings—now distinguished, we trust, from feeling states—are related to the experience of being rational and reasonable. To begin with, feelings are neither inherently rational nor irrational, yet a feeling has a reason for being.

Certain kinds of interactions can lead the individual to attach irrational meaning to his feelings; they can often even make him believe that the feelings do not have a reason for being. Further, too much interference (rather than too little) or inappropriate interference with the experiencing and expressing of feelings is ordinarily what leads to feeling states and consequent irrationality. Also, it seems that often it is the interference by others that is irrational rather than the feeling as originally experienced by the individual. Yet the feeling, experiencing individual "learns" that his feeling is irrational rather than that those who interfere with him may be unreasonable. The problem becomes the child's by means of an adroit, interpersonal transfer, thus perhaps temporarily relieving a parent, for instance, of the problem which his own irrationality created in the first place. The parent, in one sense, gets rid of his problem by giving it to the child. Yet, of course, the parent does not often truly rid himself of his problem or conflict. A common ultimate consequence is that parent and child become irrational together, and each keeps the same problem because neither can resolve it.

SOME PHENOMENOLOGICAL PROCESSES IN THERAPY

Our prior discussion of feelings, impulses, feeling states, rationality, and irrationality enables us to write more directly about phenomenological processes as they may occur in therapeutic interactions. In this section we will focus our attention on the probable necessity for certain phenomenological changes and consider something, too, of how the changes may occur. We will call attention to the phenomenological "phenomena" which occur within the therapist. These internal happenings are, in part, interactive between the client and therapist and may or may not prove useful to the therapeutic venture, as we shall try to show.

To communicate we shall need, in addition to the concepts we have already developed including timing and set, some new concepts. "Sensitivity" is one. Sensitivity, as a concept which helps us to understand something of the nature of human beings, has some interpersonal as well as rational or objective connotations. But we are concerned at this time with the phenomenological aspects of human sensitivity.

Ambivalence and Seeking Help. Let us return, for the moment, to the consideration of how a client may think and feel within himself about the prospect of changing himself—particularly when he approaches us for help. A client who seeks help with his emotional problems is necessarily ambivalent, as we have suggested earlier. His ambivalence may be expressed by honest efforts to engage us, the therapists, in such a way as to enable him to change, to feel better, to be more alive, and so on. Yet at the same time he is very likely to resist our efforts to help, sometimes immediately, certainly as the relationship develops.

Resistance to our efforts to help is experienced by the client, and by us therapists, too, in some ways that are primarily phenomenological. Therapists resist, too, and either client or therapist may be phenomenologically aware of the therapist's resistance. In fact, it is not uncommon, we think, for the therapist to attribute his resistance to the client. Further, clients can sometimes clearly perceive that a therapist is in some ways denying or resisting a phenomenological awareness in himself.

Sensitivity: A Reciprocal Matter. We propose, first of all, that sensitivity has several aspects. Further, we suggest that clients as well as therapists are sensitive. Also, we think that sensitivity can be used facilitatively or destructively by either or both participants in the therapeutic relationship. We can best describe our understanding of sensitivity and its phenomenological nature by discussing some sequences which occur in interactions between clients and therapists. In doing so we will utilize the concepts of set, timing, resistance, ambivalence, feelings, and feeling states, as well as sensitivity.

The set by the therapist to understand, accurately reflect, and clarify the client's phenomenal thoughts and feelings is, as we have suggested earlier, a basic way in which we therapists can

facilitate the development of a potentially therapeutic relationship. However, we have also suggested that such a set and its
implementation are often insufficient to lead to the changes the
client needs and ambivalently wants to make. Further, we therapists have the expectation, even the need, to help the client
change. We do not like to settle for less. Yet the change must
occur in the client, and it is most difficult to force change upon
our receptive, needy, but sometimes ambivalent and resistant
client. The change must be phenomenologically "his," although
we can assist by proper timing and sensitive awareness. Sadly
enough, our greatest therapeutic wisdoms may be of little use
unless we can find ways to use our sensitivity so that the client
can have the phenomenological feeling of choosing, making, and
owning the changes he desires.

Generation of a Conflict and an Impasse. Now let us turn
to some sequences of thoughts and feelings to see if we can illustrate how the paradoxical and sensitive accomplishment of
helping a person to make his own changes can take place. A
sequence, simplified for purposes of illustration, may go somewhat
as follows. The therapist may become increasingly aware that his
client is often depressed and that the feeling state of depression
functions to prevent phenomenological awareness in the client
of another feeling such as sadness, hurt, pain, or anger. But the
therapist's awareness that his client's depression may be defensive
comes rather late in the sequence, we think.

What are some of the prior steps in the process? We hypothesize, first of all, that for the client his depression is phenomenologically real and that the probable defensive or denying
component is not real or known to him. Further, he has a powerful need to convince us that he is depressed because that is the
only phenomenological awareness available to him. In a certain
sense our client can be a person to us and to himself only by
being depressed. Put another way, the available alternative to
depression for the client may be an experience of "nothingness,"
which is even more frightening. What happens then?

Several possible alternatives for the therapist exist, but very often it seems that we experience our own personal variant of depression. We may, for instance, feel hopeless, constricted, and quite internally undifferentiated much as our client does. Such a state of affairs may continue for both client and therapist for some time. We are inclined to think that long duration of such a symbiotic and distressing relationship is nearly always therapeutically undesirable. However, we do think that a client and a therapist experiencing depression together, each in his own way, serves dynamic purposes.

These are at least twofold. Client and therapist, if they both experience depression, have at least experienced something together, and that may facilitate the relationship and be both reassuring and distressing. The reassurance, we think, grows from the sharing and the sense of commonality. The distress, too, is shared, and this sharing can be peculiarly comforting. Further, the sharing and similarity may be dynamically reminiscent of past and present relationships with significant others for both client and therapist. In this symbiotic relationship intimacy, closeness, sharing, and commonality are present and felt phenomenologically, but separateness, coping, adaptiveness, and change are not felt.

A conflict is thus often generated and may become an impasse. Yet embodied in the dynamic reenactment, powerfully felt by both participants, is the means for phenomenological enlargement and differentiation. Either participant, or the two of them together, may recognize both the futility and the opportunity they have recreated together.

Sensitivity and Resolution of the Conflict. Clients cannot necessarily be expected to know how to rectify a relationship so that change and differentiation can ensue, but in our functioning population it can and does happen. We are happily (if somewhat uncomfortably) reminded of the client who said, "I wish you'd quit trying so hard to help me. I'm not as depressed as I was, and, besides, it's only a game I played with mother. She only liked me and paid attention to me when I was depressed." But while most clients cannot be so clearly and directly helpful as the one just cited, they do usually tell us something of how we, the therapists, may need to be.

How we hear, react to, and are sensitive to what the client says or does can make a critical difference in whether the eventual outcome is continued impasse or change and differentiation. For instance, while our depressed client may be comforted and our relationship facilitated by sharing depression, he is also likely to complain and to be critical of us, the therapists, because he is not changing. Criticism from a client can be a shock or at least a surprise. Because we have been deeply involved with our client, which has been necessary in order for the relationship to develop and the conflict to generate, a shock or surprise may be required to signal us that the time for change has come.

What we therapists do and feel after being shocked is, of course, most important. Commonly we think that we have erred— and so we have in a way. Yet it is our "error" which has facilitated the relationship and generated the conflict. If, as therapists, we feel unduly guilty over our error, we are likely to continue the impasse, for we may become inappropriately angry at the client or may simply try harder (the effort syndrome) in the same ways.

We think that the client's demonstrated ability to shock and to distress us is a signal to us to reassess what we are doing rather than to feel unduly guilty. We think, then, of the client's criticism as being his way of telling us that it is time for us to change the nature of our relationship with him. Further, interestingly enough, we think that the phenomenological sense of shock, surprise, or startlement provides us with the opportunity to begin enlarging and differentiating ourselves so that we may know how to set our relationship on a new course.

Whether or not, as therapists, we turn our sense of shock or surprise to therapeutic advantage depends in large part on the kinds of thoughts and feelings we permit ourselves to have, what kind of phenomenological enlargement we allow ourselves. If we think and feel that being attacked or criticized by clients is bad in some basic way, we are not likely to allow our surprise to be useful. In fact, it is not probable that we will permit our own phenomenological enlargement to occur, or to "turn on," as today's young people so clearly say is necessary. However, if we are appropriately sensitive and are able to permit ourselves to grow internally, we are likely to be able to communicate in new ways with our client and to have new effects upon him. Our client will also grow and have new, different thoughts and feelings appropriate to him. We, client and therapist alike, are also likely to feel that our relationship has grown and shifted to a new level. Too, our sense of separateness and respect for each other is likely to be enhanced.

One additional thing needs to be said about our expectations that our clients will have an effect on us. We believe that our willingness to be affected often constitutes a significant dynamic difference not present in the client's earlier significant relationships. It is as though a significant other has been affected in a way which did not occur in the past. In a sense the client may have finally changed his parent, if a parent was or is involved, in a way which may be important.

Sensitivity and Regression. Now we need to consider further some of the operational ways in which a therapist can sensitively handle phenomenological awareness in himself and his client. Generally we are inclined to think that therapeutic relationships suffer from too little of such awareness rather than too much. Sometimes it is thought that such awareness should be maximal in the client and minimal in the therapist. While we agree that the primary intent of therapeutic relationships is to help the client, we also emphasize that the practice of therapy must be a growing, changing, exciting matter for the therapist. It is in the therapist's own phenomenal awareness that this sense of excitement and constant growth are to be found. Further, as we have been suggesting, it is the therapist's ability sensitively to permit and to use his own awareness which can often be most facilitating for client, therapist, and their relationship.

Thus we have said that phenomenological awareness in the therapist is most necessary and yet that at times it may be difficult to achieve. Our use of the word "achieve" here suggests a partial answer to the dilemma. As we understand it, phenomenological awareness is likely to be blocked or truncated by effort rather than facilitated. How then, can such awareness occur most productively? In a basic way we think that phenomenological awareness often is best enabled by controlled yet free regression in us, the therapists. Too, we believe that if we therapists can be reasonably free to have our own thoughts and feelings, then by our example and the consequent interaction we have with our client, he may be freer to have his own thoughts and feelings, whatever they may be. Thus in a primary way our own ability to "know ourselves" can, in turn, be most freeing, supporting, and reassuring to our client.

Therapist Regression: A Facilitator.   But the notion of regression is frightening isn't it? Furthermore, isn't it the client rather than the therapist who regresses and in the process finds out about himself? Isn't regression anxiety-producing? Yes, of course, regression can be frightening and anxiety-rousing, and it is also usually true that clients may need to regress in order to better know themselves. But if clients learn about themselves through regressing, may this phenomenon not be useful for therapists, too? We think so, and perhaps we can make the notion that therapists should regress, understandable and a bit less frightening.

Let's use the example—a common one we have used before— of an attractive young woman seeing a male therapist. We think it is rather natural that as this relationship develops, sexual feelings may become a part of the relationship. It is generally expected and even thought to be therapeutically necessary for the young woman to develop sexual feelings about the therapist. And so it may happen. But, alas! Our therapist may also find himself having some rather strong feelings, sexual in nature, toward his client. What does he do? There are a number of possibilities, of course. He may simply deny all his feelings, and that commonly happens. Or when he finds himself partially or "pre-consciously" aware of his feelings, he may feel quite anxious. Certainly other possibilities exist, but these two will suffice for our purposes.

The therapist who successfully denies his feelings is very likely to record a failure. Further, the client is likely to feel more distressed about herself than ever. Yet she may have little notion why this is so. Our therapist, on the other hand, may well defend himself and his failure by thinking to himself that his client is a seductive, castrating wench. He may even so describe her to his friends and colleagues. Dire predictions about her further devastating effects on men may be indulged in privately or publicly as the case may be. We are inclined to agree, in such an instance as this, that castration has occurred, psychologically speaking at least. But it seems to us that the surgery has been performed by the therapist himself rather than by the client. Unfortunately the client may be all too ready to assume that she has such an omnipotent power for she has probably had similar prior outcomes in her relationships with men.

But to return to our denying therapist, what leads him to deny his feelings? There are a number of possibilities, but at this time we are primarily concerned with the phenomenology of the matter. Commonly, in our opinion, the therapist's problem resides in a fundamental self-criticalness that is both inappropriate and highly punitive, punitive first toward himself and secondarily toward others. However, to observers the punitiveness appears to be directed more toward others than toward self. However, we believe that the self-punitiveness is primary and that it is denied or projected. How many males can stand the awareness that they may be symbolically amputating their own genitalia? We also think that the self-criticalness pertains not only to sexual thoughts and feelings but also to feelings and thoughts of most kinds except possibly hostility and anger. Moreover, we note that the hostility and anger are likely to be truncated and impotent.

Basically, the problem with our denying therapist is not so much that he denies sexual feelings as that he very likely denies feelings of all kinds, including anxiety. He thinks much; in a certain sense he is very rational. Yet his very denial of his feelings is a very irrational behavior. Apparently the nearing emergence into awareness of some feeling, be it sexual or some other, triggers the denying mechanism. Nor is anxiety likely to be useful to our denying therapist, for he is very likely to deny that most useful of all feelings, too! Worse yet, phenomenological differentiation is continually circumvented because the affective avenues to internal enlargement are constantly being closed off. Such a therapist tends to do the same things to his clients that he does to himself. Hence they tend to remain phenomenologically constricted and undifferentiated just as he is. Apparently regression, in the controlled and useful sense, is largely unavailable to this therapist.

The second therapist, who at least can be anxious and cannot too easily rid himself of his tension, is a more hopeful possibility. Why should this be? Isn't anxiety something that therapists shouldn't feel or at least something they should rid themselves of as soon as possible? We think not, for we view anxiety as a signal that something else needs to be felt, phenomenologically differentiated, and rationally integrated later. Supervisory or consultative help may be necessary to this therapist, and we accept this possibility.

But let us see what our anxious therapist may be able to do for himself. The first key step in his self-help depends on whatever ability he has to be anxious and to recognize the feeling for what it is: anxiousness with its sweaty palms, dripping armpits, dry mouth, accelerated heart rate, or whatever. Further, it may be too much to expect our anxious therapist to know more than that he is anxious while his client is with him.

But if our therapist has somehow learned that being anxious can be useful, he may retain his anxiousness after his client leaves. Then, as he sits alone in his office, with the door closed perhaps, he may be able to let himself go further, affectively speaking. What feelings and thoughts come to him? Many, perhaps, but in our example he is likely to become aware that he has sexual feelings about his client. Now what? Denial may occur or at least there may be guilt and likely more than a little self-criticalness. Two primary possibilities emerge for our anxious therapist at this point. He may, with the aid of his guilt and self-criticalness, suppress and deny both his sexual feelings and his anxiety. The further consequence of this phenomenological direction in our therapist is that almost certainly the sequence of feelings just described will recur again: anxiety, sexual feelings, guilt, self-criticalness, and further efforts at denial and suppression.

But it is in this recurrent cycle of feelings that the second primary alternative begins to emerge. Our therapist, by himself or with supervisory or consultative help, may develop some phenomenological awareness that the cycle has recurred at least once, perhaps several times. Such an awareness is the beginning of differentiation. Further, with such awareness there can be hope that the cycle of feelings and impasse may be broken. How? In a number of different ways probably, but we have been repeatedly impressed by the usefulness of therapist curiosity at such a time.

What do we mean by curiosity? We mean primarily puzzlement, wonderment, and yet an inquiring bent or set which says, "I wonder why I feel the way I do? I wonder, too, why I don't feel some other ways?" Thus our therapist may begin to puzzle and to be curious about himself and even become clearly aware that his reactions and feelings are cyclical. Also, in spite of the possible affective power of his anxiety and sexual feelings, he is also probably experiencing effort and constriction. We are inclined to think that recognition of effort and constriction may be a more immediately important and useful clue for our therapist than his awareness of the cyclical nature of his feelings. What may our therapist do with his new awarenesses? He may, of course, simply continue to be puzzled, or he may try harder with the result that he simply increases his effort and his constriction. But there are other possibilities. For instance, our therapist may find it possible to relax and to "break" his effortful, constricted, attention to himself and his feelings through a conscious intent to do so.

We think that each person must find his own way of breaking his constricted awareness and of thereby accomplishing the "task" of relaxation. The male member of our team finds, for instance, that looking out his office window, sitting back in his chair instead of leaning forward, or closing his eyes are all ways of behaving which are potentially useful. We think such behaviors are facilitative both when the client is present and after the client has gone. We believe they are useful for two reasons.

Therapist Fantasy and Imagery: Another Facilitator. First of all, the intensity of the interpersonal relationship between the therapist and the attractive young woman is likely to be lessened, and the affective power of the constricted feelings also lessened. Second, relaxation may make imagery and fantasy more available to the therapist.

In a later chapter we will expand upon the notion that human experiencing of oneself often runs a course from kinesthetic sensations, to feelings (which we often label and identify), and finally to imagery and/or fantasy. What often seems to happen when "labeled" feelings are strongly felt is that the flow of experience is truncated or even fixated at the stage of the labeled feelings. When this occurs, "contact" with or awareness of kinesthetic sensations and imagery is lost or diminished.

At such a time, changing posture, looking out an office window, or closing the eyes can bring relaxation to the therapist, and relaxation tends to restore the flow of experience. Awareness of kinesthetic sensations or tensions can then occur; a wider range of thoughts and feelings becomes available; spontaneous imagery and/or fantasy can be experienced. It is as though breaking or altering the intense interpersonal interaction with the client restores separateness and enables the therapist, and his client also, to be enlarged and relieved by having their own more separate experiences instead of being controlled by each other in the intense, interpersonal relationship.

With relaxation and the restoration of separateness, more becomes available within the therapist, perhaps within the client also. For instance, our therapist, if he is able to relax and restore his separateness either while his client is still with him or after she is gone, may be astonished by what occurs. He is likely to become aware of how tense and anxious he has been. Further relaxation may ensue. More and different thoughts, feelings, imagery, and fantasy become available. In a sense, controlled regression occurs.

Our therapist may become aware, for instance, that his client does not value her attractiveness very much but that she must "use" it to ensure response from men. It is as though she believes her only worth is as a sexual object. Our therapist may even begin to know that his client feels deprived of affection even though she may deny this.

Also, imagery which suggests how this state of affairs has come to be may come to him. For instance, the nature of the father-daughter relationship may be "pictured"—that is, a mental picture or image may come, telling the therapist something of how father and daughter have interacted with each other in the past and perhaps still do. Our therapist may have two images, even "movies," of father-daughter interactions. One movie may consist of closeness, intimacy, affection, a little girl being held by her father. The other movie may involve distance, lack of contact, angriness, and possibly mutual rejection. But the girl and her father are older in the second movie. The girl is attractive and nearly a woman, in her teens perhaps. What is going on anyway? What relevance do the therapist's movies, images, or fantasies have? None, perhaps, but, on the other hand, may they not be tremendously significant?

Maybe our therapist has caught the essence of the father-daughter relationship as it developed through time. First there was closeness, intimacy, affection, body contact, possibly even sexuality appropriately expressed between father and small daughter. What about the second movie? Affection and closeness are gone and so is sexuality, or is sexuality gone? The girl is older, nearly a woman, and what is the mutual angriness about? Our therapist may well not have answers to his questions. The soliloquy may go:

> Who has the answers? No one, perhaps. But hold on a second; maybe the client does. If she does, why not ask? How does one ask? Hard to say, isn't it? Why not report the movies? Maybe the movies are just my fantasies and have nothing to do with her. But that could hardly be so, for the movies occurred in relationship to her. Surely they must have some relevance.

So it is that our therapist may find his way through his own internal operations, his doubts, his wonderment at his own associations, so that he becomes able finally to respond in some way which will be enormously helpful to his client, himself, and their relationship. He may report his movies and find that they have tremendous emotional meaning to his client. "Why that's just what happened!" she says. And a flood of memories and feelings are set loose. Warmness, closeness, loss, bitterness, anger, fear, and isolation may all be deeply experienced, elaborated, and eventually understood and integrated.

Or our therapist may be less of a gambler than we have suggested. He may not report his movies. Instead, he may ask the naive question, "You and your father seem to be awfully angry at each other. That doesn't seem always to have been true. Why is that?" The consequences flowing from such a query are likely to be less dramatic, but there will likely be some immediate effect, and ultimately the therapeutic gain may be as great as from the offering of therapist imagery.

It is also probable that the therapist could use his imagery in effective ways other than those we have suggested. Our basic concern is that the therapist is phenomenologically freer and more differentiated. Our thesis is that it is therapeutically necessary, even mandatory at times, for a therapist to have ways to free himself from a constricting relationship. Too, such freeing for the therapist is often accompanied by a freeing and differentiation in the client. Thus there can be gain for both.

PRIMARY PROCESS: THERAPY
WITHOUT RATIONALITY

We believe that effective therapy may also require a level of interaction which is less rational than awareness of feelings. It may require more than sensitive understanding, and more than warm acceptance of whatever feeling or thought the client or therapist has. We have said earlier that there needs to be the kind of understanding that the child had when he was learning about his feelings and what they meant to other important people. Also, in turn, we emphasize the importance of what the child understood about the feelings those other important people had toward him.

We have said earlier that we believe children perceive and

understand feelings accurately until someone lets them know that there is something wrong with what they feel and understand. We have hypothesized that feeling states have their origin, in part, in the child's inner persistence in feelings which were denied to him because they were not acceptable in the adult world. For example, unexpressed anger remains as hostility or depression. For these and other reasons we believe effective therapists need to have access to their childlike feelings and experiences. Besides being childlike, these feelings and experiences are nonintellectual, spontaneous, sometimes irrational, perhaps primitive, and naive. Along with many others, we have called these kinds of feelings primary process. Let us consider first a broad meaning of primary process and later how it implements therapy. We will compare it with secondary process because it is through secondary process that we can understand it.

In our thinking, then, primary process is a level of communication and an interpersonal experience, as well as being descriptive of an individual's phenomenology and/or behavior. A tension state, or a relatively low degree of anxiety, is a necessary and accepted concomitant of primary process; hence our insistence that therapists need to tolerate their anxiety. We do not think of this anxiety as a result of primary process because this would imply that primary process should be avoided as having a "bad" consequence. Socialization has tended to induce a kind of secondary anxiety, which in some people verges on panic, when primary process behavior and feelings are in the ascendance. This is the anxiety or tension state that we mean. It accounts for a large part of the discomfort some people experience with primary process experiences.

The Anxiety of Secondary Process: A Contrast. Secondary process is cognitive, intellectualized, has a rational sequence, and is founded on social acceptability. It results in a fairly controlled, predictable, interpersonal interaction. Anxiety is associated with secondary process, too, but has a different origin. It is the anxiety about not conforming, of knowing what to do and being afraid of not doing it. It is also the anxiety of not knowing when it is possible to know, not having cognitive control. As a simple example, a student who goes to class unprepared for a test is anxious over the possibility that he may make a failing grade.

Moreover, failure to accept controls learned through secondary process can be anxiety-producing. An example in reverse will be helpful. All of us have seen the way in which a conscious failure to conform becomes less anxiety-producing when not followed by some form of punishment. The habitual speeder who is not caught says he is not, and does not appear to be, anxious about breaking a traffic law. On the other hand, suppose the youthful driver in one of his first trips alone in the car exceeds the speed limit and is given a ticket. He learns to modify his behavior, to pay attention to the speed of the car and the posted speed limits, and experiences anxiety if he does not conform. We learn the controls offered by secondary process and are anxious if we do not conform. If we do not learn these controls, we are not anxious.

Secondary process is cognitive, rational learning, and it is associated with understanding. Some secondary process may presently lack rationality for one, but it is always capable of being explained. Primary process is lived. It becomes secondary when it is made cognitive; it is then under intellectual control and is understood. When only experienced, primary process has its own meaning in feelings and feeling states.

Returning to Primary Process. How, then, can we go about explaining primary process since thinking about it changes the nature of the experience so that it is no longer primary but secondary process? To put it another way, we think primary process out of existence. Let's see if we can find a way into the experience. Let's use an example.

A thirty-five-year-old woman says, "I'm bitter because I've never been married." That's a common enough statement, and to most people in the ordinary social world it sounds appropriate. The bitterness is real enough; you can hear it in her voice. Logic (secondary process) allows you to believe that never to have been married would lead to bitterness. There's an impulse to say, "Oh, don't be bitter about that; you might be just as bitter if you had been. How do you know that's what you're bitter about?" Now that's a simple notion; better go ahead and ask her. So you say, "How can you tell that the reason you are bitter is that you have never been married?" This is the naive question that a child would ask, and it may be necessary to repeat it. Her adult logic (or something that passes for logic) will lead you astray, and then neither will ever know why she's bitter, and her bitterness may forever keep her from making a close emotional bond.

Let's sink back again and look through a child's eyes: "Did someone tell a lie? That is closer to the real source of bitterness so carefully hidden lest bringing it out in the open disrupt the whole world." This last improbable notion fully reveals the child's perception of her world and her importance in it (she could disrupt the world!).

The Therapist's Primary Process. In examining the therapist's primary process activity as described above, we can pick out several characteristic steps. First is the taking note of his spontaneous response. "You might be bitter if you had married, too," which casts a doubt on the validity of the original statement. We are taught not to question adult logic, so there will be some resistance within the therapist to thinking at all in terms of doubting the original premise. Repeating the naive question helps the therapist to be and to stay simple-minded. The quality of simplicity is particularly important because if we are to understand the origins of the hurt and disappointment, we need to strip away the complex explanations for behavior which the adult world builds and see the experience through the eyes of a child. We need to know the child's hurt and bitterness.

Second, the client also needs to know the child's hurt and know it as a child in order to go on to an optimistic future. The last notion, that to express the hidden resentment will disrupt the world, is typical of a child's understanding and feeling tone with regard to the enormity of his behavior and its all-powerful effect on his environment. A little thought will recall to us how childish transgressions are exaggerated by parents and actually are made to shake the child's world, with the implication that the parents' world has also been shaken.

An example from a therapy interview will help develop this discussion further. A young woman telling her therapist about herself as a child said: "I remember once when I was a little girl, I wanted a new watch. I had a Mickey Mouse watch, but I wanted a new one because I didn't like it any more, and I asked my mother for one. She said, 'You have a watch; you don't need another one.' And, somehow—I never knew exactly how it happened—the watch came off my wrist, and I stepped on it, and it was broken. I was never punished for it, and I think I should have been."

The therapist "saw" the little girl asking for a new watch, had some feelings of the eager wanting, could even "see" the careless fumbling that resulted in the broken watch, and thought how beautifully simple and direct. If you can want only things that you need, then how logical to break the unwanted watch so that you need another. The therapist's response came out of that sequence. Its therapeutic value can never be fully known but is suggested by the fact that the client as an adult was unable to feel that she could want and ask for things easily and felt very constricted and controlled in her relationships with other people.

A secondary process sequence on the part of the therapist would recognize the guilt in the last statement, "I was never punished, and I think I should have been." Or perhaps it would include the thought that this was a spoiled, willful child intent on getting her own way. If the therapist follows the second sequence, he joins in the self-criticalness and perhaps adds to the constriction and over-control already a problem in the client's interpersonal relationships.

The first primary process reaction is a rather fundamental way of bringing back for the client the way in which life was dealt with in that family, what attitudes were taught, even what different perceptions the child had had and lost, and does all this in a shortened way that has more impact than a lot of discussion about family relationships.

We suggested earlier that one way of being therapeutically helpful involves reentering the developmental process at the point of failure or disturbance. In the last example, when the therapist permits himself to feel as the child did, he reenters the developmental process. He can use this reentering experience for different purposes, and depending upon his purpose, he will respond out of his subjective experience in one of several different ways.

Here we are approaching the matter of interpersonal impact, and a fuller discussion of how the therapist makes such a choice is reserved for the next chapter. However, we can indicate here what the choices are. The first choice is simply to note that the child learned a particular meaning of wanting, that wanting and needing are the same. This will not let the client reenter the developmental process, or if the client does, he will find himself alone in it. As a second choice, the therapist reacts out of his own childlike feelings and thus reenacts for the client a long-forgotten experience. As a third choice, he responds as a different kind of mother might have done—as though the client is again the child asking but this time getting a clearer, unconfused answer about why she can't have a new watch.

Reentering the developmental process in such a way as to let the client do so, too, requires something more than observing and noting. Some kind of reactivity to the client's child feelings is needed. Both of the last two choices involve this reactivity. We permit ourselves to be reactive to and through our own primary process experiences and are rewarded by the meaning this often has for our client.

We may be reactive in at least two different ways: out of the feelings we permit ourselves to have which are like the client's or out of the feelings we have in response to the client's feelings. If our reactivity is the first, it is likely to be primary and like the child's. If it is the second, it is apt to be like the parent's, but it may also be primary. Neither kind of response is reflection of feelings or clarification of feelings but is more active and carries greater impact. Both forms are effective, but one is followed by a different sequence of feelings and behavior than the other. Often the client abreacts and regresses. If the therapist is able to react in both the ways described above, perhaps first as the child and subsequently as the different adult, then the client will probably be able to achieve understanding and resolution in a relatively short time.

Phenomenology: Adult and Child. In this chapter our attention has turned inward. And this inner, subjective, phenomenological aspect of being human can be for the individual rich in meanings, full of feelings, replete with thought. We have tried to show something developmentally of how we can come to be internally rich and differentiated within our own skins. But the subjective aspect of being human can be constricted and monotonic, too. So we have had to be concerned not only with richness and differentiation, but also with sparseness, constriction, and feeling states rather than feelings.

We have been both sophisticated and naïve as we have written. Both sophistication and naïveté belong in this chapter, we believe. There is logicalness in the inner world, for instance. Whether the logic is naïve or sophisticated may depend upon whether we have been adult or childlike as we have sought to express ourselves. To be both adult and childlike is important, and so we have tried to be both in our writing. The inner world should be made up of both bigness and littleness, even in-betweenness, and so we have tried to be.

We have made a case for being sophisticated, for being adultly logical. Yet we have wanted to say that childlikeness is also logical, rich, varied, and not to be depreciated. We have even tried to make a case for the complementary nature of adultness and childlikeness. If we have done so, we are pleased, for we think of living as our entire lives—childhood memories, feelings, and hurts, as well as our usually less exuberant existence from the age of consent onward.

In building our case for the importance of the phenomenological world, we have necessarily used sophisticated, adult constructs. We have written about mothers, fathers, about ourselves as persons and therapists, and we have used psychological concepts and ideas. Yet at the same time we have written about children and how they are both naïve and astonishingly perceptive. The child's honesty and integrity have deeply impressed us, and we have written about that, too. Something of how a child can lose or distort his perceptiveness and his integrity has occurred to us, and so we have written on this. That human development and growing up are distressing and damaging as well as rewarding and fulfilling is also true, and we have been concerned about both. But damage and distortion can be rectified, and our discussion of phenomenological processes, adult and childlike, may have shed both developmental and therapeutic light.

In our next chapter we will turn to the world between people, the interpersonal world. From our base in subjective, internal phenomenology we will write in another way about how we help and hinder each other as we go about the business of being human. Processes and interactions go on between people, and we must write about them. But we will keep one foot on our base in phenomenology, for interpersonality seems to us always to reverberate in the internal, subjective world.

Chapter 5

Interpersonality: Vehicle for Human Development and Therapy

To be intrapsychically clear and differentiated and to know and accept one's own feelings are good, but these are not enough. It is not enough because we live in a social world, a world with other people. There are some human beings who achieve a tight little security within themselves and who can even be creative and productive within a system which neither allows nor demands a great deal of interaction with other people, but such individuals are rare.

It is paradoxical that distress and unhappiness are experienced phenomenologically yet often result from an interpersonal interchange of some kind. Thus negative feelings about oneself usually have their origin interpersonally. Even those feelings which are lonely and self-critical occur because of past or present comparisons between oneself and another person. Obviously the comparative judgment is self-made, but another person must be used as a referent.

Further, when developmental tasks are not appropriately accomplished and some psychological stress results, almost always the source of the problem is interpersonal. In saying this, we need to except those tasks in which a physical problem is involved, such as illness, a physical defect, or perhaps an intellectual deficit. Even in these instances, however, interpersonal experiences play a large part in the degree of psychological distress or impairment that is experienced.

It occurred to us as we reread the paragraphs above that they represented a problem in interpersonal communication. Perhaps a look at our efforts and the motivations behind them will add something to an understanding of the way in which people deal with interpersonal problems and why they are sometimes frustrated and unhappy with their efforts.

Interpersonality and how it can be made an effective process in therapy is an enormously complex subject. How can one go about making it meaningful to readers of a book? If the writer were a recluse and unmindful of any but feelings of personal satisfaction in having had the ideas, there would be no problem because there would be no need or effort to communicate the ideas to others—and no book. But having a need to communicate one's ideas to others can result in being misunderstood and criticized, or being too well understood and criticized for shallowness or ignorance—and so a conflict arises. There has to be some way of presenting the ideas, however. So we begin with something oversimplified and half reject it, then expand it a bit, then offer another aspect, always with the hope of having a meaningful impact.

Then comes the question, Why tell the reader what you are doing? The answer is that this is a way of relating, a style of being, which is intended to involve the reader along with the writer in this interpersonal experience. Incidentally, how it happened that this explanation became a part of the discussion is this: The writer came to a point in the writing where the effectiveness of the communication became uncertain, and he asked the other to listen and pass judgment. The other laughed and commented, "You have been doing what so many people do when they try to explain a complex thing. You began by oversimplifying it, and then you enlarged it. Why don't you tell about how you did it?"

The writer took the suggestion and felt no longer self-critical and doubtful but enlarged and expanded.

To go back a step, interpersonal experiences are a prime cause of later intrapsychic problems and are also the continuing source of present problems. Once an interpersonal failure has occurred, similar failures tend to keep recurring until help is sought with the interpersonal problem in its present form.

Let's have some examples. A timid undergraduate in a large dormitory finds himself lonely. There are hundreds of people from whom to choose friends. He knows that he needs only to approach some fellow student or to join in activities, yet he is unable to do so and comes for help. He explains that after almost three years in school he still feels inferior to the others and that if he is going to get over this feeling, he needs to do something besides wait for it to go away. Another student, bright, compulsively active, complains that he has had no more than three dates with any one girl. What is the matter with him that he isn't able to like any one girl well enough to go with her and maybe fall in love? These are concerns about interpersonal relationships and point rather directly to present interpersonal failures. Less clear is the interpersonal problem which had its origins earlier, when the timid young man learned to question his adequacy and when the compulsive youth learned to substitute activity for emotional closeness.

In these two examples we understand the "way of being" which has now become a problem as a once useful, perhaps necessary way of coping with an interpersonal relationship that was extremely important. We will develop some ideas about the interpersonal impact of important others, adults usually, in the growing-up process, impact which facilitates or impedes the accomplishment of the developmental tasks. We will also suggest how certain common problems may have developed and what past circumstances may underlie them. If in initiating therapy we are able to anticipate the nature of the earlier interpersonal problem, we can often hasten its confrontation and resolution.

DEVELOPMENTAL TASKS
DONE AND UNDONE

Let us think, then, about the usual interpersonal experiences of the developing child. We go back to the earliest relationship which a person usually has, that of an infant with his mother.

The child's first developmental task is to learn his separateness from others: that his feelings and needs are his and that there is a world outside of himself. The baby's earliest cooing and gurgling as well as crying probably occur in response to his own inner experience, but they are also responded to by his mother. He then learns to laugh and make expressive sounds at the sight of his mother and other members of the family. He is also responded to by them. Many babies react in the same way to friends and even to strangers who have no relationship to those with whom they are familiar.

There comes a period in the development of most children when they no longer respond to strangers and won't go to just anyone who wants to hold them. The baby's mother may explain that he is getting shy, and she may be a little distressed and wonder if she has done something harmful to her formerly outgoing, friendly baby. However, usually the child is only learning to distinguish himself and his feelings from others and their feelings for him. Frequently the child who is called shy has made an outgoing gesture which is responded to, and he then retreats, turns his head, and appears to be shy. We think of this as interpersonal self-consciousness. For the small child it is an experience of his own impact, with the accompanying distress which comes from an awareness of separateness.

A second type of interpersonal experience through which the developing infant learns to know his own separateness occurs when he begins to crawl and toddle, becoming able to go to unsafe places and to reach for and grasp objects which he cannot have. When he is frustrated by his mother in getting or doing what he wants, he frequently wails loudly. Here again is a distressful experience in which he becomes aware of his separateness from his mother and the physical world. Mothers frequently offer a child a substitute for the object he wants but for some reason cannot have. The intent is to limit the frustration and make it manageable by the small child. However, we hope that the child does not learn from this that mother knows what he wants better than he does, because an important lesson in separateness would then be lost.

Language and Development. Learning separateness and personal uniqueness is an interpersonal phenomenon because the learning takes place through the child's ongoing daily encounters with the other members of the family. This accomplishment, in turn, contributes to another developmental task: learning to talk, which has so many implications for other learning. It may well be, for instance, that a child learns to talk not only because he becomes maturationally able to do so but also because he "needs" to do so in order to express himself more completely. Let us speculate for a moment about what may happen to a child whose mother too readily understands his nonverbal behavior or the child's first efforts at verbal expression. Such a child may learn to talk less fluently and rapidly, and he may also be slower in developing interpersonally. In a sense, then, we are equating interpersonal development with the development of verbal expression. To our way of thinking, human behavior does not become truly interpersonal until language becomes available as a primary vehicle.

Thus, we repeat, a mother who too readily understands her child may thereby help to handicap his verbal development and, more importantly, his interpersonal development. While it may be possible for mother and child to communicate much nonverbally, communication with others—father, siblings, other relatives, other people—is usually more dependent on the child's ability to verbalize. This may be a most fortunate state of affairs, for these significant others usually insist on increasingly intelligible language, whereas mother herself may not necessarily do so.

May it not be true, for instance, that the schizophrenic did not experience clearly the expectations about his learning to talk held by people other than his mother? How easy is it to produce a truly schizophrenic personality when father and significant others are genuinely interested in a child's verbal behavior? Much current thinking about schizophrenia suggests the strong probability that communication of a sort develops between mother and child but that a notable failure occurs in verbal and/or interpersonal development in the child's relationships to others.

While a mother may be very interested in her child's verbal development, father, grandparents, siblings, aunts, and uncles oftentimes do more to facilitate this development as well as interpersonal development. Father's intentness upon the child's learning to say "daddy" may have more significance than that fathers are just silly!

Why do we use the word "silly" to characterize the behavior of some fathers toward their children? First, of course, there comes to mind the societal attitude that fathers should be and are often powerfully involved with their children affectively. Such involvement, whatever the internal motivation, can certainly result in a powerful need for the father to communicate with his child. Whether father's behavior is, in fact, "silly" in the derisive, negative sense depends upon a complex of interpersonally interactive phenomena. Some examples will help illustrate this complexity and at the same time demonstrate that complex, interpersonal phenomena can have understandable origins.

If, for instance, the mother has a fundamentally warm, affectionate, and reasonably healthy relationship with the father, she will be at least tolerant, if not actually facilitative of father's efforts to communicate with his child. The maternal attitudes and feelings do not compete seriously with the father's, and so the father-child relationship grows, and they genuinely learn to talk with each other. Simply put, the child learns to talk and relate interpersonally with a man as well as with a woman. In the same way such a mother will condone and even facilitate her child's development interpersonally and verbally with siblings, other relatives, friends, and even casual others.

As we see it, however, since mother's relationship to the child is primary, she can and does retain a veto over the child's relationships to others, a veto which is powerful in its function and, we regret to say, too frequently exercised. We can assume, however, that mother's naysaying capacity is not universally absolute in its application both because her power is not the same in all her relationships to others and because all others do not react in the same way to being vetoed.

If, for instance, the parental relationship is more negative than the one just described, the furthering of the father-child relationship may depend upon the father's ability to persist rather than give up when negated and diminished. Yet the price for the father's persistence may be rather high, for the child may have to choose one parent or the other and in the process feel he loses the one he does not choose.

Such a competitive relationship between parents is often highlighted strikingly in multiple therapy. It manifests itself in a determined, client effort to talk and relate to one of us and in an equally powerful effort to exclude the other. Usually, of course, as the history unfolds, the relationships of the therapists to the client parallel the relationships the client had with his parents and significant others.

Another kind of example comes to mind out of the many possibilities. A mother and father have a negative relationship, and the father is effectively removed psychologically by maternal veto power, the child's choice, or both. Yet the mother has a positive relationship with the child's grandfather. In such an instance the mother may tolerate and even facilitate the development of the interpersonal, talking relationship with the grandparent. We have noted with interest that the client who speaks warmly of a grandparent in early interviews often has such an interpersonal history.

Rationality as a Developmental Task. We have discussed two developmental tasks which are important in becoming a person: learning one's separateness and learning to relate to others by talking to them. Both are dependent upon and either facilitated or hindered by an interpersonal process with one or more important people.

We need to mention at least one more developmental task: the growth of rationality. We will give it some detailed attention in the next chapter, but at this point we wish to point out that rationality, too, is an interpersonal experience. While rationality and cognition are important in many aspects of living, we will think of them now primarily in relation to feelings and interpersonal experiences. The child who has grown up in a family in which feelings are talked and thought about has an entirely different way of approaching his problems than the child who has had no experience in talking about or giving verbal meaning to his feelings.

Additionally, we believe that family attitudes and beliefs are communicated whether talked about or not. The child develops ways of knowing about them which may or may not be useful in his other interpersonal experiences. We need only to mention the kind of person who has learned to understand feelings and attitudes by watching the expression of others (in lieu of receiving verbal explanation) to call to mind a type of individual who has particular problems in living. This person is so dependent on others to clarify his emotional experience that he is likely to be seen as dull and uninteresting.

What one can talk about is clearly communicated in families, and sometimes what one can think about and even feel is also made clear. We see, then, that the interpersonal experience of growing up can be limiting, controlling, and inhibiting of personality and the self. Or it can be expanding and encourage adventuresomeness and creativity. We enter the developmental process with our clients in order to facilitate the latter and to undo some of the prohibitions.

And Some Problems—in Personality, That Is. We have sketched the framework of a theory of interpersonal personality development. We can now look further at some of the problem areas. Probably no one who asks for therapeutic help does not have a problem in being dependent. It may be that the problem is the attitude that to be dependent is to be subjugated. Therefore dependency must be avoided totally, and every relationship must carry a guarantee that a safe emotional distance will be maintained. At the other extreme are those who see any relationship as an opportunity, sometimes an obligation, to be totally cared for and, incidentally, controlled. And there are gradations between these two extremes of the ways in which people in distress seek help and accept a relationship which involves dependency on the therapist.

We and our clients can understand a great deal about what important parental relationships were like, as well as what some of the problems of growing up were like, if we pay a little attention to the client's way of being dependent or independent. We believe that a part of the interpersonal relearning involves learning a more comfortable way of living dependently as well as independently, and that it can be accomplished in the relationship with us. One might ask, Doesn't this mean that therapists must know and understand their own needs with respect to people who are dependent on them, as well as their own problems in being dependent? The answer, of course, is obvious. The therapist's concern is actually no different from that which therapists from other orientations must have, since the problem of client dependency is a problem only when the therapist's needs are unconscious. However, our interpersonal way does imply a quite different method of relating to client dependency than the ways some orientations prescribe.

Feelings of dependency are no more nor less real than any other feelings. We see dependency that is a problem as similar to other feeling states, that is, not necessarily reactive to or growing out of the present interpersonal relationship with the therapist. We expect the client, then, to experience and live out his real dependency feelings during those times when comfort and support are appropriate, for example. Further, we expect him to learn that some feelings which he expresses as dependency may in fact be something quite different, such as stubborn resistance or covert hostility or other kinds of distortions and displacements which we have seen occur in feeling states. We see reactive independence as a feeling state in the same way and for this reason as a dependency problem.

We have been concerned about dependency not only because it is a problem to clients but also because it is an important aspect of the relationship between every client and his therapist. We insist that the only appropriate uncovering therapy is done in a relationship in which the client trusts the therapist and the therapist trusts the client in a somewhat mutually dependent experience. The therapist may be a bit less dependent on the client since he also trusts and depends upon himself in some of the ways that he ultimately hopes the client will learn. And we feel certain that he cannot permit the client to explore and resolve feelings which he, the therapist, cannot trust himself to have. He will prove himself undependable in this instance, even though he may also demonstrate that he is human and real.

But to go back to the issue of dependency and uncovering therapy, we believe that in a functioning population it is usually inappropriate to do anything to force uncovering prior to the establishment of a trusting relationship between the client and therapist. If the relationship is one of trusting dependency, there is less need for forcing and more spontaneous access to feelings and memories. Thus we understand that at first it is more important to work with the relationship than to try to get the client to fill in the blanks in his memory. In the early stages of therapy we are more concerned about developing trust between therapist and client than abreactions, for example, because we feel that the client's defenses against experiences in depth are important in enabling him to continue to function. A good therapist-client relationship alleviates at least some of the need for these defenses.

Additionally, many of the client's interpersonal problems will be dealt with as he works out his relationship with his therapist. As one young person said during the termination interview, "I used to tell you only the middle of some things and think that if you really cared about me you'd know what it was all about, but you wouldn't let me get by with that." This was a really profound yet simple recognition of the meaning that being unclear had had for her. This had never been interpreted to her. It had simply been lived out and discovered in the relationship.

INTERPERSONAL TRANSFER OF
FEELINGS AND TASKS

There is a phenomenon that is as important in human development and therapy as dependency but not so clearly recognized, perhaps because many therapeutic orientations have actively limited the interpersonal relationship in therapy sessions. We have called it the interpersonal transfer of feelings. It has been clearly recognized in infants when anxious mothers communicate their anxiety to babies with resulting nutritional and sleeping problems, as well as problems in physical development. The child develops protective defenses as he grows older so that he is not made consciously anxious by the anxiety of everyone around him, but the phenomenon persists.

We find it occurring to a greater or lesser degree with respect to other feelings in many people of all ages. It is not uncommon for one of a married couple to say of the other, "I'm happy if he is," or "I can tell whether I'm going to feel good the minute I step into the house." Strangely enough, married partners sometimes feel when they protect themselves from the other's feelings that they are somehow denying themselves some of the pleasure of interpersonal intimacy, or that they are not being loving in some way. Transfer of feelings also plays an important part in the person's developmental history and is frequently so hidden that it is difficult to recapture.

Perhaps we can say that feelings are transferred in two ways or under two types of conditions: when the behavior causing the transfer is observable and when it is not.

Transfer Due to Observable Behavior.   We all have had the experience of having our spirits lifted by a person who is obviously happy. The person expresses his feelings clearly, and they transfer to a greater or lesser degree to those around him. We even say that his cheerfulness is infectious. This is a clear instance of the fact that feelings can be transferred interpersonally. In part the transfer occurs because one is willing to be cheered, one permits the transfer.

The transfer of negative feelings may occur just as obviously, though there may be more natural resistance to permitting it to happen. If a person has an encounter with someone who is hostile, he may find himself countering the hostility by being frustrated and finally actually angry, too, and reacting angrily to the hostile person. The hostile person then has a meaning to attach to his own anger, that someone frustrated or attacked him. In the case of transfer of hostility we have an implication of the purpose of the transfer. The hostile person has been able to change his hostile feeling state into a feeling of anger with a reason, which is more bearable. That the person continues to be hostile even after endless encounters with others in which angry feelings are expressed only attests to the need for a better understanding and resolution of his hostile feeling state.

Guilt and its transfer, particularly within a family, have a rather nasty, destructive effect. Suppose a father has sexual feelings for his adolescent daughter and expresses his concern about having them by constantly admonishing her about her boy friends and accusing her of impropriety with them. She begins to feel guilty about going on dates and yet protests that she hasn't done anything she is ashamed of. She becomes angry and alienated from her father and perhaps learns that all men are to be distrusted and tested endlessly. Or perhaps a mother feels guilty about her inability to give one of her children the attention she thinks he needs. She may then give attention to his faults and misdemeanors so that he feels the only contact with her takes place when he is bad. Thus being around his mother becomes a guilty, anxious experience. If he, in turn, learns to say to her, "You never care about anything good I do," he has learned to make her feel guilty in retaliation.

Or suppose a father feels guilty because he did not finish his education and so constantly impresses on his son that he must do well in school. The destructive effect may occur something like this: The child brings home an A report card, and the father looks at it and says, "Now see to it that you keep it up." The child feels that he has not done well enough because he does not get the expected reward of pleasing his father; he feels guilty that he hasn't done enough somehow. He will also feel guilty if he doesn't continue to make good grades.

The guilt feels real to the child, yet it is not something of which he can make sense. If the father elaborates his concern over his son's grades by saying, "I know because I didn't finish school, and you can see how hard I have to work, and I don't want you to have to work this hard," the son may then feel guilty about his grades as though they were responsible for his father's having to work very hard. It is a strange irrationality that father and son become enmeshed in. While we can only *guess* that the father does actually feel guilty, this is suggested by the way he makes the son feel guilty.

Transfer Due to Unobservable Behavior. In the second kind of transfer of feelings which we have witnessed in ourselves and in our clients, manifest behavior that could be given as the cause of the transfer is missing, although there are cues and sometimes even clear verbal expressions of the feeling. It is the kind of transfer which seems to occur between an anxious mother and her baby, referred to earlier. It may even be true that anxiety is the only feeling transferred in this way, but we have some evidence that other feelings may also be.

A typical example occurs when a client is talking about something which makes him anxious and describes how upset it makes him. The therapist listens and recognizes the anxiety but does not feel it. Then subsequently the therapist becomes intensely aware of being anxious himself and usually notes that the client has relaxed somewhat. If at this point the therapist remarks that the client seems very anxious, the client again becomes anxious.

In another kind of client—particularly highly verbal, compulsive ones—the therapist may feel very anxious, and upon asking the client whether he is anxious, be told that he doesn't feel and hasn't been feeling anything. The therapist finds himself musing, "I pick up his anxiety," or, "I have his anxiety for him." We have had such experiences as this in which anxiety is passed back and forth. We want to emphasize that the therapist must be willing to let himself be anxious. We will discuss the efficacy of the interpersonal transfer of feelings as a therapeutic process in a later section of this chapter.

Compulsivity: Defense Against Transfer of Anxiety.   We must assume, however, that interpersonal transfer of feelings on the second, or nonovert, level occurs between people other than therapists and clients. If we look back at the developmental sequence, we can hypothesize some developmental consequences of such transfer, particularly the consequences involved when a negative feeling state characterizes the home.

We are suggesting that some feelings are so painful as to require defenses against them and that a child develops defenses against being overwhelmed by feelings belonging to important people in his environment, as well as defenses against being overwhelmed by his own feelings. The fact that such defenses are themselves a kind of distortion adds to their complexity and to the difficulty of maintaining open, clear, interpersonal relationships. If the child, for instance, must protect himself from his mother's anxiety, he loses some of the emotional closeness and nurturance which he needs and which she perhaps has to offer him. The conflict between his need for nurturance and his need to defend against her anxiety becomes unresolvable. It remains unresolved and active in every relationship he has with women. We can now be more specific about the nature of some of these defenses that the child constructs against the transfer not only of parental anxiety but also of parental guilt.

Obsessive-compulsive types of reaction, we believe, are defenses which have their origin and expression in this kind of interpersonal context. Suppose we think of the small child in an adult world which is dealing with real problems. The parents are anxious or upset and are trying to keep the child from being involved in their concerns. These efforts may be appropriate in their intent, but they are often not successful.

The child may be told, "Go play; everything is all right," but the tone of voice expresses the anxiety or irritation which clearly says everything isn't all right. The child plays, but he is also driven to go back and try to reassure himself that his world is as safe as he needs it to be. The parent or parents, still preoccupied, try to offer him another substitute for the interpersonal reassurance he needs. "You're sleepy; it's time for bed," or "It will help me if you will pick up your toys." The falsity of the proffered solution does not escape the child even though he may try to make it effective. No matter how obediently he does what is suggested, the tension remains that seems to him to say, "You're not important," or "Mommy [or Daddy] doesn't care about you," or "There is something here that makes me feel bad."

There may be a difference in the subsequent development of the person if the parent in dealing with the child's concern says, "Everything is all right," as contrasted with, "You can help me by. . . ." In the latter case the child is assigned a task and perhaps learns that problems are solved by doing something, and more, that he has a responsibility to carry out the task. Thus he becomes intimately involved in helping with the parental problem. The problem does not go away, but he finds a method of protecting himself from parental anxiety and feeling useful and needed at a distance from it.

An interesting differentiation occurs when the parents we have described as anxiously engrossed in a problem have two children instead of one and assign the responsibility of taking care of one child to the other. The child who gets the task assigned may develop a high, unremitting sense of responsibility, which protects him from the transfer of his parents' anxiety. But the other child may wait for years to learn that he is "supposed" to be self-sufficient or even that he has tasks that are his to perform. Hence the only defense against anxiety left to him is compulsivity.

There is a kind of lack of integrity or honesty in each message from parent to child, which the child senses and perhaps expects to have corrected at some time. The lack of integrity is most clear when parental guilt is involved. Testing these impressions then becomes important.

The child wants to test in order to be sure. If the message is, "Everything will be all right if you just do well in school," the child may compulsively do well in school and even believe he is loved and appreciated for doing so. If the message also has in it the threat, "If you don't do well in school, our whole world will collapse," the child may compulsively want to test that. He will almost fail but never quite risk going that far because he cannot tolerate proving either the falsity or truth of what the parent has always said.

In the college student we see clearly expressed this need to test the consequences of failing. The problem is exaggerated when failure tends to confirm rather than disprove the original parental statement. Not infrequently a student will say, "I can't do anything because my father has a bad heart, and I mustn't upset him." There is enough reality so that the student can't test the thing which he most wants to: whether his grades mean as much to his father as the father has always said they do, a claim the student doubts. He may say things such as, "My father likes for me to make good grades so he can brag about them at the club." The last is a rational statement and is likely said without feeling. Yet the student may be actively engaged in testing the falsity of the earlier implication that the parent's well-being is tied to his success. Somehow the child/adult knows better and is caught between maintaining the untruth and wanting to disprove it. The compulsivity is found in the method of dealing with the untruth. The falsity lies in feelings within the youth that are unfelt or distorted into feeling states or transferred from the parent. The falsity is paralyzing because it inhibits action.

Then there is the situation in which although the child is so young that he does not participate in the family problems, he knows the tension and anxiety but has no verbal cues by which to understand what the tension is about. A striking example is seen when a parent becomes ill and has to stop playing with a child abruptly, and never again resumes the former playful relationship. The household changes, too, in its feeling tone. The child remains unsure of whether he is responsible for the change in the relationship to his parent and continues to try to reestablish it.

Because the child is too young to understand or for some other reason is not told the meaning of the parental illness—although the family pattern of living is established around it—the youngster develops certain compulsive ways of coping with what he does not understand. He may, for example, become very skilled in reading the feelings of others and adjusting his feelings and behavior to theirs. He learns to protect himself from bad feelings and to have only those feelings which are acceptable. It is as though he can know the reality of his feelings only by sensing those of important others and then behaving in terms of them. If those important others are anxious a great deal of the time, he may learn not to feel at all.

The compulsive inability to reach a decision and to carry through to completion unstructured developmental tasks, along with his great dependence on authority for evaluation of his performance of the tasks, suggests the degree to which learning to do things is inhibited by interpersonal, emotional uncertainty. It is often true that the important missing element in the ability of a compulsive to make a decision is knowledge of his own feelings about the thing being decided. The problem occurs because such knowledge has been lost; the feelings have been done away with to protect the self from transferred feelings.

For some it is probably true that in order to free themselves from the neurosis of compulsivity, regression must take place. The person must risk the regression in a manner so primitive as to reexperience the feelings of fear, anger, need for love, and loving that were part of his original commitment to the compulsive behavior. He needs to know that all of his feelings were real, that they had a reason and were therefore appropriate.

We have considered some of the reasons why compulsives behave the way they do and seem to lack well-differentiated feelings. In a later chapter we will deal with the other aspect so characteristic of educated clients—the commitment to intellectualizing.

We have had a great deal to say about the interpersonal aspects of the development of feelings and the emotional aspects of interpersonal experiences. We believe that they are inseparable and that human problems have their origins in these relationships and, in turn, find their solutions in a like manner. Thus we are describing a therapy in which the phenomenal, or intrapsychic, and the interpersonal aspects of being human are intimately interrelated.

INTERPERSONAL PROCESS
AS THERAPY PROCESS

In the immediately preceding section we have outlined how developmental failures can occur. We have also described some of the particular interpersonal ways of relating which create human problems both past and present. Now we turn to describing how we enter into the interpersonal relationship with our clients in order to help them with their problems.

Impairment in affection giving and getting is a common interpersonal problem. Such a problem may be expressed in a number of different ways. Usually, however, there are deep internal doubts in the client about whether he is lovable. Less obvious but also present are doubts about his ability to love or care for others. Thus while the concerns are experienced internally, because the problem involves giving and getting affection in relationship to others it clearly has an interpersonal aspect.

Naturally enough, we first concentrate on forming a relationship with our client. Much of our early attention and effort are also focused on helping our client to know more clearly what his problem is, what his thoughts and feelings are, even what other fears and wishes he has for instance. Thus, hopefully, our client begins the process of internal differentiation.

If these initial efforts have some success, conflict, a paradox, often begins to emerge. As our client grows more and more differentiated and as he knows and experiences more and more of the nature of his needful thoughts and feelings, then his hopes and wishes, and his doubts, too, accentuate. Just as his needs to give and get affection grow clearer and clearer and are more sharply and clearly experienced, so his fears and feelings of hopelessness tend to increase. By forming a relationship with our client we have helped him in one way, even made a promise in a sense, and while he may know more of himself and his needs, he may now know equally well that the needs have long gone un-satisfied. Hurt, pain, and hopelessness may well become almost devastatingly real. But, as we said above, there is likely to be hope, too. Because we are well involved with our client, which has been necessary in order to get this far, we may become, in turn, puzzled, bewildered, frightened, or hopeless ourselves. And so we should, perhaps, for the relationship is interpersonal and reciprocal. We have effects on our client, and, in turn, he has effects on us.

There is a therapist soliloquy which goes about as follows:

> We promised something, too, didn't we? And what was it that we promised? Powerful affect, interpersonally expressed, can confuse us as therapists, even make us feel guilty and inadequate. But, again, what was it we promised? Should we feel guilty and inadequate about our inability to meet our client's needs? Was that what we promised? Or did we say we would help and that it would be painless? No, that's not right either, for emotional realization of what one has missed or had too little of is always likely to be painful. Oh, it's what he didn't get enough of that he's hurt and angry about. Did we promise to make that up to him? No, for that would be a lie, and he's had enough of those. Being lied to by others about making up for past deprivations has kept the hopeless hope alive. No, we can't make up to him for the past, but perhaps we can give him something now. Or perhaps he can give us something. He was deprived both ways, so perhaps either or both may be right. But if he is comforted too soon, that may keep the lie alive, too, so perhaps we'd better wait a bit.

The immediately preceding paragraph is an effort to write as vividly and realistically as we can about how interpersonal conflict is often expressed and experienced. We included probable thera-pist reactions, thoughts, and feelings to demonstrate that the relationship is reciprocal and can be powerfully real for both persons. We carried the therapist's reactions to a point which suggests clarification of the meaning of the interaction for the therapist. Yet some uncertainty about the eventual outcome remains. We left the outcome uncertain because we also wish to convey the fact that human relationships are complex, uncertain, even risky, as well as the fact that they may be helpful, growing, changing, and somewhat predictable.

An analogy will help us to explain more clearly why we believe human relationships, particularly in the interpersonal sense, are complex, somewhat uncertain, risk-filled, and only partially predictable. Yet at the same time we will try to convey that ways through the unknown, the half-known, can be found.

We have used the word "venture" several times in this book in discussing our understandings of human development and of therapy processes. Our use of the word is not accidental, for we do regard therapy as a venture, even an adventure, for both client and therapist. How is this, and what do we mean?

We turn now to say something of what we think the therapist's set, or direction, should be, particularly in regard to interpersonal aspects of therapeutic relationships. We think, first of all, of the word "direction" in a physical, geographical sense. As we use the word here, it does not have to do with control or managing, although that may be part of the meaning, but rather with a sense of direction. But the sense of direction is general, a way to move rather than a precise, measured matter which can be reported in degrees and minutes and then followed equally precisely.

For instance, we may know that movement should be either toward or away from the sun, but we do not know that the direction should be twenty degrees north of due east. Or perhaps we know or believe that we should head north and that the sun will be on our right if it is morning. But, again, we do not and should not ordinarily know our direction more exactly for two reasons: First, it is unlikely that knowing precise direction in interpersonal, human relationships is possible. Second, we think that efforts to make direction unduly precise are managing, controlling, and highly likely to be faulty, unhelpful, and untherapeutic. Our client will ultimately feel betrayed, and the betrayal is likely to be true if we have promised exactness we are not able to actualize.

Let us bring a client and a therapist along with us now in our analogical thinking. We think, first, of the early interviews, the first encounters. The relationship begins to develop, but since our therapist is curious and wishes to be helpful, it is inevitable that he will at least speculate about dynamics, content, the nature of the client's probable conflicts, even probably about directions the relationship will take.

For instance, our therapist may think that it is important for the client to talk about and to know more than he does about an allegedly warm and loving relationship with his mother. Our therapist will implement his sense of a proper, general direction in several ways. It is likely, for instance, that he will slant his responses to his client—be they reflections of feelings, questions, or whatever—so that the client talks and feels more about his mother than his father. Yet our therapist, if he behaves in terms of a sense of general direction rather than preciseness, will walk generally north (toward mother) with the client rather than either lead or show him down the broad, paved expressway marked MOTHER.

If our therapist and client go on with their venture together in the general, somewhat directional manner we have suggested, then both client and therapist may be surprised by where they get to and what occurs. They may find, for instance, that they are on a dirt road which dead ends in a swamp. Or they may become lost and panic ensue. Or they may come suddenly to a road marked FATHER, BROTHER, or SISTER. What happens then? Father, brother, or sister may be talked about briefly and with increasing affect. Then a pause, broken by the client's return to talking about his mother. It may seem to the therapist that the client seems relieved and less anxious as he talks about his mother. Why is that, and is it true? Can it be that mother is a refuge from other more threatening members of the family? Why is that, and what does it mean? Or the therapist may report his observation to the client and ask if the client is aware of what he has done. The client may or may not be aware of the shift.

Put another way, a number of factors may help determine how a client reacts at such a time. We will mention some of them. For one thing, the client's response will depend, in part, on the nature of the prior relationship which has developed between the two of them. If some trust, for instance, has developed, the client may well take the observation seriously in some way, no matter what his level of awareness about his behavior may be. If, on the other hand, sufficient trust has not developed, the client may only reject the observation and probably will have public and/or private thoughts and feelings about his therapist's shortage of wisdom.

How the observation is offered may make a considerable difference in the client's defensiveness, acceptance, and/or level of awareness about his own behavior. If the therapist makes a flat, assertive statement, the nature of the client's acceptance and use of the observation is likely to be different from what it will be if the therapist "offers" his observation.

Too, the client's response is likely to depend on which behavior the therapist makes his observation about. The therapist may comment, for instance, about the pause, breaking the pause, talking about mother or about father, the shift from one to the other, the apparent increase in anxiety, the relief, and so on. Or the therapist may incorporate several of the above in his observation.

We are not prepared to say, incidentally, that one mode of therapist behavior is necessarily better than another. But we do suggest that therapeutic, face-to-face relationships are fluid, dynamic, changing, partly predictable, partly unknown, and always reciprocal. Further, we suggest that while an ultimate therapeutic destination may remain quite constant, the routes for arriving there are as many as the points of the compass. It is true, of course, that some routes are more direct, and we should strive to find them. Some routes may end in an impassable swamp or an unclimbable mountain. We accept those possibilities, too. We are inclined, however, to think that routes to a therapeutic destination are seldom impossible unless therapist and client combine together in some way to avoid the destination.

Relationships, Real and Unreal. We will consider the relevance of some other interpersonal factors which help determine a client's response to a therapist's behavior, statement or observation. We note, for instance, that the sex of the participants in the relationship is often important and determining. Cross-sex relationships, male therapist with female client or female therapist with male client, develop somewhat differently than do same-sex relationships. The reasons for these differences are at least twofold, we think. First, the past interpersonal histories of both client and therapist are almost certain to affect the way in which the present relationship develops through time and also what may happen at a given moment in the relationship. Second, at least in the case of face-to-face relationships, both participants are in the present, real relationship, which is not in the past except as it becomes so.

Thus we emphasize that a male client's reaction to a male therapist may be partially a consequence of the kind of relationship he had with his father. However, his reaction is also, in part, a reaction to a here-and-now person who is not his father. Moreover, both participants probably have awareness that the two kinds of reactions are occurring. Also, we think that often an important part of the therapeutic task is that the participants separate and differentiate the two kinds of reactions.

Clients can frequently help, but we are inclined to think that the therapist carries the primary responsibility for this important work. What do we mean? We mean essentially that therapeutic, face-to-face, interpersonal relationships need to be regarded and utilized by therapist and client in two complementary, yet different ways. We think of therapeutic relationships as usually having a past orientation and emphasis, but we also believe that the present, real relationship is of equal import and that it ultimately is the source of whatever may be therapeutic. Said still another way, conflict arises and generates out of the past and is experienced and resolved in the present in order for the future to be different.

The preceding sentence is a summary of our view of the importance of time—in all its known dimensions—in therapeutic relationships, especially in the interpersonal sense. We want to convey fully our conviction that it is necessary to ensure that all three time dimensions occur and are experienced in certain ways in order for the relationship to be therapeutically changing.

Attention must usually be given to the past for many reasons. The failures in development which presently plague our client and seriously impair his view of the future have occurred in the past. Thus it is usually necessary to develop in the present relationship the nature of that past. If we are successful in this portion of our venture together, then old, past thoughts, feelings, and memories come to be experienced more sharply, clearly, vividly, and painfully, too, for, as we have seen, pain and hurt are part of the substance of emotional problems.

It is even likely that the client will see the therapist as the source, even the cause, of his increased discomfort, distress, and pain. The client's suspicions are right, too, for a part of our intent is to facilitate his ambivalent, reluctant, but necessary reexperiencing of his past in the present relationship. We think that such is usually necessary in order for an emotionally troubled person, even though functioning, to have the chance to change and make his future life different from and more satisfying than his past life. Thus we as therapists may have a different view for a time than our client does of the meaning of what has occurred. But it is in the recapture, reexperiencing, and ultimately the owning of one's past that a different present and future life becomes possible.

Yet if we as therapists are too long and too much preoccupied with the recapture of the past, our very preoccupation with it may operationally and psychologically deny to our client what we have been attempting to help him to have—a present and a future. Thus we do our client a service by helping him to know and own his past, but the meaning of present relationships must be real and owned, too.

We Are Real Persons, Too. We choose face-to-face relationships with our clients in part because face-to-faceness better facilitates for us the directness and realness of the encounter and does not prevent the development of necessary past and symbolic meanings. Operationally, how do we, together with our clients, find our way through such a complex, paradoxical, multi-leveled relationship to change, growth, and development? In a basic sense we think of the conceptual way as relatively simple, although the carrying out of the conception may often be difficult, and it certainly is likely to take time.

Our male client and therapist will help us to state again in a somewhat different way our conception and something of how the conception may be carried out. Our notion is that the feelings, thoughts, reactions, and attitudes present in a relationship have meaning for that relationship itself and also that the relationship has symbolic meanings for past relationships. Further, we repeat that it is the therapist who carries the major responsibility for implementing the realness, the hereness, the nowness, the significance, of the present relationship, as well as for facilitating awareness in both persons of the symbolic meanings of the relationship.

What do we say and do as therapists to carry out our conception in practice? Let us return to our male client and therapist again. If, for instance, the client feels and expresses anger toward his therapist, we think the therapist should recognize, accept, and respond to the anger as directed to him. Furthermore, our conception of the reciprocity in human relationships is germane here in the sense that our therapist needs to recognize and accept that something he has said, some way he has behaved, has been a direct stimulus for the client's anger. Our therapist may find himself saying something like, "I wonder if you felt that I was critical of you? May that be why you are angry?" It may even be that our therapist is guilty—but only slightly, we hope, for to be unduly guilty will diminish him, his client, and their relationship. Who will bear the guilt then? Our therapist may, and if he does, the relationship will suffer and will perhaps become ineffective. Or perhaps in the way we have described in our conception of transfer of feelings, our therapist may manage to transfer the guilt to the client. If that happens, then not much that is good, useful, and therapeutic will usually occur either.

But, more happily, other possibilities exist. If our therapist can feel the guilt but have it pass as feelings do rather than hold or transfer it as in a feeling state, he and his client can go on to be both real and symbolic to each other in the ways that are necessary for a therapeutic result to occur. Generally we think that therapeutically appropriate behavior by the therapist will lead to clear recognition and acceptance by both persons that their relationship has real, present, "in itself" significance and also that symbolic, irrational, although relevant aspects of past relationships are present. Further, we think that if the relationship proceeds as we believe it can, it will grow more and more real and less distorted and symbolic of the past. Eventually termination will occur, for the client and therapist together will have accomplished what is needed. They will have reached present significance, or meaning to each other. They will know separateness, too, feelings rather than feeling states, clarity rather than confusion, and flowing, changing, more satisfying relationships with others, rather than the terrible stability of repeated distortion.

Conjoint Dynamic States: Depersonalization and Regression. Two other related dynamic concepts have led us to choose face-to-face, interpersonal relationships for our therapeutic work with a functioning population. They are depersonalization and regression. We treat these dynamic concepts together because they frequently occur together. To us these concepts are especially germane as we develop our views of human development and of the therapeutic treatment of human problems. We think of the psychological phenomena characteristic of depersonalization and regression as occurring intrapsychically, or phenomenologically. But as we observe and attempt to deal with the behaviors, thoughts, and feelings which lead us to say that a human being is depersonalized and/or regressed, we note that these dynamic psychological states within persons always seem to have powerful, past and present, interpersonal referents. Both depersonalization and regression occur originally in relationships with other persons.

The very term "depersonalization" implies "unpersonness" or "non-personness." It may be true, as some existentialists and others suggest, that aloneness, despair, a pessimistic view of life, even non-personness, are a given in the human condition. We also think, however, that depersonalization is a consequence of some of the ways we treat each other interpersonally. We believe that once the lessons of being depersonalized and/or regressed are well enough learned in relationships to others, a human being can so manage his later relationships with people that he maintains the state of being depersonalized, regressed, or both.

Being depersonalized or regressed seems to have a peculiar defensive, coping quality. It is as though the depersonalized person says: "I may often feel very little like a person. There is some misery and emptiness in my condition and I complain loudly about it, but that misery is a dull ache as compared to the terrible risks I must take and the awful hurts that will ensue if I attempt to change my relationships with people. What do you have to offer that's any good to me? I don't like it where I am, but I'm safe."

The regressed person seems often to say something like the following: "I know I often behave and feel like a child. I know I should be more grown up, and I often would like to be. But being grown up involves responsibility, making choices, and that's too much burden for someone as small as I. Why should I? Besides being little gets me attention pretty often, and that comes close enough to being what I want. Anyway, I won't grow up. I don't like what happens to grown-up people."

By utilizing the language which seems often to be characteristic of the ways depersonalized and/or regressed persons express themselves, we have done two things. We have defined the developmental conditions as we understand them to occur. We have made it possible for the reader to draw from the examples given, some of the reasons why we choose to do therapy as we do. We are deeply concerned, for instance, that our ways of being persons and therapists should not needlessly add to our clients' problems, particularly since these problems may be related to feelings of being depersonalized or regressed. We recognize, incidentally, that we cannot necessarily prevent our clients from feeling so. We even accept that their being or feeling depersonalized or regressed is often a part of the relationship we have. And, further, we recognize that the realness of human conflicts necessitates that such feelings be real to the clients in their relationship to us, the therapists. We are concerned, however, about the degree or amount of such feelings that must occur in the interpersonal relationship with us in order for change and growth to occur in our troubled but functioning clients.

We choose face-to-face relationships because to us face-to-faceness is usually real and human and does not ordinarily prevent the necessary generation of conflicts or feelings of depersonalization or regression if these must be dealt with. In fact, we think that face-to-face relationships tend to generate conflicts associated with depersonalization and regression rather quickly and in ways that can be turned to therapeutic advantage if we can be as we need to be for ourselves and our clients.

We do not wish to minimize the difficulties of doing therapy as we do it, nor have we chosen face-to-faceness without trying other ways—hypnosis, for example. We have found that the other means we have tried have often proved effective to some degree. Yet as we have found our path to the means, the conceptions, the attitudes, we are describing in this book, we have dropped from our practice those ways of treating our functioning population which seemed to us to prolong therapy.

It is likely, too, that the ways we have developed and now find most useful are less depersonalizing to us, the therapists. If by our behavior and our methods we further needlessly depersonalize another, then may not the reciprocal effect be to depersonalize us, too? Certainly one very important reason for our interest, pleasure, and satisfaction in doing multiple therapy has been the beneficial, personalizing effects on us as well as the help our multiply-seen clients have received.

We Set an Example. One more interpersonal aspect of practicing therapy as we do has relevance both operationally and conceptually. We speak now of modeling, perhaps even identification.

But what is modeling to us? It is only partially clear, but we do know some ways in which the conception is useful and some in which it is not.

Let's begin with the negative so that we can end with the positive. We do not think of modeling as either mechanical or totally imitative, although some of both may be involved. We think of it as being more daring, more venturesome, than either imitativeness or mechanicalness implies. We do not ask or expect our clients, ourselves, our students, or anyone else with whom we relate to imitate us, although that may happen, and it distresses us if it continues for long. But we do ask something. It is more nearly a wish or hope, realized often enough to keep us going, yet not often enough to make us grow too complacent. What is our wish or hope? It is that we will be stimulating as human beings who think, feel, take risks, are often anxious, are afraid sometimes, that by our example we will help our clients and our students. To do and be what? Perhaps what they need also to be—individuals who are thinking, feeling, risk-taking, anxious, and afraid in their own ways. Thus it is, we hope, that those we work with may find us useful.

Perhaps first it will be imitation, efforts to be like us; but eventually—if our example is good enough, clear enough, honest enough—separateness, innovation, independence, even creativity, may come to be.

How Can We Be Both Real and Therapeutic?   We have said that we want to do two things with our clients. We want to be real people to them, and we want to help them to repair or resolve problems which have occurred as a result of some developmental failure. There is something almost paradoxical in this. The client has had a growing-up experience with real people, and we are proposing to offer him both a chance to know another kind of interpersonal experience which will presumably be better, will not add to the damage already done, and will, in addition, let him understand and be repaired. Certainly we want him to know us as real and human, capable of making mistakes, perhaps even the same mistakes his parents or other important people made with him. He surely has the capacity to repeat his past interpersonal failures; in fact, it is this very repetitiveness which has most probably brought him to us. Are we not presumptuous to think we can make a difference to him, even bring about changes in him? We cannot really answer the questions posed here, but we can think a bit about what some of these paradoxical problems are as we have experienced them.

Let us consider our emotional investment in the client. We have implied that we believe it is necessary to like a client in order to help him and that in the beginning we spend a good deal of time building the relationship. We and the client make concessions and adapt ourselves to the needs and limits of the other. In a sense we go about developing the relationship on a mutually adjustive basis, with the therapist sometimes conceding to the client to the greater degree. This is done, however, with the expectation that those ways in which the relationship is voluntarily limited, those things which cannot be shared, will ultimately be shared and the relationship expanded. This seems not too unlike other relationships in some ways. In fact, it is different in only a few ways: for example, it has a regular time for taking place, and the matters talked about generally concern only one of the participants. And as the relationship continues, it grows and deepens, and genuine caring develops.

What is this caring between two people? How real is it? How real can we permit it to be? Here we find a possible paradox because we have said that we as therapists want to be real people and wish to present ourselves as having real emotions. Do we mean that our caring for the client is also real? How can we care deeply and not feel that we must protect our client, prevent his doing things which will harm him, even have goals and aspirations for him, and do so knowing that we finally have to give him up and send him on? Weren't these the aspects of being cared for which he has had to fight out in his past interpersonal experiences and which have left him tied and handicapped, less of a person than he is capable of being? Aren't these the costs of being cared for which he has declared are too high to make the interpersonal investment worthwhile?

The answer to all these questions is yes, paradoxical and contradictory as this may seem. In the process of the two of us living out the relationship, the meaning of the conflict becomes clear to both of us, and the decision is finally the client's. How can a caring therapist hear a client's confession of a homosexual episode for example, one that occurred not in the distant past but recently, since the client has become an important and loved person to the therapist? We can only answer that the therapist will hear it with real pain and regret, and furthermore we hope that he will be able to express his pain and regret honestly for what it is, yet not punitively. We hope, too, that both can go on openly to explore the meaning of the incident both to themselves individually and to the relationship, including its meaning in being cared about and in caring about the other. We feel that it then becomes an experience lived out with all the meaning that is implied in caring—including the fact that some behavior of each participant can be genuinely hurtful—because the client, too, may learn that he cares that he has given pain to his therapist.

When the time comes to separate, for the client to go his own way, this is another point at which the meaning of caring becomes clear and another conflict is resolved. If the relationship has been real and the caring genuine, then separation can occur. There is honest sadness but also an honest sense of having been cared about, which the client can take with him when he goes.

What of the other feelings which are a part of caring, such as having hopes and aspirations for the other person? Can the therapist care in this way, or must he somehow keep himself from wanting anything for his client, since the client perceives such feelings as the obligations and burdens of being cared for? Here, again, is a place where we would choose to be real and complete as persons. If our client confronts us with our hopes and ambitions for him and his inability or unwillingness to accept them, we have to stop and think with him about how caring deeply does include some wishes and hopes for the other person. But it does not mean that the client has to fulfill these or be controlled by them in order to continue to be cared about. And another important problem has then been confronted and lived out.

We began talking about paradoxes, and we have pointed to the resolution of each in the course of a real, deeply human, caring relationship which allows the conflict to occur and the problem to develop, and be confronted as honestly and fully as possible. This presents the greatest paradox of all. How can we be as humanly imperfect and incomplete as we are and yet still accomplish the necessary therapeutic tasks with our clients? In all honesty we must say that we often cannot. It was out of our wrestling with just this problem that we began to do multiple therapy. It was out of recognizing that clients can talk about but not live out in a real and human interpersonal encounter, the problems which arose with the parent or others of the sex different from that of the single therapist. Furthermore, clients sometimes had difficulty in working out their problems concerning the relationship between their parents. So, as we will describe in later chapters, we joined our therapeutic efforts and worked and learned together as multiple therapists, two therapists of different sex working with one or more clients.

Some Questions We Have. As we come to the end of this chapter, we pause to wonder and assess whether we have communicated to our readers our beliefs and attitudes, our feelings and experiences, as persons and as therapists in helping people to grow and become more completely human.

Is it clear we believe that to be truly human is to be less than perfect? And yet that being human means also always to hope and strive for something better and to need to understand and forgive interpersonal transgressions and failures? Have we made it clear we believe that human beings can grow and achieve a degree of completeness only in relationship to other human beings, even as we believe that the failures to grow and the damage which occurs along the way have their origins in human interrelationships? Have we said clearly enough how realness and face-to-faceness, for instance, enable us and our clients to grow and change together?

As we reread what we have written in this chapter, we are both anxious and satisfied. We will continue to be anxious, perhaps because we cannot have face-to-faceness with our readers. But we are also satisfied because we think that some who read us will be affected by what we have said and the way we have said it. Being realistic about expectations and aspirations enables us to quiet our anxieties and to move on to our next chapter.

Chapter 6

Rationality: The Mastery Process

As we understand ourselves and others, an individual needs some sense of mastery or control of the direction of his life. We think of phenomenological and interpersonal processes as being part of such a sense of direction and control. Yet we find that we must posit a third kind of process—the rational, intertwined with the other processes—in order to account more fully for this sense of direction, control, and mastery so important to us all.

In this chapter we will discuss thinking, rationality, and its place both in human development and in therapy. We, along with many others, learned in "our growing up as therapist years," that intellectualizing was to be avoided, that it would trap us in our clients' defenses, that thinking kept us from knowing our feeling experiences, that to be rational was to fail to understand the primitive, childlike experiences which kept our clients from being and feeling adult. Thinking, or as usually put, "intellectualizing," hampered our therapeutic efforts. And so we learned to pay attention to the feeling experiences which we and our clients had and to ignore and deny that "bad" intellectual process which went along with feelings. And who can escape the condemnation, perhaps even contempt, so clearly expressed in, "Oh, he intellectualizes everything; he hasn't had a feeling in years," and like comments about this best-known defense among intellectual and educated people.

It was in the comfort and security of our shared therapy experience, multiple therapy, that we finally were able first to look at rationality and then to begin to think about it and wonder what its therapeutic meaning might be. It was after we had worked out many aspects of the phenomenological and interpersonal processes that we began to think about the times in multiple therapy when one of the therapists sits quietly. We saw that we had experienced the quiet periods not as detached, withdrawn periods but as a form of participation in the therapy, although not an expressive one. We concluded that the best way of designating the quiet therapist's function at such times is to call him an observer.

RATIONALITY:
A THERAPY CONSTRUCT

The observer is attending to many different aspects of the therapy. He or she is observing the interaction between the other therapist and the client, the relationship process. The observer may be involved in the phenomenological experience either of the client or of the other therapist. This may be experienced as, "Oh, I understand how he feels," and may refer to either the other therapist or the client. A third area of observation is the observer's phenomenological experience. This may begin as, "I wonder what I feel about this," then become, "Why do I feel it?" Additionally, the observer attending to his own inner self may become aware of a fantasy or recurrent thoughts or even a single fleeting idea and then work to capture the idea and bring it into focus by verbalizing it. We differentiate this attending to self from outright withdrawal because we perceive the stimulus for the inner experience to be the on-going therapeutic process and the experience itself to be an interactive though quiet participation in the process.

In multiple therapy the observer process is easily recognizable, and in a later chapter we will talk about how it is introduced into the therapy. What about dyadic therapy? Does the therapist ever become an observer? As we thought about it, we could clearly recognize that this is a function the therapist does carry out but with less facility because it means disengaging himself from the interaction or perhaps attending to several experiences at once. There seem to be three levels of attention. The first is listening to the client's words. The second, attending to the feelings being expressed. And the third, attending to one's own thoughts, feelings, and fantasy. The therapist observer in dyadic therapy probably cannot give the amount of attention to these observations that the observer in multiple therapy can and at the same time continue the dyadic interpersonal process.

For greater clarity, let us consider an example. Suppose the client attacks the therapist and the therapist responds hostilely. The interchange becomes a real life living out of the expression of angry feelings toward each other. If both the therapist and client feel guilty because they have fought and do nothing to understand it, their guilt will damage the relationship. But if the therapist can stop and observe his own and the client's behavior and also his own feelings, and then think about what has occurred, he may be able to continue the interaction in a mutually helpful vein, and the client may benefit from an honest, direct, interpersonal interchange mutually experienced and understood. Here we introduce another aspect of rationality, that of understanding through an intellectual assignment of cause-and-effect relationships. The therapist says, "I answered the way I did because I felt criticized." So rationality, as we have conceptualized it, consists of making observations, understanding cause-and-effect relationships, and abstracting.

Rationality: A Mediator.   Another way to elaborate further the rational process is this. A client says, "I like my professor in existential philosophy, but it just tears me up when he talks about not being." And the therapist responds with concern and warmth in his voice, "But you know there is in existential philosophy some-thing that can relieve that because they say you can know not being only because you know being." Certainly here intellectual concepts are being dealt with, and a rational way of solving a problem is offered; but the problem is presented emotionally, the response also is given affectively, and the intent is interpersonal. There could hardly be a more abstract, intellectual content than existential philosophy. Another kind of therapist response might be, "I wonder why you are so concerned about not being." This is a clear invitation to think about the problem and a suggestion that thinking about the cause of the feeling offers relief. And that is certainly a rational procedure.

We have thought about the meaning of thinking and ration-ality in the human condition, with the intrapsychic and inter-personal processes playing interactive parts. We have concluded that rationality is a mediator, a catalyst, and a control on the interaction between the phenomenal self and the social, inter-personal being. No one process should long continue alone, for serious disturbances occur when there is an imbalance among the three. Rationality is most often recognized as useful and is actually implemented interpersonally. Thus we know that to get along with our fellow human beings we need to think alike about many things and to have common attitudes. We might consider that while all people have the same potential for feeling and its phenomenal experience, we can relate to each other only when we share accept-ance of the ways of expressing these feelings. The process by which this kind of commonality is achieved is rational and involves education. Let us turn, then, to some thoughts about the develop-ment of the rational process as it occurs in personality develop-ment with emphasis on the dimensions which we have found useful in therapy.

RATIONALITY:

A DEVELOPMENT TASK

How then does the rational process occur in personality develop-ment? What is the nature of personality difficulties which result from some impairment in the balance between the rational process and the phenomenological and interpersonal processes? We think of the rational process as understanding in a conceptual, thoughtful sort of way. We think of it as the way in which human beings gain mastery over their world. To stop and think is the device or method by which children are taught that they can take responsibility for what they do and that they can expect others to be equally responsible in turn. We begin to teach reasonableness early. We say to the baby, for example, "Don't touch; it will hurt the baby," when we keep an infant from touching something hot. If a parent says only, "Don't touch," the human capacity to know reasons for things is ignored.

The cultural patterns may determine whether reasons and explanations are given along with demands and prohibitions—and also determine the cultural outcome. The giving of reasons is the essential difference between teaching a child and training an animal. To be able to understand and to expect to understand are both essentially human. As human beings we are able to trust our interpersonal and social environment because we know our environment and our fellow human beings are reasonable and rational. Can we, then, concern ourselves about the nature of rationality from our experience as therapists?

OBSERVING: PART OF THE TASK
OF RATIONAL DEVELOPMENT

To begin with, there are at least two dimensions of the rational process. One dimension has to do with making accurate observations and the other, with adequate, appropriate conceptualization, explanation, and reasoning. We will think first about observation and develop some ideas about its meaning in personality theory and in therapy. We have been saying that rationality has a coping function, that it helps us to feel secure with ourselves and with our environment.

Perhaps the reverse is also true. Irrationality makes us anxious and fearful. Why or how do we experience something as irrational? Take the example of a young man who comes for help because he is frightened by his own feelings of violence. He says he has recently had feelings of wanting to kill a lot of people. A few questions reveal that these are not people he knows, just people, and he is worried. Since he is so concerned, the therapist does not try to show him that this is irrational by pointing out realities, for example, that since he has never been angry enough to kill before, why should he think he is now? Instead, the therapist may say, "Can you see yourself doing it, and how would you go about it?"

The client begins to recount his hostile fantasy. In order to do so, he makes an observation of his fantasy and stops it long enough to describe it. The fantasy may be totally irrational, but the client's prior effort has been to give it meaning, to explain it, sometimes even before he is able to describe it. Somehow it is the irrationality of the feelings that seems most distressing. And because they are irrational, the tendency is not to want to observe the fantasy. But with urging he begins to describe an elaborate plan for getting a lot of people in a confined area and developing highly technical weapons with electronic controls. Suddenly the young man says, "I can't do that. I can't make the weapons. I don't understand enough math." He visibly relaxes and his anxiety is abated. He has observed his fantasy, seen why he cannot carry it out, and regained mastery of himself where before he had known only panic. That he may have other hostile fantasies until he understands the source of his general hostility is also true. But a degree of relief has been afforded by a clear observation and recounting of his fantasy.

Where mastery of overwhelming feelings is the issue it seems that usual efforts at rational control are ineffective. Think, for example, of the ways in which people try to deal with their fears. The injunction "Don't be afraid" is relatively meaningless; and "It's silly to be afraid" may only add to the problem. But if there is some way to explain the fear, if only to recognize that there is something to be afraid of, then the fear becomes manageable. The person has a sense of being able to master rather than a feeling of being overwhelmed. In this latter instance the frightened person makes the observation that there is something to be afraid of. Then when he has "seen" that much, he knows that to be afraid is not irrational, and he can begin to perform appropriately. We are convinced that observing, or seeing, is an important aspect of understanding and of mastery.

As we have thought about the observational aspects in rational process, we have been led to search for dimensions and constructs, ways of assigning meaning in our own personal experiences as we understand ourselves as therapists and as people. As we frequently do, we questioned each other: "What is it [thinking and fantasy] like for you? I have visual images, do you?" We made an interesting discovery, which we would like to report along with some inferences we have drawn.

The question was, "Don't you have visual images?" The reply, "I haven't really thought about it." Further thinking and attention to thought processes brought the report, "I think I have so taken for granted the fact that I can describe something or talk about something because I have seen it, that I have really been unaware of using an image or having had one. It's as though it is always available, and so it does not have to be considered. . . ." Now, that was a most interesting contrast to the questioner's experience, which was consciously to try to produce an image and then to think and verbalize about it. We understood that we differed in the conscious manipulation of images and the degree of awareness of their usefulness.

We made a tentative assumption that images are a part of thinking and learning for all people and that the degree to which images are conscious and the freedom with which they can be consciously manipulated may vary. We began to think about how children are taught at home and in schools to use visual imagery, or to suppress, limit, or control it in useful as well as maladaptive ways. We thought, too, about children as observers and were reminded of the old story, "The Emperor's New Clothes," along with the child's observation that the Emperor was wearing nothing at all. Then we went on to consider the meaning of children's fantasy, and also the meaning of adult fantasy and its usefulness in therapy. We also gave some consideration to imagery and how it can be useful in therapy. And we speculated about how rationality includes verbal abstractions derived from the varying kinds of observation processes and how these same abstractions may be either creative and productive or distorting and maladaptive when they are a part of interpersonal communication.

The Child as Observer. Now, after this overview, we want to focus on children as observers. Children are active observers of the world around them and frequently disturb their parents by the clarity of their understanding of what they have observed. Sometimes the naming of their observations is faulty because they do not have the background for this kind of abstraction. Take as an example a little girl who, riding down a highway at night, saw a reflectorized highway marker which said "DIP." "Oh," she exclaimed, "there's a smiling man."

Much parental effort goes into shaping children's interpretations of their observations. Sometimes giving an observed fact a meaning or an explanation obscures the observation. Sometimes the obscuring may be intentional. Children's observations of sexual activity are such an example. For whatever reason, whether because the adult world cannot tolerate the clarity of children's observations or because interpretation complicates meaning, children can grow up to be adults who are less sure and less clear about what they see than they were as children. They grow up to be adults who respond to their interpretation of what they observe rather than to the observation.

We believe that the simplicity of the child observer process is available to the adult but not always readily useful. Let us consider, first, what has happened to it. If interpersonal communication were confined to reporting what one sees as a series of factual observations, our conversations would be sterile and quite meaningless. After all, as complex as our world is, the number of things to be seen and reported is limited, and these would soon be exhausted as a source of interpersonal contact.

Suppose we contrast "Johnny's pants are four inches above his ankles," which is an observation, with "Johnny's growing fast these days," which is an abstraction from the same observation. The latter is not only more tactful but also permits more interaction about the fact, if we assume that the intent of the observer is to establish interpersonal contact. The infant who points and says "cow" has reached his limit of interpersonal conversation with but not of interpersonal meaning for the older person with a wider vocabulary and more verbal ways of interpreting him.

If we watch two infants together, we realize that each has ways of communicating his personal meaning to the other who has no greater skills in conversation than he has. They communicate about things other than observations. It seems evident that for one person to mean something to another, feelings, attitudes, values, actually all kinds of intrapersonal experiences, need to be communicated, and that they may be communicated about an experience of observing or about an observed thing. Simply to recount an observation does not achieve the desired interpersonal contact, and even babies playing together show us that this is true. Thus we have a basis for explaining why observations become modified, interpreted, enhanced, abstracted, and even distorted in the interest of interpersonal meaningfulness.

And yet we hypothesized at the beginning of this chapter that rationality is a primary basis by means of which we human beings are able to sustain any interpersonal relationships at all. Are we inconsistent, then, to point out that the observer aspect of rationality is inadequate to accomplish interpersonal relationships, that, in fact, observation must sometimes be obscured and changed? It seems also true that distortions in the observer process are the origins of maladaptive behavior in some cases.

Fantasy as a Part of the Observation Process. Let us think a bit about fantasy and see where that takes us. We believe that observation precedes fantasy and imagery. Fantasy is sometimes a projection of intrapsychic experience which can make the phenomenal world observable. A fantasy of going up to someone and kicking him can result in a surprised, "Oh, I didn't know I felt like that toward him."

In a child's world fantasy can include even more than a projection of phenomenological experience. Sometimes there are imaginary people and animals, and even experiences with them. Much fantasy is played out with other children, and the verbalization is with their playmates. When children play together they seldom confuse fantasy with reality, because there is a tacit or often overt understanding that this is "play and pretend." On the other hand, children seem to need for adults to maintain a kind of reality to which they can refer. They carefully separate, even when playing with adults, what is fantasy from what is reality. This suggests that parents and other adults have a significant part in the way children use fantasy and play as a developmental experience.

Let us examine some ways adults relate to children's fantasy. We believe that here lies a source of future neurotic conflict in the children, or if the relationship has been an appropriate one, a source of secure independence. Small children playing together often makes plans (fantasy) which require parental consent to be carried out. Sometimes the consent hasn't been sought, and parents find themselves interfering in the acting out of a fantasy which is well along in its development. We do not suggest that there is a general rule about whether parents interfere or not, rather that the meaning of the interference will be different depending on how the parent becomes involved in the fantasy.

An example will help to clarify. Three small children, two little brothers and a little girl who lived next door, decided they would have a "camping trip" and sleep out in the back yard. The boys went home to make preparations, and when they approached their mother about their plans were told they couldn't do it. The little girl went in and packed a bag with all her clothes and gathered up her bedding. She talked about it to her mother and father, and they talked about it with her. They asked her what you did when you went camping, how you eat, how you sleep, etc. She told them as she continued to make plans and to get ready. They all went out in the back yard, and the little girl took all her things along, thus continuing to play out the fantasy. Finally, the father and mother went back into the house and continued to be concerned about their own affairs. In a very few minutes the small girl came back in carrying all her things and announced that it was too cold to camp out. We regard the parents as observers in the fantasy rather than as being involved in it, although their questions might make it appear that they were actively involved. Their questions and the child's answers became a part of the verbal experience of the fantasy.

In the case of the mother of the two little boys, we suggest that the fantasy was cut off because she became involved to the extent of believing—to the same degree they themselves believed—that they would carry it out. She was not an observer because she became immediately involved to the extent of having to forbid the fantasy as well as the proposed "acting out." We do not intend to suggest that children should always play out their fantasies with no adult interference. This would be to deny the validity of greater experience in recognizing the risks involved. We are proposing, however, that parents may often need to be observers rather than participants and that being an observer is a very important kind of involvement.

Another incident will further illustrate children's need for adults to be observers rather than participants. Two little fellows were playing in front of a house when the owner came home. Each had on a red fireman's helmet, and they carried sticks as though they were nozzles of a fire hose. One said to the other, "Go over there and turn on the fire hydrant." Then they ran down the walk in front of the adult toward the front door, holding their sticks so as to direct them toward the house. The adult said, "Where's the fire?" One little fellow answered, "It's your house." And then he turned around and anxiously added, "It's just pretend. There really isn't any fire." Apparently the child understood the adult's question, "Where is the fire?" as meaning that the adult participated in the fantasy, and the participation made the fantasy too real to the child to be tolerable.

We are suggesting, then, that when adults believe or participate in the fantasy, it can lose its value for the child or perhaps distort or damage its meaning. We even believe that it can be damaging to the child's development. In this connection we should point out that in families children are not the only ones who may have fantasies. Adults may, too; they may even lose contact with the fantasy as fantasy and begin to believe it. In such families we would expect the children to have difficulty distinguishing fantasy from reality. We believe that some of these children grow up to be adults whose reality contact is impaired.

Suppose, for example, it is very important to a set of parents that they love each other and present to the world a picture of a happy, harmonious couple at all times. Let us further suppose that, by definition, a "happy" couple doesn't fight. The children hear their mother complaining about many minor things but always adding that it doesn't really matter. The father may be very busy and have so many things to do that he never has much time to spend in this happy relationship with his wife. The children must never doubt the happiness. Everyone is dedicated to it!

What can these children do to bring reality into their lives? One child may settle for unreality and live in an unreal, schizophrenic world. Another may be hostile, fighting everyone, and a behavior problem in school. This second child certainly challenges the "happy family" fantasy and at a serious cost to himself, but the parental happiness fantasy does not appear to be disturbed. A third way of dealing with the fantasy is exemplified in the last child, who has many friends and seems happy but who somehow never settles down to anything and can't make decisions. As he grows older, he is not able to be really close with anyone. The parental fantasy goes on, and the parents wonder what was wrong that the children didn't turn out as they should have.

Fantasy has acquired a negative connotation for many people. Some parents have believed and some professional people have taught that fantasy in children and adults should be discouraged. We think that the concept needs to be better defined and its meaning clarified in order to make an accurate decision as to its efficacy. Children who play out their fantasies often have a very useful learning experience. They play at being a doctor or nurse and give meaning to their present or anticipated real life experiences. They look at pictures in books and movies. They watch television and develop sources for imaginary experiences. The richer a child's life as an observer has been, the more sources he has to call on to give content to his imagination. So the child observer lays the foundation for the child who learns mastery of his world by imaging with the verbal content of what he experiences. Fantasy played out also has verbal content. Fantasy in which there are images and verbal explanations we have thought of as imagery.

Imagery: Part of Fantasy and Observation. An element of control, of mastery, is present when a mental picture can be called up, seen, described, and talked about. An example will help to illustrate this mastering effect. Let's consider moving to another town and compare two ways of fantasying about it. The stream of thought in one instance goes like this: "I won't do it. I can't. I hate it. What will happen to us? I'm helpless. I don't feel good. I'm useless." It also includes variations on the theme of the difficulty of the task and the feelings of inadequacy and self-criticism. The images, if any, are gray or black and unformed.

In contrast, a fantasy which we would consider has coping elements might have unhappiness in it, but it would develop more along this vein: "I hate to move. It's so much work. All those books. Guess I'd better start collecting some boxes. I must remember to ask at the store, etc." The element which makes the difference, as we see it, is the concreteness of "I hate to move" as opposed to "I hate it," and we hypothesize that there is present a stream of images of tasks, which in turn suggest how they can be accomplished.

We cannot be certain, of course, that this is a universal process of mastery, but it has been useful to us as therapists and explains certain kinds of experiences we have had with clients. We have been suggesting that fantasy with images has particular power because images can be observed and understood in a way which means mastery. We are sure that many clients we have seen have been helped, in part at least, by our urging, even insisting at times, that they image about a task or situation rather than simply recount their repugnant, avoidant feelings.

Interpretations and Abstractions: Making Rationality Interpersonal. We need at this point to discuss the interpersonal aspects of rationality. We have dwelt at length on the observer process and its derivations: fantasy and imagery. We will have more to say about them when we describe some other therapy processes. Earlier we pointed out that simple observations do not necessarily suffice as an interpersonal mediator. Consequently, in order to relate meaningfully to each other, our reports of observations—whatever kind they may be, whether observations of our own emotions, our companion's emotions, our past thoughts, present experiences, or fantasies about the future—are all changed in some way. This makes them no longer simple verbal pictures but more or less complex abstractions. These abstractions communicate interpersonally and carry the burden of making us meaningful to each other.

It is in this very process of achieving interpersonal meaningfulness that problems arise. As each one of us listens to another telling about his interpersonal and extrapersonal experiences with their accompanying distortions, interpretations, enhancements, extrapolations, and embellishments on what the speaker has observed or experienced, we, the listeners, go through an equally complicated process of making the speaker meaningful. Sometimes listening results in confusion because the meaning simply cannot be sorted out. Sometimes the listener becomes confused, stops listening, and responds without having heard. Sometimes the listener's interpretations are so intrapersonal to him that the original speaker is confused or feels misunderstood, even depersonalized by the response. This latter kind of interpersonal failure is so common that it seems important to be explicit about it.

People who share a household or live in families are usually able to interpret each other fairly appropriately. But we have all heard adolescents living at home say angrily, "I don't see why my mother [or father] acts the way she does about my dates. I don't do anything." The hurt is clear, and we understand that the parent's anxiety has somehow impugned the adolescent's integrity. In therapy relationships, where there is much less time for mutual testing of motivation, the risk of misinterpretation is even greater.

Suppose a coed comes to see a young male therapist because she has a problem with her roommate whom she likes but who has a habit of masturbating, which offends her deeply. She has thought of all the things she might do to change her roommate and has been unable to bring herself to do any of them, so she seeks a therapist to pour out her frustrations about the roommate's behavior, perhaps with an unconscious hope that he can do what she cannot do. If he interprets her feelings as being inappropriate, thinks perhaps she is over-reacting and overtly offers to help her change her feelings, she feels criticized. She may respond with anger and more stormy frustration. We will assume that he genuinely wants to help her and that his suggestion of how he can help is in good faith; the result is that he, in turn, is affronted by her misinterpretation of his good intention. Their interpersonal encounter then has resulted in mutual hurt and rejection because each has partly misinterpreted the other's motivation. Each feels a less worthwhile person because the misinterpretation has criticized something very important. Interpretation has obscured the ability of each to make a simple observation of the other's intent.

Imagery and Therapy. We have been considering some of the reasons why interpersonal communication may have little contact with the simple, child-observer type of imagery which we believe can be a source of clear understanding between persons. The notion that the ability to observe as simply as a child can be helpful in interpersonal experience needs further exploration. Perhaps it has utility only for therapists. Let us consider what it might mean to the young man to whom the distressed coed has come. What would he see?

Let us reconstruct what his imagery process would likely be. He would see a very upset young lady talking about behavior in another young lady and feelings about that behavior which he does not understand. He would see himself wanting to help her. He would perhaps feel it kinesthetically. But somehow when he tries to picture what goes on in that dormitory room it is less clear—the scene is blurred. He sees himself turn away from the closed door of the room to pick a book from his shelf and run down the table of contents looking for a topic that seems to fit.

> Ah, here is one. I'll try it. [*He then looks at the coed and shakes his head.*] No, those words don't seem to have anything to do with what she feels; she is alive. I'll have to try something else. I wonder if I could possibly know what this means to her. I am not a girl, I have never been a girl. Perhaps she could tell me if I let her know I really do want to see into that room and know her in it.

So he turns away from what he knows, to learn from her; and perhaps as she tells him—who doesn't know but sincerely wants to—she herself is able to "see" the scene more clearly and what it means to her.

We are suggesting that the therapist's imagery can give him knowledge of himself and better ability to make choices of what he can do and does not want to do in an interpersonal encounter, even though the imagery may not tell him what the other person has experienced. However, sometimes the imagery does tell the therapist exactly what the other's experience has been, and so the therapist is able to communicate, "I have been there with you, and I know what it feels like, even though I don't experience the feeling in exactly the same way you do." His imagery can also add another dimension, which is, ("I am seeing this experience quite clearly up to this point, but I'm somehow not clear about why this other thing happened. Can you tell me?") And the client, intent on sharing with the therapist, supplies something which had previously been missing even to himself.

We want to make clear how this attention to imagery makes it possible for the therapist to be conscious that he makes choices. Let us consider again the young man and the coed. No doubt he was aware that the picture was blurred when he said, "I can't help you with your problem with your roommate, but I can help you with your feelings." It is not as clear that he knew he had made a choice.

Suppose he looks at the closed door in his image of the girl's dormitory room, knows about the vague, confused images inside, and says to himself, "I have no business going in that room, I don't belong there." If he tells the young lady and makes it clear to her that this is a private world of girls which he respects, she will feel enhanced as a woman and feel much less rejected by an outcome which still leaves her with the problem. On the other hand, she may recognize that she didn't want him, an outsider, to do something lest it hurt her roommate. If the therapist and coed do follow this fantasy each in turn, the coed now perceives what her choice would be about having him actually do anything. It is not intended the foregoing should imply that the emotional stress of the interview is immediately relieved. But the therapist has at hand a means by which both of them can live through and work out in imagery what has been an unmanageable experience for the client.

Incomplete Images Are Related to Problems. We believe that imagery is frequently a part of people's struggle to solve problems which they are not able to cope with and that it does not lead to a successful resolution when the imaging process is not carried to completion. In such an instance the imager stops the process before he has reached a point where he can see that he made a choice of action. It is possible that talking permits the imagery to be carried to completion, that is, to the point of clear recognition of choice; talking may even assure completion. Certainly telling another person and making him understand often clarifies the issue for the speaker and helps to sort out and specify the fantasied possibilities. An example will help us here.

A young woman sought out a therapist because she was concerned about her premarital sexual activity. Some discussion revealed that her parents and particularly her father believed that she was an inordinately "good" girl, and the therapist sensed some pressure within the client to disabuse the father of the idea. The therapist said, "Let's imagine how you would tell him. Start at the beginning, and we'll go through the whole experience." The client with some direction by the therapist then began to imagine the experience. As she described the scene and began the conversation with the father, she suddenly said, "I can't do that. It would kill him."

An interesting bit of feedback came from a friend of the client who reported that the client had been talking about how much better she felt following the interview. We hypothesized that the young woman had been having a partial fantasy about telling her father but always stopped short of the point where she could clearly see what it would mean to both of them. Perhaps completion of the imagery in such a case could be achieved only when another person is present to urge the completion.

FEELINGS, FANTASY, IMAGERY:
A MODEL FOR MASTERY

Let us go back now to a further consideration of the dimensions of fantasy and its relationships to other psychological experience. In the developmental process we have talked about the relationship between children's fantasy and play. It seems that fantasy is part of planning play as well as a source of motivation for play. Play, in turn, builds experiences and makes fantasy and thinking meaningful in many ways. The child learns what an imagined experience is like, what the physical, behavioral parts of the fantasied activity may be. We think that play produces some emotional experiences but that those have more to do with playing itself than with the fantasy being played out.

A little girl playing nurse does not learn how it feels to be a nurse though she may learn ways of coping with her own fears of encountering a nurse in the doctor's office. Sometimes a play experience acquires an emotional tone because of some distressing emotional incident associated with it, as in the case of the older child or adult who is afraid of all dogs because of an unfortunate but forgotten experience while playing with a dog. However, it is probably more common that the learning aspect of played-out fantasy does not include the learning of emotional states that become a part of the adult experience.

It seems important to make a distinction between the physical concomitants of emotional experience and the kinesthetic aspects of fantasy. If we can indeed make such a distinction, it will help to clarify the way in which imagery can function in helping people to master a situation or cope with their emotional states.

People frequently report a muscular tingling associated with thinking about a physical activity. For example, thinking about playing tennis can include a feeling in the muscles of the arm which suggests swinging the tennis racket. In contrast to this kinesthetic experience, pleasure associated with playing tennis is experienced more as a general feeling in the whole body; and if one attends to it a bit, it can be experienced separately. If one continues to sit and think about playing tennis, it is possible to see the whole experience, the image of grasping the racket and serving, and even to work on various ways of holding the racket and serving, moving the arm so as to produce an arc with a maximum of power or direction. This is an example of the way in which fantasy can help an older person learn and master when the emotion involved is largely a pleasant one. The kinesthetic experience and the emotional experience combine to enhance the concentration on imagery and may ultimately lead the person to act out the imagery and become involved in a game of tennis.

In the case of unpleasant emotional concomitants, the imagery may never occur even though there may be many kinesthetic experiences present in the truncated fantasy. The fantasy is totally involved with the physiological aspects of the kinesthetic and emotional components, and the more controlled and directed imagery simply does not occur. The person may say, "I cannot think because I feel so much," and in a way this is an accurate description of what happens. We have found that if we as therapists make suggestions about how to image, people most often find that they can "think" and are able to cope with their feelings and experience relief.

A common phobic experience, fear of high places, affords an example which can demonstrate the process. Let the reader imagine himself on the edge of a cliff looking down. Feel the weakness in the leg muscles as though they could give way and perhaps the conscious tightening of the muscles to be sure they don't. Feel the tightness in the chest, the pounding in the heart, the need to grab something and hang on. Now look down at the bottom of the cliff. Can you see yourself there? Yes, and you still feel scared and need to hang on.

Now watch yourself fall. Do you turn over and over in the air? Do you twist your body and fling your arms around? By this time having looked at the picture of yourself falling, you probably no longer feel as afraid, no longer have the muscle twinges and the physiological signs of anxiety. This attention to the visual imagery in the fantasy has relieved the emotional stress because the kinesthetic components are no longer applied to the emotional aspects but to the visual imagery. Attention has shifted, has become directed, and control is restored. We emphasize that it is necessary to see yourself fall because only feeling the fall will increase the panic. The latter experience has in it only the kinesthetic and emotional components of the fantasy, not the imagery.

Another type of person, one who characteristically acts out his fantasy, often finds that he has done things for which he seems to have no explanation except "I felt like doing it." Fantasy is incomplete for him, too, but in a different way. We have hypothesized that this kind of person has the kinesthetic but not the emotional experience of the fantasy, and he does not have visual imagery. We think that, impelled by his kinesthetic experience, he acts out the fantasy and that its emotional component is either not experienced or is changed by the doing. When the emotional component is ambivalent, the acting out may serve to obscure the ambivalence but probably does not resolve it. That it is not resolved is suggested when the acting-out behavior is repeated, even though it is not a satisfactory or enhancing experience. We believe, then, that our general proposition can explain some impulsive behavior and also help to manage it.

We have sought to understand why fantasy gets interrupted before being carried through to imagery and a point of choice. As we think about it, it seems to us that anxiety in some intolerable form must intervene to interfere with the transfer of attention to imagery. We suspect, too, that the anxiety may not be of a personal, reactive type but perhaps has its origins in earlier relationships with important adults. It is as though some strong voice says, "You must not think about this any more." When we consider sexual fantasies, it is clear that this is what happens in many instances. It may also happen when the playing out of fantasies by children brings parental interference. "You can't do it so stop thinking about it" is the probable injunction. There must also be some less clear, more subtle prohibitions. The child's story which is interrupted with "That's silly talk" (and the voice is harsh with anxiety) may be another form.

Then there is the child who tries to participate in family problems that include a high level of family anxiety which he does not clearly comprehend but which prevents his carrying his understanding of the situation to any reasonable conclusion. As an example, we can think of the small boy who has learned to look forward to his father's coming home in the evening as a time to romp and play and be close to him. If the parents are in conflict and divorce follows so that the father no longer comes home in the evening or else comes less regularly, before the actual divorce occurs there may be a period of time when first the play and then the anticipation are accompanied by anxiety in the father and/or anxiety in the mother that finally becomes the child's.

The parental anxiety may be unclear to the child and may be experienced by him as a "bad" feeling, but it can eventually interfere so that he no longer is able to complete his fantasy in anticipation of playing with his father. He may grow up with a memory of his father in the form of a fantasy which he stops at the feeling of loneliness without being able to complete the fantasy to understand what other feelings entered into his loneliness. The memory is lost or remains unformed because that past play time with his father could not be thought about. It made people too anxious.

Our general thesis has been that rationality and reasonableness are human attributes which help people to cope with their interpersonal and intrapersonal lives. We have made the general assumption that understanding which includes a sense of the choices which are available is an essential part of the way in which human beings cope with and master their life experiences.

Our work with the population in a university setting has placed greater emphasis on this mastery aspect than would be true in a therapy population of lower educational level, but this emphasis on mastery would not, we believe, negate our therapy's functional value with less educated people. We observe that clients who come from homes where there has been no emphasis on thinking about problems may not know how to do so, but we also note that they can learn to think in ways which are useful to them.

Much learning in school is closely related to the development of imagery through a kind of directed fantasy, in our opinion, the educational process itself contributes significantly to this kind of mastery and control. Education's contribution may not always be positive, either.

We further hypothesize that a good deal of educational failure stems from not learning to capture and manipulate imagery so that the learning of subject matter can occur with a reasonable economy of effort. Educational experiences may even contribute to cutting off fantasies. We believe, then, that the job of helping our university client population is easier because they usually do know something about imagery experiences and how to manipulate them inasmuch as they have been relatively successful in school. However, even in this population, a great deal of variability exists among individuals. We are not prepared to say whether facility with imagery or the lack of it is related to intellectual ability, socioeconomic factors, emotional stability, or some combination of these. We are convinced, however, that rationality that includes imagery can be a powerful coping device.

Rationality Misused. Some of the most unhappy, disturbed people we know have reasons for everything. They can even think out solutions to all their problems yet solve none of them. Do they somehow negate the theory of mastery by rationality? Let us listen to them. A common example is, "I have a good husband, nice children, everything I need, really, but I don't understand myself. I can't make myself do the things I ought to, really want to. I've no reason to be like this. I am not myself. I cannot understand myself." The effort to understand and to cope by being rational is very clear, yet it does not produce a change. Another says, "I must be mad at my roommate. I hit him and knocked him down. But I don't have any reason to be mad at him; he really hasn't done anything. I can't understand myself." This boy thinks and worries over his behavior. Rationality as he utilizes it does not offer any relief. Still another says, "My wife says I must be mad at my mother. But that can't be true because I've always loved her. She's done so much for me."

Apparently if one says, "I feel because," that ought to make a feeling reasonable. If it doesn't, the perplexity and distress that follow bring the person to a therapist for help. Or there is the troubled young man who says, "I know I shouldn't, but I can't make myself stop looking at dirty pictures." And there is the woman who says, "I'm so depressed. I cry all the time. I don't have anything to be sad about. I've thought of everything. I just can't do anything about it." These people are all struggling to understand themselves, believing that somehow understanding should mean relief and resolution. Here is no lack of striving for rationality. What might be wrong? Why are they not successful?

If we think of our fantasy model with its mastery and resolution outcome, we can begin to make some hypotheses and to direct our therapy procedures with a little more sophistication. First, we note that these are all thinkers. Some of these people also feel, but do not accept their feelings. They experience their feelings but cannot make sense of them. And here we depart from some of our colleagues who believe that acceptance of feelings results in resolution. We agree with our clients that there is something inappropriate about the feelings being experienced. We have designated these feelings as feelings states. They include the unexplained depression, the too great anger, and many others.

Second, among these persons who do not understand themselves are some who guess at their motivation and feelings by observing their behavior. Frequently we hear them say, "I find myself doing [something or other]." They are concerned about their behavior, sometimes even frightened by the intensity of the emotion expressed by it, but totally unable to explain it. We believe that they simply act out the kinesthetic experience of their fantasy and have no time to discover either the feelings involved or to plan—that is, they have no time to image the process to the point of making a choice or understanding its meaning.

A third group of "thinkers" without mastery are those who "feel because" and those who do not feel even in the midst of an intense expression of feeling because there isn't an appropriate reason. These persons present a particular kind of distortion of reality with respect to feelings, a distortion which results in the denial of feelings which do not have an acceptable reason for being. Or perhaps feelings which have very different valences are mixed together in such a way as to block rationality. How can I be angry with someone I love? Such apparently opposed feelings are simply not reasonable to these people. In the model of fantasy to imagery and mastery that we have been theorizing about, the feelings are cut off because the fantasy has a fixed end, that is, there is only one way in which it can end.

We will call the last statement a rule or generalization. As an example, let us consider the lesson the small boy learns about being angry at his sister, when he is punished for hitting her with a toy. He is told, "Boys don't hit girls." It is very difficult to keep separate the act of hitting and the feeling of anger, and the rule may change for him from "Boys don't hit girls" to "Boys don't get angry at girls." An even more common rule is "Children love their mothers." Any angry feeling toward mother violates the rule and can be turned into a guilty fear that anger toward mother means that the child does not love her. The experience of feeling angry does preclude an affectionate, loving feeling for that time period. The rule about loving mother makes it difficult to know that anger is a temporary, reactive feeling and need not preclude affectionate feelings when appropriate, since feelings are to be experienced according to a rule, not reactively.

All too frequently the angry fantasy is cut off by the rule and is not carried to an image of what one might do to mother. Sometimes it may even end in an image of what one must do oneself for being such a bad child. The child forbidden to be angry may grow up to be the woman with no reason for feeling so depressed when she has such a good life or the young man frightened by the intensity of his anger toward his roommate. In such instances the fantasy simply does not develop in the adult. In the case of the depressed woman, the fantasy stops when the emotional experience of her anger comes under the influence of the rule. In the case of the young man, action occurs in response to the kinesthetic experience of the fantasy, and neither his angry feelings nor his hostile feeling state is experienced clearly.

But the sequence of fantasy and its interruption need more explanation. One other kind of thinker should be considered: the person who has learned to image the fantasy to its conclusion but has lost its kinesthetic and emotional components. This person will sit and tell his therapist, placing great emphasis on the *do*, "I have thought of all that; what I need is to *do* something." We hear him talk on and on about his feelings, but we wonder what they may be because he gives no other evidence of actually feeling them. Perhaps he has learned the mastery process too well because he seems to have only control from his fantasy. There are no planning and motivation. We also notice that his repertoire of experiences to be talked about is remarkably narrow, his life rather dull. He carefully limits the scope of his fantasy. It is largely a verbal experience, with little that is pictorial. If we ask him to stop talking, he becomes visibly anxious. We are led to ponder whether talking has become a substitute for our hypothesized, imagery type of mastery, and whether talking only controls his feelings and does not really express them.

We wonder what his family was like and how he learned to sit and think about things he would like to do but doesn't do; how he learned to talk about his feelings but not to have them. If we examine the sequence in our model, we can identify the fantasy and the planning, perhaps even the imagery. The missing components are the kinesthetic and/or the emotional experiences, which we have seen serve as motivators to action. What could have become of them? What made them drop out? The answer seems to lie in what the client says about why he doesn't "do" what his fantasied planning says he might or should. When pressed he says, "I can't. I don't know why, I just can't." Often he hasn't even asked himself why he can't; and if he has asked, he has no answer which is satisfactorily rational to him. For most people like him, that unknown reason lies in the forgotten past.

Therapists Are Sometimes Rational.   These incidents we have been describing suggest some ways in which therapists may use a part of the rational process to help clients. We can describe some other ways in which therapists may be rational and in so doing be useful to their clients. The person whose feelings are real only if he can account for them will be totally frustrated by and frustrating to a therapist who suggests that he must have some feelings that he doesn't know about.

Such a person is the very bright young man who came asking for help saying: "I'm not doing well in school, but that is nothing new. I'm a senior, and I haven't made good grades since I was a freshman. That doesn't worry me. What really worries me is that I no longer care. I don't care about anyone, and I don't care whether I study, and I don't care whether I stay in school. That really bothers me."

To the questions about how he gets along with his parents he answers, "Just fine. We're a close family." And then he reveals that he is heavily in debt and enumerates some additional personal deficiencies. Still, he insists that he is scared only because he doesn't care about any of these admittedly real problems. The therapist makes a statement, as a simple logical deduction, that it doesn't seem that the client's relationship with his father can be just fine when the client does so many things which can only be hurtful and punishing to his father.

Weeks later this client returned to report what had happened to him, including a number of major changes in his feelings and in his life. He said, "The more I thought about it, the more I knew you had to be right. There was something wrong with my relationship to my Dad. I went home and talked it over with him, and I made some changes in it." We can't know with certainty why this client was helped except by what he tells us, but the incident is reported because it illustrates in at least two ways what we are proposing.

This young man had been thinking about his problems. He was using rationality as a coping process, but somehow this thinking had become circular and irrational in its sequence. It was irrational because it was illogical. To break up the sequence and point out its irrationality is not as easy a matter as logic would suggest. We believe that he had to become aware of great intrapsychic need for change, of some kind of intrapsychic pain or distress, because a very basic, interpersonal relationship was involved. We think that his need to defend the nature of his relationship with his father was so great that to have asked him to give up rationality would have added a problem rather than helped him, and would have caused him to feel confused. We, therefore, entered into his mode of coping and were rational right along with him.

We have found this last notion useful in working with a functioning population for the very reason that they do usually depend heavily on reasonableness. To permit them to do so helps them to continue to function. Another way of putting it is to say that we sometimes join and utilize clients' rational defense rather than attack it in a direct way. The result is, hopefully, that they are able to see their own irrationality and to deal with it appropriately.

Certainly this kind of approach does not always work, but we would choose it as a way of beginning with some clients. We might say, for instance, "I see you are the kind of person who thinks about his problems. Can you tell me how you have been thinking about this?" The client can feel complimented by having his thoughtfulness recognized, and he can go on to recount his own thought process and perhaps to recognize how the sequence has been illogical. Whether this is sufficient to resolve the problem will depend most on where in the developmental sequence the distortion and failure occurred. We assume that the young man in the earlier example did not need to reexperience a developmental failure at an early age but rather needed to make changes in his more recent relationship with his father.

Developing rationality and learning to use it effectively is a task which continues into young adulthood and perhaps much later. We consider that failures in this task are evident in much the same way that failures in other developmental tasks are. We sometimes see people who say, "Thinking is something I do in school. I hate school, and I never think about anything outside." We call them immature and sometimes feel rather frustrated and helpless about how to work with such retarded persons. If we go back to think about how rationality develops, beginning with good observing, this suggests how to work with this kind of person. We believe that making accurate, independent observations of self and others is the area in which the developmental failure has occurred. Whether this client also has to reconstruct and understand why he didn't learn to do so is a question to be decided individually. Perhaps in observing his childhood experiences, he will come to assign reasons for their having happened, or he will begin to desire to know reasons.

And Therapists Are Sometimes Not Rational.   We should not leave this discussion of thinking and rationality without saying something about the kind of people with whom therapists are not rational, reasonable human beings. We believe that because being rational is so easy and natural for most of us, we can readily be trapped into being only that when it is actually not the way to be helpful. If we find ourselves being rational and intellectual with a fellow intellectual, we will often find ourselves finally bored and vaguely discontented because the therapy is going nowhere. So we try to foretell this. And having recognized that here is a client whose whole life experience is well thought out, whose every relationship is an intellectualized interaction, we avoid being cerebral with him.

Instead, we call up more primitive, interactive, feelingful ways of relating. We try in every way possible to prevent him from understanding what is going on and from drawing us in some way into his depersonalized, unemotional, intellectualized way of keeping himself alone and unknown. We hope he will learn from us that there is a safe world in which he can be without his having control over every facet of it. We assume that his need to control and his overdevelopment of the mastering powers of rationality also tell a story of fear and uncertainty in early relationships. We believe that only thinking about those early relationships will not let him learn another way of being safe with his fellow human beings. In the two preceding chapters we have written about the kinds of things we as therapists do with him.

Terminations with Understanding and Rationality. This seems to be the right place to say something about what clients are like when they terminate. We have had something to say concerning people who need to learn the value of thinking about themselves and their experiences, as well as something to say concerning those at the other extreme, who actually think themselves into nothingness. By implication we have said that there is an optimal way for human beings to live rationally. In order to think about an optimal kind of rationality, we now turn to our clients when they terminate.

It is often true that they want to talk about what the therapy experience has been like and to tell us what they think was important and meaningful to them. This seems to us a way in which thinking about the therapy experience, sharing their thoughts, mediates a mature, perhaps equalitarian relationship with us, the therapists.

They will say so, too, that they know they will have more problems but that they feel fairly confident about knowing how to meet them. We have understood this kind of statement to mean that thinking is no longer simply a device for mastering but has become so much a part of them that it can be talked about as though it were a feeling, carrying with it the sense of security which mastery affords. Thinking has indeed become a mediator for interpersonal relationships and a source of control for feelings that otherwise might be overpowering and feared. In terminating, clients will sometimes reward us with glimpses of their truly exciting and creative ways of conceptualizing their experiences, ways which are now their own individual methods of seeing the world.

How to Be Rational About What We Have Written. In this chapter we have tried to accomplish something in particular. What is it that we have tried to do? It is evident, of course, that we have written about observing, thinking, fantasy, imagery, feelings, rationality, and irrationality. We have even suggested a "model," which embarrasses us a bit, for such a way of conceptualizing and writing is not our usual way of doing, thinking, and being. But then models tend to be logical, at least they appear to be so, and we have found logic and rationality useful in working with our clients as well as in hypothesizing about human developmental success and failure. Yet while we have wanted to be logical and rational, and to convey something of the importance of these functions in human affairs, at the same time we have wanted to remain speculative.

Above all, we have wanted to suggest and to stimulate, rather than to define. Our model, we hope, suggests a sequence, mastery, coping—yet also openness, imagination, and change (rather than definition and closure). If we have accomplished our purpose, the reader will be stimulated to image, to fantasy, to wonder about self and clients. Did we make sense at times and not at others? Hopefully, we have done both. If we have made sense, then we and the reader have something in common. That is good. But if we have also not made sense at times, the reader has something different to work with. We invite him to complete his own fantasies in his own ways.

Chapter 7

People Are Unities

We have told and behaved a small lie in our immediately preceding three chapters. We don't believe the lie and neither, we hope, do our readers. In fact, we have said that we don't believe the three kinds of processes we have described—phenomenology, interpersonality, and rationality—are separate, distinct, and unrelated in human beings. Still the act of writing separate chapters on them may have led us all to think that human beings are more compartmented than they really are. So, we find it necessary to write something of how the processes, while they may be described and conceptualized in ways which make them have some separate and distinct meanings, do not occur so neatly, separately, and distinctly in functioning human beings.

All of us have a more or less rich, varied, useful, phenomenological aspect to our lives. But it is only an aspect, for we also live and interact with others, unless we are hermits, and this interpersonal life affects both our rationality and our phenomenology. Further, all three processes are interactive and reciprocally modifying as a human being grows, changes, learns, and is uniquely human. The possible combinations, interactions, and modifying effects approach infinity; thus we can be assured that we are all different and separate. Yet we can all have the necessary experience of commonality and belongingness since our modes of thinking, feeling, and interacting have similarity.

We have an ideal, too, although probably none of us achieves it. Simply put, we think of an ideal human being as one for whom the interactive, reciprocal, modifying effects of the processes, each upon the other, are unimpeded. The processes are "balanced" because of the ever-present, modifying reciprocity. Yet there is constant change, for the effects and modifications are constantly going on. Our ideal person is recognizable and knowable, yet he is constantly changing and stimulating as we know him through time. He is balanced, but not static or the same..

But we have suggested that the ideal is perhaps never accomplished, and we do not wish to advocate that it should or must be. What do we wish to advocate or say then? Shouldn't we strive to be ideal? Perhaps, but the very notion of striving suggests something of a problem, particularly since striving sometimes is only effort, in our view, and often leads to frustration and even to impasse. So sometimes we strive, but sometimes we can do something else.

Here our experience in writing this book provides us with an example. Certainly, writing is a rewarding and fulfilling effort but a frustrating one at times, too. Very rewarding also has been our occasional ability to be passive, receptive, quiet—in a way, to let an experience "tell us its own meaning." As it is with us, the therapists and writers of this book, so it seems to be with our functioning but troubled clients. We often help them in much the same way we help ourselves. The striving, frustrated ones we help—sometimes, at least—to be quiet, receptive, to "listen to" or "hear" their own inner life. Perhaps, even, we help them to know something of how their striving and frustration affect others and to modify some of those effects.

With the ones who know and express their feelings strongly,

who in a way know their inner emotional life too well, we are sometimes able to help them think, to be rational. And, too, we may help them to know something of why their strong, well-known feelings do not necessarily get from others what they most desperately want.

And so in our own way we come to the topic of assessment. Simply put, how can we know what is needed by another person which may help him to be more of what he wants to be? What is missing or distorted? What is too much or too little? What isn't being changed when it should be? Is there too much thought and too little feeling? Closeness with others is wanted and needed, and how can we help with that? Or perhaps there is too much closeness with someone, even symbiosis, and how do we know that? Even if we know it, what can we do to help?

Utilizing our process conceptions in an integrated way helps us to answer these questions, arrive at assessments of what is needed, and thereby further the therapy we do.

ASSESSMENT THROUGH THE PROCESSES

To us, assessment by utilizing our process conceptions is exciting and useful for several reasons. One is that assessment is a part of the developing relationship. Thus a sense of psychological distance and depersonalization, sometimes the consequence of diagnosis, does not ordinarily trouble us or our clients overly much. Also, since assessment is part of the relationship, our ability to observe how the processes develop in the relationship tells us both about the nature of the relationship and something of what we need to do to be helpful. Assessment, then, for us is investigative, conceptual, and satisfying. Also, it helps us as therapists to be effective in our work.

Reciprocity: A Basic Principle. But, more concretely, how do we use our process conceptions to assess and understand? And how do we translate our assessments and understandings into therapeutic effectiveness? To answer these questions we begin by stating a useful, general proposition: Human beings have troubles with which they may need help because the reciprocal, modifying, balancing effects of the three processes upon one another is deficient, lost, or perhaps undeveloped. Incidentally, loss of or a diminishing of one or more of the processes and consequently of reciprocity is a rather different matter from the failure to develop them, in our view. A person who has less of the ability to think, feel, or relate interpersonally than he once had and hence less of the vital, modifying function of reciprocity is at least aware—perhaps frighteningly so—that he has lost something he once possessed. But ordinarily in such cases in our functioning population, although the sense of loss is frighteningly real and devastation and further deterioration are most threatening, restoration of the damaged process or processes and of the reciprocity function are therapeutically easier than is assisting processes which never were, to develop.

Yet we are not pessimistic about helping a person who may seem at first to be undeveloped phenomenologically, rationally, or interpersonally with the consequent incapacity for reciprocal modification which lack of development of one or more of the process areas usually means. Our optimism is based upon two considerations. First, we have had some therapeutic success with such persons. Second, we observed that in our functioning population, what appears to be an undeveloped process is more likely to be a diminished or interrupted one. In fact, as the therapeutic relationship develops, it usually becomes apparent that the process did develop but then truncated more or less abruptly. It is even possible to know with some precision the age level at which the truncation occurred.

As we have suggested in other places, in such a case the therapeutic task may be to reenter the developmental sequence with the client and "grow up" with him. Therapeutic failures often occur, we think, because of therapist unwillingness or incapacity to reenter the developmental sequence with the client. Failure can occur, too, when a therapist too readily believes that a recently lost or diminished function is lost forever, perhaps as the client does. In such instances, it is often as though the therapist is engulfed and rendered hopeless by the client's desperation.

Assessment Foretells Therapy: Intellectualizing. With the aid of our general proposition regarding the importance of reciprocity among the processes, we can turn to some assessments we often make and to what we do to make them functional in therapy. Let us utilize some common, recognizable examples. In our bright, functioning, late adolescent, young adult population we can conveniently divide those who come to us for therapy into two general types: those who think too much and those who feel too much.

Let us consider now the first type, the thinkers, the eminently rational. They are accustomed to ordering their world and are usually distressed, at least by the time they reach us, that the world is not more orderly, more rational. They tend to talk about feelings, about internal, phenomenological life, but it is talk "about." The talk seems to be an effort to ward off feelings, to avoid, in fact, the phenomenological differentiation which they talk "about" as though it were real.

They are the ones who are likely to have "insight," and yet at the same time they complain rather bitterly that even though they "understand," it doesn't help. They are even likely to doubt that therapy can help them, for they already understand what is the matter. Their insights and understandings often prove to be quite accurate, interestingly enough. But they use the insights defensively to ward off feelings or to avoid direct, interpersonal encounters in areas or ways which make them anxious and uncomfortable. Furthermore, they attempt to engage us, the therapists, in further intellectual, rational, "insightful" discussions of both their troubles and their insights.

We may engage in such discussion or "go along" with the client for a time for three reasons. First, we need to confirm our assessment, and we find that often the most exciting, fruitful way to do so is by participating directly in the relationship. Such participation even helps us to know the probable futility, which the client also knows in his own way, of continuing the relationship on the purely intellectual, rational basis. Second, as we have said elsewhere, a relationship must be built, and we utilize what is most readily available to do so even though we recognize that the nature of the relationship must change in order for therapy to occur. Third, our willingness to be intellectual and rational with our client in the beginning better enables us to know and to feel how, in what ways, we must change the relationship in order for the client to make the changes he needs to make.

When we have gone along with our client long enough and when our assessment is confirmed, what are we likely to do? As we start to use our process conceptions, what general directions may we follow? Conceptually the answers seem simple enough, although in practice what needs to be done may range from relatively easy to difficult. First of all, it is often evident to us that the client is phenomenologically differentiated in some ways but quite undifferentiated in others. Usually in such a client as we have been describing the lack of differentiation has most to do with the experiencing of feelings and emotions. When the feelings seem to be absent, our therapeutic task is more difficult than it is when the feelings are only truncated or warded off, a fact we referred to earlier. Thus part of the continuing assessment task may often be testing whether a particular capacity to feel is really absent, or undeveloped, rather than distorted, truncated, or warded off.

Fortunately in our functioning population a particular capacity to feel is rarely absent or totally undeveloped. We find that much oftener feelings are highly controlled, inhibited, distorted, or displaced; or we may even find that thought has been substituted for feeling. Our optimistic view of our clientele, coupled with our usual finding that capacity to feel is impaired in some way rather than absent, enables us often to move rapidly in our therapy. As a consequence of our assessment, our focus is on facilitating the direct experiencing of the feelings which are inhibited or otherwise impaired. Please note that we are saying we want our clients to experience their feelings, not just to express them.

Another aspect of assessing intellectualizing clients involves becoming aware of the feeling state or states which characterize them. Commonly, we find that with such clients a characteristic feeling state is hostility although any awareness of it may be more or less successfully denied. Usually our awareness of the hostile feeling state comes through the interpersonal effect our client has upon us, the therapists. He bores us, perhaps, or we may bore him. Or he may be patronizing to us or we to him.

Fear used defensively is also common. Fears are often talked about by the client but usually do not seem very real since the talk often does little to relieve or change them. In fact, often the client clings tenaciously to and talks about the fears to avoid either feelingful awareness of their origins or the experience of other kinds of feelings. With such a client it is as though he learned that to be fearful was acceptable and that the experiencing of other kinds of feelings was not so acceptable to him and, probably, to significant others.

That a fear or fears can function as a feeling state and a defense is evidenced when a therapist has the good sense, for instance, to recognize that a fear is being clung to and eagerly talked about without any change occurring. Frequently the therapist gathers the clinching bit of evidence when he notes that the client eargerly, even anxiously, returns to the fear when something else is being discussed and another kind of experience is becoming imminent. The eagerness with which an intellectualizer talks of his compulsions and how they trouble him and how eagerly he returns to talking about them when he seems threatened illustrate this point.

Guilt or guilt-riddenness is also a common characteristic of intellectualized clients although recognition of it may be difficult for both client and therapist. References to guilt are often oblique or well justified if they are direct. If such a client's references to guilt are direct, he has many "good" reasons for being either guilty or not guilty as the "case" he makes for himself may be. Such a client seems often to use talk literally to "wash away" any real feelings, guilty or otherwise, which he comes close to experiencing in a direct, primary sense.

There is, we believe, a further curious aspect to the intellectualizer's experiencing of feelings. It is probably evident from what we have said thus far that we think of the intellectualizer as eminently rational, overly so, in fact. Further, he has interpersonal troubles, again often with little awareness partly because he is monotonic in his mode of self-expression and hence may become boring, uninteresting. And there are other reasons why he may have less than satisfactory effects on others.

But what may not be so clear is our notion that to minimize or truncate feelings leads to the accumulation of these reservoirs of feeling—guilt, hostility, fear, or whatever—that we have called feeling states. Thus our intellectualizer is likely to be mightily startled, if not downright frightened, by occasional bursts of powerful, uncontrolled, and frightening feelings. Such episodes are often the stimulus which brings him in to us. Further, he commonly reports that these episodes are "unlike" or alien to him. So, in fact, they are in a way, for he has been busy denying or short-circuiting his feelings but not really ridding himself of them. Thus we go about assessing the intellectualizer.

Interpersonal Impact and Naturalness in Therapist. There is yet another aspect to our way of going about this business of assessment. We prize this aspect, and it is perhaps particularly germane to assessing and working effectively with the overly intellectual and rational. We refer here to a special low-level kind of "self-consciousness" that we experience in working with such persons. While we observe, assess, and are otherwise rational in working with them, we find that during the therapy we are unselfconscious, even unaware, of many assessments we make. Also, it is not until later that we become aware—if at all—of the ways we may have been effective in our therapeutic encounter, what we have done that was helpful. At times we are even astonished at what we have done—how loose, how natural, we have been.

It is also most interesting how our intellectualizing client may grow angry, even exasperated with us; yet at the same time he is usually relieved, even pleased, that we are not as he is. Moreover, his anger, if that is what he feels, is likely to be experienced strongly, directly, and expressed to us. We can then be pleased, accepting, and rewarding, and a change can occur in the client and in our relationship.

As we think about our naturalness, our spontaneity, we are struck by the probability that this is an important technique we have learned which enables us to have the necessary interpersonal impact. Also, this way of being insures that we therapists do not become overly intellectual and rational ourselves, thereby perhaps contributing to our client's problem rather than helping to resolve it. Thus part of our assessment is a rather unself-conscious assessing of ourselves, the therapists. If, for instance—and this does happen—we find ourselves being less spontaneous, less natural, than we should be, we relax, disengage ourselves, think less, or otherwise "free ourselves up." Sometimes this may even take an effort at first, but we find that it can be done and that it is good for us and for our clients. Multiple therapy has taught us much about the importance of this phenomenon, and we will say more of this in later chapters.

Undercontrolled Emotions. We have already uneasily suggested that our clients—a functioning university group, you will recall—may be roughly classified into two general types: (1) those who think too much and feel too little and (2) those who feel too much and think too little. We have observed, too, that both types are likely to have interpersonal problems but manifestly different ones. The intellectualizer, whom we have discussed in some detail in the previous two sections, is likely to be concerned about "distance" in his relationships with people, although he may not state or be aware of his problem in these terms. The persons who feel too much, on whom we shall now focus our discussion, are likely to be much more concerned with the probable fact that people "go away" from them. Thus their experience, fear, or concern is not so much with distance from others or alienation or barriers between themselves and others. They are distressed that they have been or will be abandoned. They tend to be bewildered, if not devastated or very frightened, by the fact that their relationships are extremely variable. They report and genuinely feel episodes of closeness and intimacy which are usually followed by the feeling that they have been abandoned, that they are terribly alone, that no one cares.

There is likely to be an insatiable quality about such persons. They want and need very much; yet they are constantly troubling to themselves and to others since it seems that they can never be satisfied. In a sense the insatiability is childlike, and it is not well mediated by much capacity to accept what is possible or available. In a way the assessment of those who feel too much is relatively simple, yet some erroneous conclusions can be reached rather easily, too.

The feelings, the demands, the hopelessness, the apparent insatiability, will ordinarily become apparent to the therapist in two primary ways. First, talk and feeling about those who have already gone away is likely to come strongly and quickly. Rejection and abandonment are frequent and immediate themes. Second, the therapist may quickly find that the client sees and reacts to him as someone else who promises something and will also go away and abandon him. Such clients are ordinarily quite appealing, for they are evidently needy and neediness appeals to therapists.

Further, the therapist may too readily believe, as does the client, that the latter is truly insatiable. If a therapist is too quick to believe that the insatiability is real and powerful, he may too readily accede to client demands and make promises that he will have trouble later in fulfilling. Or he may beat a hasty emotional retreat that confirms his client's worst fears. Either course makes it appear that the therapist believes in the insatiability just as the client does.

However, it is important that the therapist know and even feel that the client feels insatiable (and hopeless), for that enables the therapist to understand how his client does truly feel. Such awareness is important for assessment since it aids the therapist both in understanding the nature of the problem and in building the relationship. It also suggests what must be learned by the client, what must be changed or corrected. Such a client must learn to interfere with his feelings, to break them up, to recognize that there are other persons and things besides those immediately in front of his nose and eyes.

We regard insatiability as a feeling state rather than a feeling. And our intent as therapists must be to treat it as such: real and unchangeable for the client, real yet changeable for the therapist. The ability on the part of the therapist to believe that insatiability can be changed is most important. If he does not believe this, alternatives are closed off for both client and therapist. What are these alternatives? Essentially we think they can be understood as belonging to thinking, rationality, judgment, some control of feelings but not inhibition or denial of them. Simply put, our client must learn to think, to be rational, to be aware of choices. Further, he must see that he can learn to make some of the choices he learns to think of. If our client is able to learn to do this in his relationship with us, his other interpersonal relationships will also change. He will be less frightening to himself and others, and he will less and less often be abandoned as a consequence. Once some ability to think and choose is established in our too feelingful client, change often occurs rather rapidly. In our view, the reciprocal, modifying effects of the processes upon each other have been set in motion and will continue to interact.

One final aspect of the importance of choices—whether clients are feelers or thinkers—needs to be mentioned. Here we refer to the different meaning that choices, or alternatives, may have depending upon which type of person the client is. In the instance of the thinker, it is not that he cannot *think* of alternatives. Our observation is that he can think of many, too many usually. His problem is more likely to be emotional starvation because he cannot choose. He does not feel strongly enough about one alternative to be able to choose it. In one way, then, our task as therapists is to help this kind of client to know and experience his feelings well enough so that he has an emotional basis for choosing as well as a rational one. The feelings, fantasy, imagery model is useful here.

Our too feelingful client may emotionally starve to death for quite another reason. His problem is not in having too many alternatives but in having too few, perhaps only one. And these are likely to be ones he cannot have or attain. As he learns to be more rational, more attainable choices become available, and thus in another way our work as therapists may near its end.

Defenses: Our Own and Others. We can say something about the way we go about handling defenses, our own as therapists and our clients'. The term "defense" is a rubric well understood by psychologists and one which we expect will communicate a common understanding. But in therapy how often would we say the word or even think it before going ahead and maneuvering around to try to overcome the limitations which defenses put on our relationship with the client and on his ability to understand himself and to change? The answer is seldom.

In order to think about defenses, one must pull back, stop relating to the other person, separate oneself from an ongoing process. In therapy to think about defenses is to have to recognize an interpersonal frustration or impasse. It is itself a defense against the frustration. So in the therapy hour, there is often not a great deal of conscious concern about defenses. There is much more spontaneous dealing with them—frequently by circumventing them, sometimes by confronting them. But the action is not really thought out, calculated, intentional.

Then why mention defenses at all? The answer is that spontaneity is not always sufficient. When this has been so, we have had to stop and think, and consequently over a period of time we have arrived at some useful conclusions which have helped us in such instances to go on to interact spontaneously and/or meaningfully and to prevent the frustration. What are some of these conclusions, or discoveries?

We found that one way of handling a defense is to understand the defense mechanism and to make it understandable and sensible to the client. If the therapist is able to think of defenses as having a meaning and a purpose which are uniquely appropriate, he can deal not only with his client's defense at any given time but also with his own. Frequently a therapist feels frustrated or irritated by the client's defensive maneuvers. If the therapist is able to recognize his feelings and to believe that there is a reason for them, he will, in turn, be able to think about the client's defense as reasonable and understandable as something more than a defense; and he may be able to make the client see it in the same light. This way of reacting has a meaning appropriate to the ongoing interactions.

Suppose the client asks a question that is somehow unanswerable. The therapist, wanting to give the client what he asks, feels a momentary confusion and replies by asking another question about the meaning of the client's question. Since the original client question had a defensive intent, this will increase the client's need to defend, and he may respond by remarking that psychologists never answer questions. If the therapist can then be open enough to admit that he wanted to answer the first question but found he couldn't without understanding it better, then the client can risk looking at what the therapist wanted and perhaps make his question clearer. The reason for the unclear question may become apparent, and its defensive nature may then have meaning for both.

We are suggesting that defensiveness may produce defensiveness. In a similar way openness may encourage openness.

We believe that with the client population with which we work, it is important to think of defenses as meaningful rather than as always pathological. If we think of defenses as pathological, then they are something to be overcome rather than understood and made useful. A little thought about the devices often recommended for dealing with defenses will clearly show that such devices assure the therapist that he can maintain his defenses and that there will be no need or opportunity for reciprocal openness. Even the reflection-of-feeling response to a personal question, such as "I guess you would like to know more about me," does not invite a reciprocal openness and exploration of the defensive question. The therapist is able to remain hidden and unresponsive to the client, who is left with his question unanswered. The client is also likely to feel that it is meaningless and that he is himself less meaningful. A statement by the therapist such as "Your question or your statement seems defensive" can only convey to the client that this was a bad thing to have said, and neither the therapist nor the client is likely to deal with the matter any further.

The Intellectualizing Defense Again. A second discovery we made regarding defenses is that the same defense needs to be dealt with differently in different people. In fact, a particular kind of defense is not even handled the same way with the same person at different times. As an example, we can consider intellectual defenses.

Since a typical intellectualizer has little access to his feelings and talks volubly about his concerns, yet gives no evidence of anxiety and is even puzzled if asked about anxiety, a therapist is often tempted to try to make him anxious. This is usually rather frustrating, and the client often denies that he feels anxious, while talking on and on about the things that concern him very much and about which he really should have anxious feelings. It is generally acknowledged that such talking is a powerful and difficult defense with which to work. One way of penetrating it is to ask the client not to talk; after he has been silent for a few minutes, he will find himself terribly anxious. Thus a beginning will have been made in having him experience his anxiety.

As a therapy continues and such a client continues to talk without anxiety, frequently the therapist begins to feel anxious. If the therapist will say to the client, "I guess you must be feeling anxious," the client will often stop and seem to think a minute and say, "Now that you mention it, I am." It is then often possible to relate the feeling to the content, and the client gradually learns to look for and know his own anxiety.

Another point. If the therapist is being deluged with talk, a good indicator that the talk is defensive is that it involves a great deal of only partially relevant detail and requires the therapist to be very attentive in order to make sense out of what is talked about. The therapist will probably feel that he has to pay such close attention to what the client is saying that he does not have time to think about his own private thoughts. Such therapist concentration is a good clue to the way in which the client is controlling the relationship between them and should at least make the therapist wonder why that kind of interpersonal control is so necessary.

We advise the therapist to remove himself from that control, even if in so doing he stops hearing the content. If then out of his detachment he has a fantasy or a spontaneous reaction to the client, let him respond out of this, and the defense is likely to be well disrupted. If it just so happens that the client in leaving the interview tries to walk out through the wall instead of the door, the therapist can then feel sure the client is attending to his feelings!

With some intellectualizers, then, we think that the therapist should avoid being caught up in the content and should respond out of his own world, minimally controlled by the client's talk, in such a way that the client is frequently disrupted. Such a way of behaving makes very great demands on the therapist because he needs to have a relationship and it takes real effort not to accept the client's terms for relating. Also, we think that a therapeutic procedure in which the therapist specifies the terms of relating does nothing to help the client's defensiveness because the client only learns and accepts a set of terms, adopted as his own, which, in turn, may give him a sense of being in control of the relationship. He has not really learned that a relationship can be an expanding, reciprocal experience through which he can grow and become effective.

The last statement suggests an important aspect of defenses— that they prevent change. Consider for a moment the importance of stability, lack of change, to such people. Think how fearful they are that they may make a decision which will change their lives. Consider how indecision is couched in terms of fear of making the wrong decision. Yet the decision to procrastinate may also be very wrong. It seems that the fear is mainly of changing. Thus as therapists we offer such clients a changing relationship. We prevent their being able to learn just how to relate to us, just how to please us, and gradually they learn that change is tolerable, even pleasurable, and to be sought after.

We need to say again that the therapist must forego his usual palpable relationship and believe—and act on this belief—that he is relating to a person not visible to either one of them but somehow hidden under the intellectual facade—a real person, and a feeling person with capacity to grow and change, having hidden surprises for both of them. The therapist's timing of this kind of interaction is important because it needs to occur before the therapist has become so accustomed to relating to his intellectualizing client that both he and the client are convinced this is the only kind of relationship they can have. Yet it also needs to occur after the client is committed to therapy. If it occurs too early, the client may become so frustrated, frightened, and disrupted, not knowing that his therapist can help him, that he may leave therapy and feel very rational and justified in doing so.

The way in which the relationship between the therapist and the intellectualizing client is controlled needs further discussion. We mentioned earlier that when the therapist finds himself so busy listening to the client that he isn't aware of his own thoughts and feelings, he is being controlled. He is also being controlled if he cannot say anything to the client which is meaningful to him. The client may respond by agreeing, yet it is obvious that the agreement is really intended to placate the therapist, to fool him into thinking that he is being useful, and at the same time to immobilize him. About the third time a client politely says, "That's interesting," to a therapist's comment, the latter should conclude that his impact is minimal.

Reciprocal Impact and Emotional Defenses. We believe that change occurs as a result of the reciprocal impact of the therapist and client in the therapy relationship. And, further, we believe that defenses serve to prevent change by preventing this impact. There are ways which clients have of preventing this impact other than intellectualizing. Intellectual defenses are the most sophisticated, but emotional ones can be more deadly to the therapist, immobilizing him more completely. A flood of tears may mean that what the therapist has said has been very meaningful and that the client will find himself changed as a result. It may also mean that the client has found a way of stopping the therapist, of showing him that he must be more careful, must protect the client, must stay away from that subject. A therapist would be foolish to draw such a conclusion from the first experience of tears in his client. But if they are repeated often, he would be equally foolish not to consider the possibility that they are defensive.

The same consideration needs to be given to overt anxiety. A client's statement, "That makes me anxious," may be more wisely responded to by some kind of reassurance that the anxiety is appropriate and bearable than by the immediate cessation of the anxiety-producing interaction.

Probably the most difficult emotional defense that therapists have to deal with is hostile attacks. All of us tend to defend ourselves against hostility whether we understand its reason or not, and therapists working with clients who are initially hostile often have great difficulty staying with them long enough to make a relationship. Hostility later in the therapy is another matter entirely because it is usually something the therapist has been working for and is a sign that the client is changing. An indication of maturity in the therapist may be his ability to welcome a hostile attack from a client who has been depressed or for some other reason unable to express what he feels.

Defenses That Foretell Termination. Let us go back to the proposition we made earlier that defenses are meaningful and have their own unique function in the individual. If somewhere well along in therapy, we find our client being defensive, we naturally assume that there is something to be defended and we wonder what is troubling him. We often feel rather sure that somehow an earlier conflict has been regenerated, that something has happened which places the client in the position once again of having to deal with something which makes him feel unsure, inadequate, and lonely.

We need to think and ask ourselves what part we have played in this apparent regeneration of conflict. Are we—as therapists working with the client for a better life for him—somehow recreating that insatiable need for perfection that made life so unfulfilled and frustrating during all the years of growing up, for instance? Is there something about the client's implicit expectation that therapy is the place to work out problems and talk about pain, which makes it impossible for him to feel loved and cared for in the therapy unless problems are present? Is to be troubled and somewhat inadequate the only way he can maintain this good, warm relationship? Maybe. But if that is true, we as therapists have somehow made a false, unreal promise about what the relationship can mean. We have deluded our client in the way he wanted to be fooled, of course, and it is up to us to correct the mistake. But in thinking about the reciprocal effects of the relationship, we have concluded that it is a mistake which needed to be made. The client needed to know that even though he had long felt deprived of love and caring, for him to feel bad and troubled in order to have such care is too high a price to pay for it.

So when we come to this realization, we begin to suspect that things are going rather well, that the client is in some way aware that the relationship is coming to an end. And we help him to know that we, as well as he, can rejoice in his growth and that we care for him even more as a stronger, coping person.

Thus we recognize that even troubles may have a defensive purpose, a defense against a change in the relationship which can mean separation. We believe that it is the therapist's responsibility to recognize the meaning of some recurrent troubles and to know that however real they may be, they may have a meaning within the relationship which is understandable—and not necessarily in the terms which the client has assigned to them.

What we have just said seems to present a kind of paradox. On the one hand, we believe that a client's behavior, feelings, thoughts, have meaning to him only as he understands them, owns them, if you will, and is responsible for them. Yet we are saying that here is a case in which the therapist must take the responsibility of knowing and understanding for his client. How, then, can we expect our client to leave us and be capable of taking responsibility for his part in a relationship with other people? Indeed, it is a paradox. But we are talking about a real relationship in which there is more clarity, perhaps, and more willingness on the client's part to share our motivations than in most therapeutic relationships.

We have not promised him a permanent home, and although we can share his hurts and disappointments, we cannot prevent them. We can teach him that they can be understood. We can show him his part in them, and this we do so that he can know he can be responsible for them, rather than overwhelmed by them. We believe it is a more real way of life if our client learns that he does not have to bear total responsibility but can depend upon us for some things, and, in turn, be depended upon.

So we talk it over with him, speculate with him, express our beliefs, may even live out with him his exasperation with us that we have had such an idea. We know that our interpretation of his recurrent disaster is correct if he comes back after thinking it over and tells us that he understands what has happened. If he puts it in his own way with nuances and details which only he can add, we are additionally sure that growing up has occurred.

Growing Up Is Giving as Well as Getting. In an earlier chapter we had something to say about deprivation, and we pointed out that such clients are deprived not only of love and care but also of the knowledge that their giving and helpfulness are meaningful. Here we must consider how therapists as helping people are making maximal use of this dynamic quality of helpfulness in themselves but how at the same time helpfulness may be a therapist defense.

Let us think a bit about this. In being helpers and always thinking about and even searching out the needs of others, we can carefully ignore our own needs and their effects. We can and do feel uncomfortable and almost affronted by an offer of help from another, and we feel quite justified in rejecting the offer because we are so convinced that all we need as people is a chance to help someone else.

If our client is one whose dependency is burdensome, we may try to set up some kind of limits so that it is tolerable to us, or we may describe it as hostile. It is very hard for us to think that sometimes the hostility is justified in the present, and we ascribe it to a past, interpersonal relationship and try very hard to help our client remember his anger at those others.

If some unplanned incident occurs whereby the client has an opportunity to be a gracious giver, we are pleased and feel that he is making progress. Or it may come as a surprise to us that this helpless person can for a short time be a helpful person to us.

But let us look at this last instance a bit more realistically. In the growing-up process, one learns that to do things for others is a way to be meaningful and loved, and even makes growing up worth while. To be able to do something for the older members of the family and to be valued for it are enhancing. Yet here in therapy we have a relationship in which the helping is the province of only one person, the therapist. No wonder the helpless and dependent are with us so long and improve so slowly!

Let us consider further some aspects of the problem and some ways in which the result just described may be minimized. The client gets the idea out of the realities of the relationship at the beginning of therapy that the only way to maintain the relationship is to continue to dredge up problems. We think therapists need to be alert to this possibility. To counter this kind of thing, the therapist should be as enthusiastically responsive to good things that a client reports as to problems. Think for a minute of the meaning of "That's good; now what shall we talk about?" as a response to a client's happy report of some success as he begins the interview.

On the other hand, we do not concern ourselves unduly with what are called "flights into health." We do recognize the defensive nature of premature termination, and certainly at times we recognize at termination that there are problems a client has not dealt with and even that these may need to be dealt with. However, because we feel that defenses are reasonable, we are inclined to take the attitude that the client has done what he could at the time and can seek more help when he feels a greater need for it.

Perhaps it would be helpful to explain that we think of therapy as a special instance in the development process, that the changes a client needs to make will usually only begin in the therapy relationship and will continue and even be accelerated after therapy is ended. Sometimes changes are only dimly experienced while therapy is in progress and become dynamically apparent as the person actively involves himself in living. For some people therapy is in a way a defense against living.

The Decisions We Make in Therapy. To round out our description of what therapy as we know it is like, we wish to say something about decisions we make in therapy. Of course, there are many decisions and choices simply because this is an interpersonal experience. Many are made in order to maintain the relationship. Many are made intuitively, and we know about them only afterwards as we think about what has gone on between the client and us. We have the impression that the spontaneity, the unplanned character, of these decisions usually enhances their effectiveness, and frequently we feel that we couldn't do as well if we had thought it all out ahead.

These unplanned choices we make are characteristically decisions about our interaction with the client. The offer of a hand, a pat on the shoulder, an angry retort, have impact if they are spontaneous. They seem contrived and not appropriately reactive if they are planned.

Our kind of behavior will depend on whether we react to the client with feelings or with feeling states. If we are able to express our feelings for the client reactively, we are helping him to differentiate feelings—if for no other reason than that we differentiate them. If we discover that we react to our client but that we have not been aware or expressive of the reaction, a therapist feeling state is likely to be developing. As therapists, we cannot plan a way to express the reaction as a feeling because it is not a feeling except as it occurs reactively within the relationship.

As an example, suppose a client is subtly attacking, and the therapist becomes aware that he is angry in turn. But he doesn't discover his anger until after the session. If he makes up his mind to tell the client he is angry at him, he may find himself in the next session being hostile, not reactively, but for something which is now past or perhaps which hasn't yet been repeated. Thus his feelings are inappropriate to the present interaction. We do not want to imply that it is not appropriate for the therapist to discover that a client can help to set up an interactive feeling state. It is of great importance that the therapist become aware of what is happening so that he can take steps to prevent it or limit his part in it and to extricate himself from its effects. His decision has to do with "I frequently get caught in this, and I intend to keep out of it" rather than "I will do so and so when the client does . . ." whatever the interactive maneuver has been.

Another problem occurs in the therapeutic interaction when the therapist finds himself feeling responsible for his client's life. The client's part in it is often quite clear, but the therapist's motivations for taking such responsibility for his client are often more obscure. To make the decision to be less responsible may do nothing to help the therapist avoid the client's ploys, which suck him into what can only stalemate the therapy. More than an overt decision is required in this case, though awareness of taking too much responsibility may be helpful to the therapist. Essentially we are saying that the therapist's insight and decision to change may not be enough to permit him to change. We will be discussing this in more detail in later chapters. We will stop here with the recognition of the problem.

There are, however, some other decisions we do make overtly and carry out. These are made partly as a result of the assessment process we described earlier in this chapter. We may choose, for instance, to be rational and intellectual with a client who is only too aware of his feelings and reacts out of them with little or no understanding of their meaning. For this kind of person we may make a conscious decision not to become immersed in feeling with him except as we may need to in order to understand and name what he feels. With him we would talk about feelings and do so quite consciously and purposefully.

With the person who talks about feelings or talks about things which should generate feelings but don't, we carefully avoid being drawn into the discussion and try to be more reactive than rational. This may require a great deal of conscious effort, but the intent is often rewarded by really dramatic changes in the client. For example, if a client is talking calmly about being the victim of some childhood cruelty and the therapist enters into the experience reactively by swearing angrily or crying or by some other feeling reaction, the reaction will often shatter the calm and let the client know the feelings he might have had about the experience.

Whether or not to touch a client is another instance in which one can make a choice consciously rather than intuitively alone. Perhaps one learns the meaning of physical contact with clients by trial and error. Maybe it is not possible to offer dependable, useful rules about it. Let us say, first, that we think the therapist should touch a client only in reaction to his own feelings toward the client. Touching should never be contrived, planned, or done because someone else does it; rather it should be done only because the therapist genuinely and spontaneously feels like it.

Given that the therapist has an impulse to give the client some physical comfort or reassurance, most often a moment of consideration about what it will mean follows. This is the trial and error mentioned above, and perhaps most people learn to trust the impulse to touch or not by doing it, because this is really all they have to go on, and the results are unpredictable.

One useful thing to think about is whether the impulse to caress the client stems from the fact that he is emotionally a very young child needing comfort or from the fact that the therapist really wants to encourage or prolong the regression. Sometimes it is more useful to say something comforting than to touch a very regressed client. The hug or reassuring pat may then be given later when the client has regained emotional control and is more his own age emotionally. On the other hand, if regression does seem important, touching the client can be a very effective way of bringing it about.

Sometimes what is needed is a chance for the client to recognize that he or she has confused affection with sexual feelings. The experience of being touched by the therapist may be regressive to the point of generating the conflict between the client and the opposite-sexed parent with whom the confusion originated. To accomplish an appropriate separation of sexual and affectionate feelings in the client, the therapist needs to be clear about his own feelings lest the client's confusion be reinforced and magnified. If the therapist is confused and unclear, it would be a mistake for him to use the client to try to clarify whether his feelings are sexual or affectionate.

We would also like to suggest that therapists who have strong personal prohibitions against physical contact should not try to override them because there is no way to be sure that the therapist's ambivalence will not in some way be communicated to the client and add to his problem. We think, too, that usually some discussion of the meaning of the touching should take place, some mutual verbal sharing of the feelings which both client and therapist have experienced, in order for the client to gain the most from the experience.

Deciding to Set Limits.   We give conscious consideration, also, to whether we should set limits for certain clients. Clients who complain about some behavior, and come in because they are distressed about it, invite us to forbid the behavior. If we do, they will engage us in a battle of wills as to whether they will continue the behavior or not. This may be a way of making the conflict real, but we have felt that it is not possible for us to give much help while participating in the conflict thus. This is another way of saying that we first must try to understand what meaning the given behavior has to the client.

If we are able to see that the behavior is defensive and that it keeps the client from experiencing feelings, then in that case we think it is appropriate to ask the client to give up the behavior to learn what is hidden behind it. In such an instance the therapist needs to feel able to tolerate the client's breaking the limit set. Otherwise he may be drawn into the conflict and have to reject the client, which is often the client's expectation.

For example, a girl who is compulsively sleeping with every boy she knows may even welcome the therapist's suggestion that she stop so that she and the therapist may have a chance to discover what it is all about. If they are able to work together, they will almost inevitably come to a point at which the relationship breaks down. Then a little inquiry will disclose that she has broken the limit and feels guilty about it. She will reveal that she expects the therapist to terminate the relationship and to stop caring about her and that she also expects other kinds of consequences which more clearly belong to the primary family relationship. The therapist may feel disappointed and may even feel that the client has rejected him. However, if he understands that this is the client's reliving or reexperiencing of the primary conflict, he may be able to understand better and deal with it in an appropriate way.

Sometimes it is effective to say something such as, "If you can control this behavior, we can work together," with appropriate explanation of why it is necessary. The client then makes a commitment to therapy and to change, which is helpful to both. Sometimes the struggle to maintain the limit is evidence for both client and therapist that the client wants to change and is a first step in resolving the client's ambivalence in being committed to change. Gaining the client's cooperation in furthering his own therapy in this way means that he is working with the therapist to achieve a less helpless and purposeless feeling in obtaining aid.

We do not set limits without careful consideration with the client as to whether he can be somewhat successful in maintaining them and whether the behavior is one which if continued would in some way disrupt or damage the therapy.

Sometimes with a particular kind of compulsive, self-defeating client we have limited the duration of therapy. As a basis for making this decision, we have taken note of the fact that our fantasy about the client says that "this one will take a long time" and that it will be "tough" to get him to move. Recognizing that we are somewhat reluctant to undertake the therapy, we have thought, "We'll limit the time and see what he can do in, say, twenty interviews." Frequently such a client is able to make real use of a fixed number of therapy sessions—to organize himself within the time given him and to make changes that make him feel better. This is the kind of client who will not solve all his problems or deal with everything which is important, but he is also the kind who could get so compulsively involved in therapy that it could go on indefinitely.

We have had a particular intent in discussing the decisions we make about the therapy process because we realize that to discuss therapy as an interpersonal process implies an oversimplification. Indeed, it is too simple to say that we enter into a relationship with our client and try to be as real and human and honest as we possibly can. We are those things and more: we are therapists and psychologists who from long experience in working with troubled people have learned some things which have been effective in helping them. We think about what we do, and we are willing to experiment and try different things when we find ourselves frustrated in helping someone. Out of our thinking and experimenting we have learned that sometimes it is useful to decide to behave a certain way, to structure the therapy in terms of the needs of a particular individual. Because we do give ourselves this freedom, which also means that we give ourselves permission to fail, our therapy is never static nor boring to us. It retains its challenge and its excitement.

The Ever-Changing Unity of the Human Being.   What makes a human being human? Some say it is because we have souls or spirits. Perhaps we do. Others say it is because man can think. Yet another thinker will maintain, and rightly so, perhaps, that human beings are such because they can feel, care, and love. Another theorizer, a psychologist perhaps, may argue persuasively that human defenses, or pathology, are uniquely human. Another psychologist, experimental in bent, may be fascinated by the possibility that much human behavior can be explained by reflexes, rewards, and punishment. Instincts, or an innate predisposition to develop in certain ways, seem likely to be part of our humanness, too. A geneticist may be both frustrated and pleased by uniquely human genetic complexity. Some might even argue that there is nothing unique about being human at all. Perhaps so. Another may declare that human living is meaningless, that there is no order and all is really chaos. And such may have truth for him and for others, too.

Thus the argument about the nature of humanness goes on. Is one view right and all the others wrong? Do we have an answer, a better one, perhaps? No, we think not, but we do have some views, too, and we hope that our notions, if they have any meaning to others, can be included along with all the other wonderments, convictions, and speculations.

To us, any explanation of the total nature of human beings is incomplete and necessarily so. Yet there is pleasure in observing, explaining, and theorizing, and so we do it along with many others. One of our observations is that change is part of being human. If that is so, then an explanation, a theory, may be right at the time the observations are made, but it may be wrong by the time the formulation is made because change has already occurred. Too bad, deplorable, not good, turn back the clock? Some may want to stop time, sometimes we do ourselves. But we can't do that either, and we suspect it might be rather dull if we could. So, instead, we find ourselves both fascinated and frustrated by the ever-changing unity of the human being. And that is what we have written about in this chapter, ever-changing unity.

Chapter 8

Helping Others to Be Therapists

We come now to another unique, specialized relationship—that of trainee and supervisor. Why do we call it unique? It is so, in part at least, because each of the participants belongs to a particular kind of people, people who need to be helpful to others. Their task together also has to do with helpfulness—with how the therapist can help his client.

We have written earlier how being helpful can limit relationships and protect the helper from some of the give-and-take which more complete relationships include. We have mentioned how the therapist's helpfulness often has a defensive quality, which he may find rather necessary for his own sense of well-being. Our intents, then, are multiple when we enter into a supervisory relationship with another therapist or with our student therapists. We can put it most clearly by saying that we want to help our supervisees to be helpful but not to use helpfulness to hide behind or to defend themselves. We also want them to learn to form good reciprocal relationships, to be able to be both helpful and appropriately dependent, so that they can be freer and more complete in their interactions with their clients and others. In essence, our supervisory intent is always one of enhancing people's ability to relate to each other.

SUPERVISION AS
TASK-ORIENTED THERAPY

What we have been saying has certain implications, namely, that we want our therapist learners to change, to grow, to become more fully human. These are the same kinds of goals we were talking about for our clients, and in this sense we are therapists to our supervisees. To put it another way, we are more interested in their being "good" therapists than in their doing good therapy, although they may learn some things to do, too. We are attentive to the ways in which our supervisee's dynamics interfere with his effectiveness with his client, but we are also concerned about what his relationship to us, the supervisors, is like.

We have, in fact, as much interest in seeing to it that the supervisory relationship is developing as in making sure that the therapeutic relationships with clients are going somewhere. If a supervisee uses us only to report his progress with cases and to solve problems which may develop with them, we feel dissatisfied with the relationship. Yet isn't this the usual expectation which supervisees have? We must answer, "Yes." And we also admit that we sometimes find our supervisees resistant and resentful that we expect more of them and ourselves. Our own needs for reciprocal relationships are being expressed here, and indeed we have sometimes been accused of using our supervisory relationships to fulfill some of our own needs. So we do. How else can they be meaningful and fulfilling to us, the supervisors?

Decisions Are Made. Let us go back to the part of supervision concerned with a therapist's dynamics that interfere with his accomplishing the task of helping his client. Here it is often true that in order to effect change, a more frankly therapeutic approach with exploration into earlier important relationships may be needed. As with clients, we believe it is unlikely that change can occur if there are only interpretations of motivation and pointing out of similarities to the past. This brings us face to face with the question of how far we should go as supervisors in helping a supervisee to relive and to resolve these old conflicts. Let us say, first, that we often find that a supervisory relationship has become frankly therapeutic.

At this point we believe that the persons involved should have the freedom to choose among alternatives. Sometimes it is only when a therapist is confronted by the fact that certain old conflicts interfere with his ability to be professionally helpful that he can recognize their meaning clearly enough to want to work them out. We as supervisors may suggest he seek therapeutic help from someone else, or we may change our supervisory relationship to therapy. We may even suggest, if the problem is not one that seems resolvable, that the student therapist change his professional goals. The choice will be determined by supervisor and supervisee and by the relationship between them. Many of the same considerations which go into our decisions of whether to undertake therapy with particular clients have a part in what decision is made here. For example, can the problem be worked out between the two people involved, or would a different-sexed therapist be more helpful? Will the supervisory relationship need to be maintained, too, and is this possible? If the problem is one which can be somewhat circumscribed and handled without a total therapy experience, we are inclined to go ahead and work on it rather than refer the supervisee.

The two of us have frequently worked together with our student therapists so that they had personal therapy with one of us and supervision with the other, with the expectation that they would get what they needed as people and professionals from both a man and a woman. While we have functioned in this way partly because it was convenient, we have also considered that it is dynamically very effective. In addition, we consider it appropriate to consult with each other on the progress or problems our client or supervisee may be experiencing.

The Effort Syndrome Again. One reason why we have been willing to work with our supervisees on their personal problems is the frequency with which they become the source of difficulty for supervisees in relating to their clients. When a supervisee complains about a client who is not progressing or who is frustrating him in some way, almost invariably it becomes apparent that the therapist and client are caught up in an interaction which involves the therapist's own dynamics. What can it mean to be "caught" in one's own dynamics?

One way this can happen is through the effort syndrome, which was discussed earlier when we were describing unproductive therapy relationships. The notion that if something is hard to do, one must try harder is well established for people who work on advanced degrees. It is quite understandable that therapists are often caught up in working harder; we ourselves are on occasion. But it is also highly unlikely that the therapist's hard work is going to accomplish what the client himself needs to do.

Sometimes for a supervisor to call the therapist's attention to how hard he is working will enable the therapist to free himself and hand the job back to his client. Sometimes, on the other hand, the student therapist finds himself repeatedly caught up in working hard and is not able to circumvent his client's defensive maneuvers which produce this kind of result. In the latter case we need to look with our supervisee at what there is about the client's defensive maneuvers which triggers the therapist's ineffective efforts, what there is about the client and the therapist's relationship to him which so often result in this kind of impasse.

The instance of a therapist working laboriously with a girl who is hard to please can sometimes be traced to the therapist's mama, who was so hard to please. When the therapist ties hard work to pleasing mama, often he no longer resorts to it in trying to work with the girl client; it drops out of their relationship. We reiterate the point that merely calling the supervisee's attention to a dynamic which is operating may sometimes be effective, but when it keeps recurring, the supervisor needs to deal more with the source of the dynamic in order to free the therapist. Not all problems are as simply understood as the one just described, but simplicity is not the criterion for whether a problem should be dealt with or not.

Spouses Can Be Problems.   Sometimes a therapist has difficulty with his/her opposite-sexed client and is immobilized in the relationship because of current difficulty with a spouse. A supervisor may take the attitude that this is a problem which the supervisee himself has to work out and that the supervisee needs to do whatever he can to separate it from his therapeutic relationships. However, this is seldom possible to do because while the therapist is unhappy and immobilized in his home relationship, at least some of his therapeutic relationships usually remain static, too. The supervisor may or may not want to work with his supervisee on his marital problem, but he should certainly recognize that there will be effects on his therapeutic relationships.

Persons, Not Skills.   How then do we deal with the task of the supervisory relationship, helping the supervisee with his cases and teaching him to be a good therapist? We do not teach skills, yet we expect our supervisees to become skillful. We do not believe that there are universally effective techniques for doing therapy, yet we try new ways of working with people and their problems, and are pleased when our supervisees experiment with new things. Basically we as supervisors are endeavoring to help therapists to become effective as people—sensitive, feeling, expressive, and creative in their own way.

We feel about our supervisees the way we think they should feel about their clients: that if we take the responsibility for what they do, they will be unable to take appropriate responsibility for themselves. We do not ever want to take vicariously the responsibility for a student therapist's case load. Instead, we want to be available to help if there are difficulties, to make suggestions, to evaluate the meaning of certain happenings, and to be supportive when problems arise. To listen to a report of progress about every case would be to assume a sense of responsibility that we do not believe we should take. And to listen to tapes of every session would involve us in teaching skills and techniques in a way we do not like. This is not to say that we are uninterested in the progress of cases. And we do often find listening to tapes with the supervisee a useful practice in helping him to understand the interaction between his client and himself, which may be unclear if he only describes it verbally.

Some may ask, "How can we be sure that clients are being properly handled and that our supervisees are learning if we don't take active, specific responsibility?" We find that if we are attentive to what our student therapists talk about or don't talk about, as the case may be, we can often know where they need help or where they are having difficulties. And we feel, too, that supervisees must have the right to make mistakes and to learn from them. We also believe that when a therapeutic error is made, frequently it can be made therapeutically useful and the relationship repaired. So we are not greatly concerned about preventing mistakes. We would even permit a supervisee to make one if a valuable learning experience might accrue.

The apparently laissez-faire attitude we hold arises out of the conviction that at best our notion about what may be appropriate in any given situation is a hypothesis. On the other hand, the supervisee usually has feelings and impressions about his client which stem from the relationship and are a part of it. The supervisee's reported feelings may represent the living out of a conflict which is important to the client. Thus when a supervisee describes a situation in which he feels impassed and frustrated, our response may be, "Fine, you are in the middle of the conflict." We are supportive, but we do not often tell the therapist how he should go about living out the conflict with his client. We may make and communicate observations, but we believe that only the participants can resolve the conflict and that interference may prevent a therapeutic outcome.

SOME FACILITATIVE
SUPERVISORY ATTITUDES

We take seriously the task of helping others to learn to do therapy. Yet we believe that such learning should be pleasurable for both supervisor and learner. Thus in working with our learners we are willing to be serious, concerned, even anxious somewhat as they are.

But at the same time we find ourselves as supervisors working not only to facilitate knowledge and an awareness of the anxiety associated with the seriousness of learning, but also to leaven and help control the anxious experience. If, for instance, as supervisors we are able to be as we think we should be, then our learner should find his experience to be anxious, yet he should have some recognition that the anxiety is or can be limited. Further, times should occur when there is a sense of reward and pleasure that something has gone well, that an impasse and/or conflict has been generated and then broken through or resolved, for instance.

We think, too, that while it is most important for the learner to be pleased with his own accomplishment, it is also important that we, the supervisors, be responsive, rewarding, and clearly pleased that our learner has done so well. The basic sense of well-being about oneself and one's accomplishments may be largely internal, but nearly all of us are also somewhat dependent on others for recognition and reward.

The Dependent Learner Is Sometimes a Problem. There can be a supervisory problem, however, because many a therapist in the process of becoming, perceives his learning task to be almost entirely that of pleasing his supervisor. Such a learner attitude is usually accompanied by an apparently low level of need to be self-respecting. Awareness that he should probably be pleased with himself and his accomplishments apart from his supervisor's response to him appears to be sadly deficient, if not missing entirely.

In this particular supervisory learning problem our basic concern is with the sequence of the emotional experiences, which is the reverse of the order we believe best facilitates genuine growth in our "becoming" therapist. Our learner can value and appreciate himself only after he has been approved. Thus he remains almost totally dependent on others for his sense of well-being in general, as well as for his opinion of himself as a therapist. Our supervisory task is to reverse the order in which the sense of enhancement occurs.

The task is not necessarily an easy one, but it can be an extraordinarily exuberant day for the supervisor when such a dependent learner is genuinely pleased with his accomplishment, whatever it may be, and only incidentally needful of the supervisor's approval. In fact, in such an instance the supervisor's response to the learner changes from approval to pleasure, which can be shared by both in a way which enlarges and enhances both and yet takes away nothing from either. Separateness and independence are enhanced, and another developmental task is on its way to being accomplished.

And how can such reversal of needfulness in the supervisee come about? In many ways, probably. We do not know them all, but we can suggest some supervisory operating principles or sets which we have found useful to us and our students.

First of all, it is evident that as supervisors and teachers, we value—both in ourselves and in those who learn from us—the capacity to function independently. But how can we implement such a value or set, particularly with regard to the dependent, "other-oriented" learner we have been describing? The processes involved may be painful for both supervisor and student, but the task is not impossible to accomplish.

"There may be pain for the supervisor as well as the supervisee?" you ask! How can that be? The pain for the supervisor may well come from the eventual recognition that the eager "taker" whom he may have liked so well is remaining only a "taker" and that the relationship is unilateral, one-way, not reciprocal. Further, our disappointed and pained supervisor may find that his apparently eager learner is not even doing very well with what he takes. And why might that be? We think it is natural for our dependent learner to be resentful at some level about his own dependency. Or perhaps it may only be that "borrowed," or unintegrated, ideas and suggestions are inherently difficult to carry out successfully.

But whose adequacy is at stake? That's an interesting question, is it not? Perhaps only the supervisor's adequacy must really be questioned, for what has the learner risked? Not much. However, he may be disappointed, too, for the overly dependent learner is often, if not always, distressed that he is not doing as well as he might like. He may blame his supervisor, and rightly so perhaps, but if that is all that happens, the supervisee may never know of his part in the failure.

Our supervisor and dependent supervisee may or may not resolve their dilemma and learn to enhance each other more appropriately. But it is also true that, just as in more clearly defined therapeutic relationships, the impasse of disappointment can be turned to advantage if either or both participants recognize what they have done together. We think ordinarily it is the supervisor who recognizes the nature of the impasse and so is able to begin turning apparent failure into growth and development. But we are not inclined to sell short the ability of the learner to be perceptive and helpful about setting the supervisory relationship on a new, more productive course.

Talking About Clients Is Not Necessarily Learning. And now we arrive at another conception in regard to the supervision and facilitation of learning to do therapy which assumes the status of a principle to us. While we accept the fact that it is necessary for a supervisee to talk about his clients with his supervisor, we think that often the talk is defensive and about the wrong person or persons. What do we mean? Simply put, we think it is often the supervisee, the supervisor, or the relationship between them which deserves most attention.

It is easy to forget that it is the therapist, not his supervisor, who must be helpful to his client. The last sentence seems like a simple, obvious truth, and so it is, but it leads us to something else that is obvious and yet likely to receive little attention. A therapeutic relationship ordinarily consists of one client, one therapist, and a relationship between them. Problems may arise because a client is defensive, evasive, or otherwise difficult to deal with, and it may be necessary and helpful for the student therapist and his supervisor to talk about the client. But we also observe that therapists can be defensive and evasive, too, and even supervisors are not immune to such human problems.

Hence we believe that often attention and talk must be turned to the therapist and to what may be blocking him from forming a more productive relationship with his client and also his supervisor. What feelings may he be having and suppressing or denying, for instance? What has he not said or not perceived about himself and his client and their relationship?

A common example will help us to make our point. A male therapist seeing a female client may describe her as seductive and himself as successfully resisting her efforts to seduce him. What may actually be true yet denied by the therapist is that he is being equally seductive, thus playing a game which he must hide from his supervisor and perhaps from himself.

How may a supervisor become aware that such a game is going on? And how may he intervene to be of help? There are a number of cues. For instance, a several times repeated account by the therapist of the client's seductiveness at least suggests the probability of projection and/or denial by the therapist.

An opposite sort of cue may be equally indicative to the supervisor. Such a cue is the therapist's repeated denial, in talking to his supervisor, that his client is attractive. It is common for a therapist to allude several times to a particular attribute of his client, such as the shape of her legs, as making her unattractive. Why is it necessary for him to make so many references to his client's allegedly unattractive attribute? What may he be defending against? A tape recording of an interview can also be very revealing of the nature of the interaction between therapist and client.

But what does a supervisor do when he discovers that such a game has been going on? He has a number of alternatives, some of which seem to us better than others. He may err, for example, if he joins with the therapist in being critical of the client. If therapist and supervisor criticize the girl for her alleged seductiveness, neither may arrive at any very clear understanding of her problem or why she expresses herself as she does. Nor is she likely to be much helped by the unfortunate collaboration.

Similarly if the supervisor is critical of the therapist, not much that is good is likely to happen either. Why is that? Here we believe that the problem is one which involves a high degree of self-criticalness on the part of the therapist. Why else must he project and/or deny his thoughts and feelings? If the supervisor joins in criticizing him, he may be enabled to expiate his guilt, but expiation is likely to be only cathartic. He learns little, and he will perhaps repeat the game with the client. Certainly he will repeat it with others.

Feelings, Fantasy, Imagery: Our Mastery Model Revisited. Another conception which assumes the status of a supervisory principle to us begins to emerge at this point. We observe that therapists in training ordinarily do not suffer from too great freedom in knowing and experiencing their own thoughts, feelings, and fantasies. More commonly they tend to be too constricted, to deny and suppress these human assets. In such ways the capacity of a therapist to use himself as a sensitive, therapeutic instrument can be seriously impaired. Further, supervisor criticalness of the client, but more particularly of the therapist learner, may only exacerbate the problem.

A more productive alternative is for the supervisor to encourage and facilitate greater freedom in the learner regarding his thoughts, feelings, and fantasies. Here the "model for mastery" outlined and discussed in Chapter 6 is especially useful to us as supervisors. Also, the examples in Chapter 4 illustrating the usefulness of therapist regression show concrete ways in which a therapist can know and use himself. We have found it possible on many occasions, for instance, to intervene directly with a therapist learner and assist him or her to complete a fantasy, along with the concomitant imagery, much as described in Chapter 4.

We have found, too, that when we are able as supervisors to assist our learners to fantasy and image more freely and completely, they are then enabled to behave more appropriately with clients. Usually their more useful behavior generates quite spontaneously and does not need to be instructed or controlled by us. Simply said, the block or constriction in the therapist is broken up, and he is free to generate his own procedures with a sense of enhancement and independence that pleases both supervisor and learner.

Independence Can Be Deceptive. But what about the determinedly independent learner? While we value independence in ourselves, our clients, and our students, independence can also be reactive in a way which frustrates the supervisor, the learner, and the learning process. We are referring here to the dynamic problem which exists when independence is essentially a reactive need. In such an instance, the underlying problem is a dependency conflict not so different from that of the "clinging" dependent, although the expression of the problem is deceptively opposite.

Supervisors may react variously to such an apparently independent learner. One supervisor may be pleased to have a supervisee who is so independent, unexpectant, and undemanding. Another may constantly feel frustrated because he is unable to fulfill his need to help. Still a third supervisor may be distressed by how little he knows about what his supervisee is doing. A fourth may feel angry and hostile or perhaps think that his supervisee is angry with him and hostile. Such supervisor feelings, except in the case of the pleased supervisor, usually signal a problem which must often be dealt with directly in the relationship between the supervisor and therapist. How can this be done?

First of all, we think it is important for the supervisor to recognize that a critical, dynamic difference exists between a truly independent, functioning person and one who is reactively independent. The first person is independent in a creative, self-actualizing, nonsecretive sort of way. Further, he is able to be dependent and to ask for help when he needs it since he does not see and feel dependence as the threatening, dichotomous alternative to being independent.

Our second person, who is reactively independent, is much more likely to be angry (hostile is probably more accurate) when he feels that his autonomy is threatened. Often it is not possible early in the relationship for a supervisor to tell which kind of person his apparently independent learner is. Usually only as the supervisory relationship develops is he able to make the distinction. If the supervisee is reactively independent, the first cues to the supervisor are likely to be his own developing feelings: anger, frustration, distress, the feeling of being shut out, or whatever.

A pleased supervisor who has a reactively independent learner should be distressed, too. He probably will not be, however, since his pleasure with his nondemanding supervisee may be directly related to questions he has about his own adequacy as a supervisor. We note, for instance, that inexperienced supervisors are often inordinately pleased with a reactively independent supervisee who makes few, if any, requests for help.

What may a supervisor do when his own developing feelings tell him he has a reactive independent on his hands? He may be reactive in turn, of course, out of whatever feelings he has—be they anger, distress, or whatever. Such reactivity may prove helpful, but if he is only reactive, our experience suggests that a battle rather than resolution will develop. Supervisor reactivity may start a resolution process, but it will ordinarily be insufficient to accomplish the goal. So what else can the supervisor do? Here we wish to recall the fact that defenses have a reason for being, even though the reason may be lost or obscured and even though the defense may impede learning. So we think it is important that the supervisor should realize and then understand that his supervisee has reasons—however irrational they may be—for his stubborn, determined independence.

At this point we feel that the supervisor must make a decision. For us the decision is ordinarily simple since we see supervision and therapy not as involving different processes but rather as having somewhat different ultimate purposes. Hence we usually conclude that we need to explore with our supervisee the meanings that dependence and independence have for him. Sometimes such an exploration may go on for some time, for several supervisory sessions, perhaps. The exchange becomes frankly therapeutic in its impact although we usually try to keep clear the fact that part of the purpose of the exploration is for the supervisee to learn to do therapy.

Eventually if supervisor and learner have some success in their venture together, the supervisee can usually arrive at an emotionally meaningful realization that his reactive independence is maladaptive for him as a person and as a therapist. Further, he will recognize that on occasion he can welcome a need for help rather than always defend against it and see it only as a threat to autonomy.

A further dividend to our learning therapist from his new realizations should be greater effectiveness as a therapist. In what ways? A number of possibilities exist, but we have noted that the learner has often resolved his problems with his own dependent clients. For instance, he no longer sees and reacts to dependent clients as simply threatening to him. Further, it is even likely that our once reactively independent therapist will recognize the same quality in his clients as less than desirable in contrast to a probable uncritical admiration of fellow souls in the past.

AND THEN THERE IS
GROUP SUPERVISION

Our first intent in supervision is to enable student therapists to make good, affectively open, interpersonal relationships. To advance this intent, we concern ourselves with the way the students relate to us as supervisors: that is, we give attention to the supervisory relationship. We expect the relationship to change and develop over time and to be mutually enhancing. Group supervision is another experience in which therapists learn to be open and undefensive in interpersonal relationships.

In neither type of supervision is our intent to be protective or totally unthreatening. We do, however, expect the relationship to be growth-producing and, above all, enjoyable. While we do not deny that therapy is a serious, anxiety-producing experience for client and therapist alike, we want to prevent its appearing to be so deadly serious that there can be no pleasure in it. Group experiences seem particularly capable of providing ways of leavening the serious therapeutic atmosphere. We believe that the supervising of learners in small groups has some significant contributions to make. In fact, we think a training program should utilize both kinds of supervision primarily because different but complementary benefits are derived.

Some questions naturally arise about using both methods of supervision. Should a student have both at the same time? Won't conflicts arise when a student's group supervisor (or supervisors) is not the same person as his individual supervisor? Won't students sometimes feel that they are oversupervised? Other questions might be asked, but these will suffice for our purposes. Yes, we do think that students should have both kinds of supervision either simultaneously or consecutively. And it is true that conflicts can arise when learners have more than one supervisor. It also sometimes happens that students feel they have more supervision than they want. But neither the conflicts which may arise nor the possibility of overburdening learners concerns us overly much, and we will say why later in this section.

We turn now to consider some of the advantages and complementary benefits of the two kinds of supervision. Group therapists have maintained—and we concur—that many persons, therapists included, resist being exposed to the sometimes emotionally bruising impacts of a group interaction. We respect the resistances and believe that they have reasons for being, but we do not believe that our respect for such defenses means that we should prevent the experiences from happening.

Put another way, a person who fears exposure in a group or who finds talking in a group difficult has not accomplished a rather important developmental task, to our way of thinking. Such persons often maintain that their dyadic relationships are good and that nothing else is necessary. They may even be right that their one-to-one relationships are good. But the world of people is not so constituted that only dyadic relationships are possible for most persons. Most of us are constantly being thrown into group situations whether we wish such to happen or not. Further, each such experience can be agonizing to the one who fears them unless a good group experience intervenes to change the meaning that being a group member has for the person.

Thus some of our intent in providing group supervisory experiences for students is an effort to provide the intervening "good" experience. As we have suggested before, change and development do not often occur as a consequence of avoiding that which is unpleasant or anxiety-producing, in our opinion. They occur because a conflict is generated, is met head-on in company with others, is emotionally real as in the past, and yet is different because the present experience is different. Simply said, a person does not learn to function better in groups by being left out of groups.

Other benefits are derived from a group experience, too. Although these gains are perhaps only corollary to the more generic problem and its resolution as outlined above, they are the fruits of resolution and should be mentioned. For instance, we note that modern graduate school education is commonly seen and experienced by the student as a bitterly competitive experience. This is both true and unfortunate, but some good group experiences can do much to ameliorate the bitterness of the competition. We find that our student therapists, partly because of their experiences in groups, learn to care about and to respect each other. Friendships are formed which are deeply meaningful and often long-lasting. Group experiences seem to make a special contribution, and on the whole a greater contribution, to the development of interpersonal skills and capabilities than do dyadic relationships as a rule. Secretiveness, which can sometimes assume pathological proportions, is difficult to maintain when an intense, extended group experience is available. Dyadic relationships may promote openness in a person, but frequently a group is even more effective. Further, each group member can learn that his impact on others is variable as well as that different persons affect him differently.

Some other lessons in regard to human commonalities and uniqueness can be felt, seen, and integrated also. For instance, it may be first threatening and then reassuring when two or more group members discover that they share a common or similar problem. The reassurance comes when each begins to face and resolve his problem and, further, when each helps the other as sometimes happens. Yet each person is likely to solve his problem in his own particular way, thus achieving separateness, uniqueness, and self-respect as well as respect for others.

We note also that intense group experiences seem to have a special facilitative effect in promoting reciprocity among the process functions we have written about earlier. The intellectualizer is, for instance, likely to learn that he has genuine feelings since the more feelingful group members are very likely to "help" him. They will insist that he has feelings and can experience them. Resistance may occur, but group pressure is powerful. On the other hand, the members of a group who feel too much may be very positively affected by their encounters with the thinkers. What they can learn and incorporate is that thinking, logicality, and rationality are useful human attributes also. In such ways do group members help each other to change and to become more complete persons.

Finally considerable gains are made in professional skills and capacities as a consequence of group experiences. Some of the gains may come from interactions with the group leader or leaders. But we think that even more significant gains may be derived from interactions among group members. An important lesson to be learned is that not only an older, perhaps wiser, person can be a source of support and enhancement, but that a peer can be helpful as well.

We said earlier that we were not overly concerned with the possibility that students might derive conflicting opinions as a consequence of having more than one supervisor. Our low level of concern is due in part to the observable fact that opinions are often in conflict in the world we all live in. We think it is a part of personal and professional development for a student to find that such is so and that apparently conflicting opinions can often be reconciled. For a student to discover that two apparently conflicting opinions may both be right is powerfully educational. We have often found ourselves able to facilitate such a discovery. Our experience together as multiple therapists and as multiple or conjoint group supervisors has been particularly helpful in showing us that disagreement is not always what it appears to be.

In some instances, too, we have discovered along with the student that the student himself has generated the conflict of opinions. He may do this quite easily, incidentally, by presenting a problem in one way to his individual supervisor and in a different way to his group supervisor. This does not especially distress us, however, for if we are sufficiently alert and sensitive to what is happening, we are often able to help the student to realize what he has done. With his realization may come a significant change in his need to promote fights between authorities. We have seen a number of rather significant conflicts generated and resolved in this way.

We also said earlier that students may sometimes feel overburdened by the amount of attention and supervision they are receiving. In our experience this phenomenon is rare, for students usually want more attention, rather than less. When this does occur, however, we attend to it and try to discover with the student what the source of the distress is. Interestingly enough, we find that the effort syndrome is most commonly involved. Usually what seems to have happened is that the student somehow has gotten caught up in trying too hard to make something go better, be it his cases or a problem at home. What we are often able to do is to help lift the burden, reduce the terrible seriousness, and assist in restoring humor and some personal ease. Sometimes, too, there seems to be little we can do to help, and when that occurs, we accept that perhaps less desirable state as best we can. Occasionally the complaint of too much supervision seems justified to us and is found to be attached to some situational matter which can be changed.

A WORD TO SUPERVISEES

We think that for a student therapist to see supervision as an experience to be endured is unfortunate. This attitude cheats him of a chance to learn something which can be enhancing to him. Sometimes supervisees need to tell their supervisors how to be helpful. If the supervisee can be clear about what he wants and make himself clear to his supervisor, he can have an enhancing experience of having changed his supervisor and their relationship. Supervisees too often feel that they have no rights to learn about; sometimes they do not even have any expectations that they will learn and grow; and so they settle for simply getting along with their supervisors when they could expect and enjoy a reciprocal relationship.

Probably this kind of feeling about supervision comes out of a tendency to be so self-critical that taking suggestions becomes a source of further self-criticism. It is as though having to learn something is admitting to lack of perfection, which is intolerable. The same supervisee may be very critical of his supervisor for not offering what he wants. At the same time he may be overprotective of his supervisor and unwilling to make demands lest the supervisor be unable to meet them. If the supervisor, too, has some doubts about what he has to offer, then the overprotective supervisee and the unsure supervisor will find themselves immobilized in the relationship, discussing cases or listening to tapes. And both of them are likely to be thoroughly dissatisfied.

We hope we never become so sure of ourselves that we do not need or want to discuss our therapy experiences with others, be they students or colleagues. We believe that if we find ourselves persistently thinking or talking about a client, we are asking or needing to ask for another's observation of the therapeutic interaction. We may reserve the right to judge the value of our effort, but we always want to have available others to whom we can talk about frustrating things. Thus we set an example and encourage our students to seek consultation about puzzling therapeutic experiences. We hold that it is more self-respecting to recognize that we do not always know everything which might be known. It is better always to be seeking to learn rather than to believe we can learn no more.

SUPERVISION AT ITS BEST

Another way of expressing our basic attitudes toward supervision is to describe what is to us the most interesting, challenging kind of supervision. When a therapist has learned the fundamentals and is confident in his therapeutic relationships, he frequently wants to innovate and experiment. In this case the supervisor listens to the therapist, helps to clarify his motivation, and in many different ways thinks through with him the meaning of what he plans and how he may carry it out. The relationship becomes equalitarian in the shared thinking. There is also a subtle way in which the responsibility for innovation is shared. The therapist feels supported and not alone in a venture which he might otherwise find too risky to attempt. Two heads think through and anticipate meanings, and two heads conceptualize outcomes. When conflict is regenerated in the therapeutic relationship, the two share the anxiety, and later they also share the pleasure of success as a reward for the risk taken.

Such a relationship begins on a foundation of mutual trust and respect and of capacity for clear communication between the two. Both persons have a gratifying sense of reciprocal growth and enhancement. The supervisee has the sense of independence and maturity that comes from creative self-expression, without the often attendant isolation and aloneness. The supervisor has a rare opportunity of sharing closely in an exciting therapeutic venture in which he is not isolated by being the one who is looked up to as having the answers. Instead, he has an opportunity to learn, too.

Some might think that this kind of experience can be had only with colleagues, but we have not found this to be true. In our case most often this experience occurs with our graduate students in the final phase of their training. We have thought of it as having a meaning applied to training analogous to the dissertation in research training, as it is ideally intended to be. Often our students go away to other institutions looking for a continuation of this aspect of their experience. They are either pleased or disappointed depending on what they find.

A Bit of Heresy. In this chapter we have written about some processes and attitudes which we have found helpful and facilitative to those who are learning to be therapists. We have probably committed heresy for we have not made sharp, clear distinctions between clients and therapist learners. In fact, we have even gone so far as to say that the processes which go on in supervision and training are the same as those which occur in therapy. We have perhaps been even more heretical by suggesting that learner therapists do and should make mistakes. Further, we have admitted that not only do our learners make "mistakes" but that we may even at times help them to do so. But we have also explained that we are deeply concerned about innovativeness and creativity. To us the freedom to "err" embodies the freedom to learn to profit from errors, to learn that errors are reparable, that they may be closely related to conflict generation and resolution and thus most useful at times.

But we are contrary, too, for while we believe deeply in freedom, innovation, and creativity, we are also expectant, even demanding. And how is that? We are not demanding about the development of skills as such, although our learners do become skillful. What we do demand and expect is that those who learn from and with us grow and become more complete as persons and also become therapists. The fact is, we find a distinction between these two demands hard to make, for if personal growth, knowledge, and awareness do not occur, then becoming a therapist does not truly occur either.

Part Two

Multiple
Therapy:

Therapists in
Collaboration

Chapter 9

What Is Multiple Therapy? Some Practical and Theoretical Considerations

We begin by telling how we took the first steps to experiment with multiple therapy. Over ten years ago each of us was seeing one of a married couple in therapy. As we worked along with them individually, we conferred frequently about our problems and our progress. These were the informal kind of exchanges that are possible when colleagues have reason to be mutually interested in clients.

Our couple had sought us out by name, and each of us was working with the same-sexed partner, male with male, female with female. Each was deeply involved with his own client, and yet we both were well aware of the problems the couple experienced in their marriage. One afternoon as we were talking, almost simultaneously each of us expressed the wish that his own client could have the experience of working with the other therapist. The wish came out of the recognition that both clients had unresolved problems with the parent of the opposite sex and that these were being expressed very destructively in the marital relationship.

As we talked, it became clear that we had not been as success-ful in helping our clients resolve problems with the opposite-sexed parent as we had been in helping them resolve difficulties with the parent of our own sex. "If there were only some way that ——— could work with you," we said to each other. Next came a very tentative, "What would you think of putting them together?" Then with a mutually growing enthusiasm, "How shall we tell them?" and "Should they have a choice as to whether they will see both of us together?"

The discussion continued until we agreed that the male thera-pist would call the male client and present our proposition. How our clients were able to accept the notion we do not know. But a time was set, and we were launched on our first multiple therapy—full of doubts and at the same time rather excited about doing something new and untried. To this day we feel as though we stumbled into the experience, but we did so out of a rational discussion of what would be best for this pair of clients. It is most important that we felt successful with these people and tremendously buoyed and enhanced by the experience of working together.

Multiple Relationships Are Multiple Therapy. In the years since, we have continued to be enthusiastic experimenters. We have become more sophisticated about what we do. Many of our students and colleagues have become involved in similar multiple therapy situations. What then do we mean by the term "multiple therapy"? We mean, first of all, that two therapists work with one or more clients. Almost always the two therapists are a man and a woman. As we have thought about the term "multiple therapy" and our persistence in using it we have realized that it refers to the multiplicity of relationships which are possible.

At least four dynamically distinct relationships are possible when two therapists work with one client, and when a second client is involved, the number of relationships increases con-siderably. These relationships are: (1) that between the client and the male therapist, (2) that between the client and the female therapist, (3) that between the two therapists, and (4) the client's interaction with the relationship between the two therapists. These four recapitulate the client's relationships with his parents in their simplest form. But we can add two more: each therapist's interaction with the relationship between the client and the other therapist.

It is in the addition of interrelationships between two people through the presence of a third or fourth person that we gain the opportunity for both conflict generation and resolution, which are not so readily available in dyadic therapy. While the multiplicity of the relationships may lead to confusion and maladaptive ways of coping, most problems of this kind can be resolved if the therapists are able to keep their relationship a genuinely collaborative one. Since collaboration is so important to the success of multiple therapy, we will devote this whole chapter to it. Simply adding persons and increasing the multiplicity of relationships as in group therapy does not tell the whole story; the main point is that as a result of the addition of a person or persons, the relationships become better understood. Thus persons are added for dynamic purposes, which we will more clearly describe in Chapter 11.

Some Questions Arise. Many questions can be raised about the complex discriminations which may be involved in deciding both the appropriateness and the conduct of multiple therapy. The first set of questions which are asked of us and which we ask ourselves is: How do we determine that a given client or clients should be seen by two therapists? Are there client characteristics which indicate the therapeutic appropriateness of the multiple method? Are there clients who should not be worked with in this fashion?

A second set of questions revolves around the issue of when multiple therapy should be instituted. Should a client be seen from the beginning of the therapeutic relationship by both therapists? Or should the second therapist be introduced into a dyadic relationship and then leave the relationship at a later time? How does a client react to seeing two therapists? What should a client be told about the purposes of multiple therapy? In the following sections we will formulate and present our best current understanding of these issues.

WHEN TO INITIATE
MULTIPLE THERAPY

Multiple therapy can be initiated in a number of different ways and at different times in the therapeutic process. Some clients are seen multiply from the very beginning of their venture into the effort to change themselves by seeking help. Others are seen once or twice by one therapist, and then the second therapist is introduced usually as a consequence of the nature of the early interactions with the first therapist. Or it may be determined that a second therapist should be introduced but that for dynamic and client "developmental" reasons, this introduction should be delayed.

A fourth type of situation occurs when dynamic and/or developmental reasons for introducing a second therapist become apparent in the original therapeutic relationship after the relationship has gone on for some time. In this case the need for another person may not have been apparent or even considered in the beginning.

Finally, the second therapist may be introduced into the original one-to-one relationship when that relationship has become impassed and help is needed not because of clarity and understanding but because of confusion and despair. Such occasions for multiple therapists are usually dynamically different from the more "reasoned" situations. For one thing, the anxiety levels for both therapists and for the client are much higher because failure is usually seen as a possible imminent outcome. However, the introduction of a collaborator at such a time can work powerfully to resolve the impasse. This last reason for initiating multiple therapy has become an infrequent one since we have become more sophisticated about the process and now introduce multiple therapy at an earlier stage so that impasse does not so often occur.

INDICATIONS OF NEED FOR
MULTIPLE THERAPY: CLIENT
CHARACTERISTICS AND DYNAMICS

From our own experience and that of our colleagues and students, we have formulated some dynamic, frequently developmental characteristics of clients which suggest strongly that multiple therapy should be the treatment method. We will demonstrate our thinking in two primary ways: by developing our conceptions of the nature of the dynamic, interpersonal conflicts which underlie some fairly common problems of clients and by utilizing case descriptions to further illustrate and clarify our rationale.

One of the most common reasons for initiating multiple therapy is the recognition by the therapist that the client's life history is characterized by some kind of impaired relationship with his parents. The intent in this case is to afford the client an opportunity to interact with two parental surrogates, who will recreate the earlier conflict in such a way that the client will be able to experience the feelings which characterized the earlier relationships. Then the client, having understood the meaning of the parental relationship, will have the opportunity to make a new and better relationship with his therapist "parents." We recognize that this is an oversimplified explanation of the purpose of multiple therapy, and we want to emphasize both the complexity and the utility of the interactions in contrast to those in the one-to-one relationship.

In dyadic therapy, in which there is only one relationship, that between the therapist and the client, learning new ways of interacting is frequently a long, drawn-out process which is not always easily transferable outside of the therapy hour. Furthermore, it is not as easy for clients to maintain their resistances to change when they find themselves the focus of attention from two interested, caring individuals. Clients who destructively manipulate persons with whom they have relationships find this much more difficult to do when two persons must be dealt with. Also, often it is evident that the client perceives the relationship between the two therapists as one which he can use as a model, and he makes an effort to identify with the therapist of the same sex. To help him when in doubt about his identity, the client has one therapist of his own sex and one who offers a comparison or contrast.

Reasons for choosing multiple therapy can be found in client defenses or problems which become clear in a diagnostic interview. Hysteria in female clients appears to be a diagnosis which can be most effectively treated in multiple therapy. Among unmarried, undergraduate women we have felt that some hysteria is normal and to be expected. However, when hysteria is accompanied by childhood or lifelong emotional deprivation, there may result the kind of neurotic interaction with the therapist—especially if he is a young man—which some have called unresolved transference. Multiple therapy seems to offer a way of circumventing this type of interaction.

Also, when hysterical symptoms characterize the problems of older women, e.g., age thirty or above, and the client is no longer as flexible as formerly and has not made a satisfactory sexual adjustment, we feel that we can offer better therapy if we see her together. Usually a client such as this has preferred her father, or has been ambivalent toward him, and has a relationship with her mother which is full of conflict or is emotionally distant. Our intent with such a client is to reverse the parental experience, to enable her to accept emotional support from the female therapist, which helps her to control her anxiety in relating to the male therapist. The therapy is an acted-out reversal of the primary parental relationship. When we describe the therapy as an acting out, we mean that it is an emotional experience of closeness to the female therapist. There is also an experience of approaching the male therapist with anxiety felt and expressed in an hysterical way. There is also resolution of the conflict and a reduction of anxiety, which permits an appropriately closer relationship with the male therapist. The final resolution involves relating to the two therapists at the same time, along with a reality perception of their relationship to each other in the therapeutic process.

We have generally found that clients who express strong preference for one parent over the other, particularly when the preferred parent is of the opposite sex, are good candidates for multiple therapy. Often there is open conflict with the same-sexed parent, as in the case of the hysterical female client. It is common today, too—perhaps more so than ever before—for males to prefer and feel closer to their mothers and to feel a lack of closeness, even open conflict, with the male parent. Such clients are often most efficiently helped by seeing a man and a woman therapist together. Sometimes, if we are clear early enough, multiple therapy is instituted from the beginning. Other times the second therapist is introduced when a dyadic relationship has progressed sufficiently so that the problems and conflicts are sufficiently manifest to indicate need for the second therapist.

A client who has lost a parent is often a likely candidate for our multiple approach. The common circumstance, for instance, in our present, college-age population, is that the father was lost due to war. Such a client, whether male or female, suffers more or less knowingly the pangs of deprivation so often associated with the loss or truncation of such an important relationship. We cannot "make up" such an important loss to anyone, but we can often help first by causing the deprivation to become more sharply and clearly known, then by assisting in resolving the attendant conflict and in aiding the client to know and seek relationships which will ease the deprivation.

An emotionally labile client, whatever diagnostic formulation we may attach, is often best seen ultimately by two therapists. In such cases we often find that one of us works with the client by responding directly and empathically to the strongly experienced feelings. The other is likely to remain more detached and to take a more controlled, rational approach. By so combining our efforts, we are often able to assist such a client to feel less lonely and frightened and also to know that thinking and control are possible even though the feelings are strongly experienced.

We have been discussing instances of multiple therapy initiated as multiple therapy. In these kinds of client problems we have been able to decide that multiple therapy should be the therapy from the time of an early interview.

In some cases in which the case history indicates that multiple therapy might be appropriate, an initial interview will indicate that it should be delayed. These are usually people whose capacity to relate at all is seriously impaired. For instance, a constricted, intellectualizing compulsive may often need to establish a relationship with one therapist and learn to tolerate his emotional experiences before being asked to cope with two therapists.

In a similar way, overtly hostile clients, who have little control of their hostility and attack the therapist without enough awareness to feel guilty about it, are often so distressed in an interpersonal relationship that progress is slowed by the necessity of coping with two therapists.

And, finally, the client whose only resource is to depend on the therapist, who watches the therapist, and who can only relate by first determining what the therapist wants and then producing it, is another type of individual who may need to learn first to relate to one person. We emphasize, though, that such a "watcher" may ultimately be best worked with by two therapists. Particularly is this so if the first relationship develops and then impasses, or breaks down.

These latter three types of client, the overtly hostile, the intellectualizing compulsive, and the dependent, while they are all difficult to work with in a one-to-one therapy, they are often inappropriate for multiple therapy until they have achieved some comfort in a one-to-one relationship.

There are other ways of arriving at a decision to see clients in a multiple therapeutic relationship from the beginning, but at this point they are less clear to us. With other kinds of client problems it is more usual for the second therapist to be introduced after the client has been seen by one therapist for a period of time.

Initiating multiple therapy without prior individual therapy has been the result of our own personal, professional growth and experience, and we consider it to be our most sophisticated variation on the process. An intake interview which produces this kind of decision has to afford many intuitive decisions about the client's interpersonal strengths and include considerable insight into the way his present problems have originated.

And now what about decisions, and how do we make them? Multiple therapy calls for many decisions, conscious and deliberate sometimes, intuitive and unconscious at other times. Such matters will be the subject of the next section.

DECISIONS: WHO MAKES THEM?

In any relationship between people there are times when one or more members must make decisions, unilaterally in some instances and collaboratively in others. In multiple therapy we are constantly making decisions about ourselves separately, ourselves in collaboration with each other, our separate relationships with our client, our mutual relationship as it may affect our client, and so on. The decisions we make are at times quite conscious, deliberate, and rationally undertaken either separately or collaboratively.

For instance, in beginning with a new client we often concern ourselves with such matters as in whose office we should meet and even in what chairs we should sit. Further, we may even discuss and agree about who will take a particular responsibility for beginning the interview or for introducing some particular content. We make such decisions in a number of different ways and at different times. For instance, in a discussion following an interview we may make a decision that one of us should take a particular responsibility for beginning the next interview in a particular way. Such a decision is based on our best dynamic understanding of our client, our relationship to each other, and our individual relationships to our client.

Initially, when we have relatively little idiosyncratic understanding of our client, we make such decisions in accord with our past experiences with other clients or in terms of "cultural" norms. We usually will decide to see a male client in the male therapist's office and a woman client in the female therapist's office. As our understanding of our client grows, we continue as we have begun, or we change in accord with some new understandings we are developing.

Initially, too, we may either seat ourselves somewhat randomly, or we may be purposeful if we have some reason for thinking that "who sits where" is important. Later, as our dynamic understanding grows, we may change chairs, sit closer together ourselves, or one of us may sit closer or further away from the client. Again we emphasize that our decisions in regard to both offices and seating may be deliberate and thought through, or they may be free and impulsive.

We are generally quite conscious of time, too, and we are usually agreed that one of us will be responsible for ending the interview. Generally we assign this responsibility to the male therapist since ordinarily we see this as a male function. Particular circumstances and growing understanding may lead us to modify what we do, however.

Generally decision-making is a shared function insofar as we are able to make it so. We may sometimes consult openly with each other while our client or clients are with us. At other times we may decide about something after the client is gone, or perhaps in the few minutes before an interview we will determine how some particular specific or dynamic should be handled.

At other times decision-making must be more unilateral for any of several reasons. One of us may not be available when a client calls on the phone, for instance, and the one who is reached must often make a decision. In such an instance we are usually most concerned to inform the other about what has been done or decided.

At another time only one of us may be able to make a decision or take an action even though both of us are present with our client. Such an event may occur when one of us is deeply and emotionally involved in a particular interaction with our client. When that happens, the other, who is usually more of an observer at such a time, may bear the responsibility for deciding that the interaction has gone on long enough, that something else needs to occur, and he may then intervene, thus making a temporarily "one-way" decision. But in our work such matters as these are now more truly collaborative and are the subject of the next chapters.

RECIPROCITY AND
EFFECTIVENESS ENHANCED

We are sometimes asked how in the practice of multiple therapy we justify what may appear to some an uneconomic use of the relatively few persons who can do therapy. At first we defended ourselves by saying that doing multiple therapy is good training for therapists, both experienced and inexperienced. We also said that we enjoy doing multiple therapy and that it is good and necessary for us, the therapists. We added that there are interesting phenomena associated with multiple therapy, which we wanted to study and observe further. Finally, we usually added that our multiply-seen clients have been significantly helped by the experience, although we were often not able to be very specific about how this is so.

These reasons are still true, and we offer them as a partial explanation of why we do multiple therapy. But increasingly we have become convinced that for many if not all clients some experience in a multiple situation is necessary to accomplish what needs to be done. Thus, rather than defending our "right" to do multiple therapy for personal or training reasons, we have come increasingly to recognize and point out to others its advantages as a method of treatment in its own right.

Further "why's" and "how's" in regard to the effectiveness of multiple therapy will be the subject matter of the following chapters. But these last few paragraphs are needed to set the stage. Simply said, we believe that—and we hope to show why— multiple therapy is the most effective means known of enhancing the vital reciprocity among the three process functions—phenomeno-logical, interpersonal, and rational—for therapists and clients alike.

Chapter 10

The Multiple Therapists

Some persons may conclude from our enthusiasm that multiple therapy is for therapists and that clients benefit only incidentally. And so this chapter will seem to say, because now we will describe what multiple therapy is like from the therapists' point of view. We hasten to assure the reader, though, that we will also devote a chapter to the way in which multiple therapy serves the client.

When two experienced professional people walk into the room with their first client, it is not hard to guess what they think about. Each thinks of his great responsibility to the client. Each thinks of his obligation not to interfere with his colleague. How can the therapists be sure of making the client comfortable in a situation which is so strange to all of them? How can the therapists control their own anxiety and establish some comfort with each other? Many other things can flash through each therapist's mind, things that are a part of the repertoire of an experienced therapist. We suspect that most of us are far more aware of the independent, autonomous, responsible kinds of feelings and attitudes than of the therapeutic meaning and personal satisfaction of working with a cotherapist. Furthermore, there is little in professional therapists' training which prepares them for building a coworker relationship which can be helpful and meaningful both to them and the client.

Earlier we talked about several different relationships which are important to the therapeutic process. The relationship between the two therapists is particularly significant and has many facets. "Collaboration" is the term we have given to the primary functional aspect of their relationship. What is involved in collaboration, and the exciting, rewarding aspects of learning to collaborate as well as its problems, will be the subject we will discuss in this chapter.

SOME PLEASURES FOR
MULTIPLE THERAPISTS

We have implied many times thus far that we think the doing of therapy can and should be pleasurable as well as serious and responsible.

One of our concerns in this chapter is to write as meaningfully as we can about some of the joys we know as a consequence of doing multiple therapy, as well as about the good training it gives us and the benefits it provides to clients. How shall we begin to write of pleasures? What is a pleasure, anyhow? Laughter and humor are pleasurable for most of us, and so we can begin. We note that ordinarily for us, as well as for our colleagues and students who do multiple therapy, a multiple therapy hour provides several occasions when we find something humorous, when we chuckle singly or together, or perhaps roar aloud with the spontaneous laughter which comes when something is genuinely funny. And do our clients join with us? Can he or she laugh with us? Sometimes they can, and when that is so, the pleasure is enhanced for all of us. At other times our clients may only be puzzled by our behavior.

The Importance of Humor. For some clients we often find that there is little humor at home and that they can rarely recall seeing their parents laugh together. Other clients may think we are laughing at them, and sometimes their suspicions are true, but not necessarily in the way they may think.

An example will help to clarify some of our meaning here. Some time ago we were seeing a young, male, graduate student. The two of us had seen him in multiple therapy from the beginning because his relationships with his parents suggested that he needed to see both a man and a woman and also because in the intake interview he had revealed a considerable capacity to relate well, which he knew little about, incidentally.

Therapy with him was a very serious matter at first. His anxiety level was high, and he suffered (and we do mean suffer!) from a number of rather frightening symptoms. He was concerned about being sexually impotent. There was the possibility, so he would ruminate, that he was organically damaged. Girls seemed to find him attractive, but the possibility of sexual demands so worried him that his relationships to women were transitory and threatening. He had many other problems, too, and we all labored most seriously with them.

Laughter and humor were infrequent at first, and that was something of a burden, but we persisted and gradually something of great interest to us began to emerge. Our client had a most delightful sense of humor, but he was quite unaware, even unconscious, of the fact that many things he said and did were genuinely funny. So we began, usually one or the other of us at first but sometimes together, to chuckle aloud when something our client said, did, or related struck us as humorous.

He was very nonplussed by our behavior at first. He accused us, rather angrily at times, of not taking him and his problems seriously and of being hostile to him. But we persisted in seeing and reacting to humor when and where humor was, and we did little to explain ourselves except to show that we found some things funny. We would chuckle or laugh when we felt like it. Eventually our client grew to appreciate himself in his own way and to know and value his ability to be humorous. That this development could have occurred in some other way we seriously doubt, for he had been very little appreciated by his parents for the delightful person he is—except when he has problems.

Thus we believe that our behavior with this particular client constituted a significant "dynamic reversal," which was most important to him and to us. We add, incidentally, that along with gaining and owning his sense of humor, our client also made significant progress in solving his problems. His anxiety dropped markedly, his performance as a student improved considerably along with his attitude toward himself as a student. His fears— or wishes, as some would have it—also diminished more than a little, and some other frightening and debilitating symptoms disappeared entirely. All this was accomplished in some twenty sessions of multiple therapy, which is no mean achievement, we believe. We do not wish to imply that being humorous with our client was the only way in which we were helpful to him, but we do believe that humor was a most significant variable in his improvement.

It may seem strange that we emphasize humor as often being important both to us and our clients. But our experiences, particularly in multiple therapy, have taught us that such is so. For one thing, we are convinced that being humorous markedly reduces the probability that the "effort syndrome" will surround and overcome us. Multiple therapy, particularly, enables us to maintain and enhance this important aspect of ourselves as we go about our work with our clients. Incidentally, humor may not always directly help our clients, but its loss is almost always detrimental to us and to those we try to help.

Over the years we have come to be fascinated by how we "tend" to each other in this important matter. We have become especially sensitized to indications that too great seriousness, too much effort, too much anxiety, or deadly constriction is overcoming one of us. On such occasions the other of us, who is not so powerfully involved, is often able (and we depend on each other for this) to intervene in order to lift the seriousness, lessen the effort or the anxiety, or break up the constriction. Often our means for accomplishing this is humor in some form.

Feelings, Fantasy, Imagery Again. But we labeled the heading for this section "Pleasures," so are there not more things we do or are in multiple therapy which give pleasure and enhancement to us and our clients? We think there are, and we will write about some of them. The reader will recall the "feelings, fantasy, imagery" model we presented in Chapter 6. We could not have seen, understood, and explained that model as clearly as we did if we had not had certain kinds of experiences and observations as a consequence of doing multiple therapy.

For one thing, having a partner enables us to feel, fantasy, and image more and to do it more easily. How can this be? We mentioned earlier that in dyadic therapy it is possible for the therapist to free himself so that he can attend to and complete his own feelings, fantasies, and imagery. But this is not always easy to do. A client can be powerfully engaging so that the therapist does not necessarily even know that a better therapeutic result might occur if he broke the interpersonal interaction and attended more to himself. In multiple therapy, since one has a partner it is nearly always possible at a given time to attend more completely to oneself and to see, understand, and utilize what one is really thinking, feeling, fantasying, and imaging.

For example, the one of us who is puzzled and vaguely aware of something going on inside may say to the other, "Something's puzzling me. I guess I'll see what it is." The one addressed then expects to carry the interactive effort with the client while the puzzled one retires to discover what he can. We are often most pleased with the result, for the one who retires is often able to complete a fantasy along with sharp, clear imagery, which is most helpful in indicating a new therapeutic direction.

An example will serve again to clarify our meaning. Some time ago we were working with a man who was articulate and who generally seemed to have good access to his feelings. Yet as we worked along with him, we were puzzled, for somehow a particular meaning, a nuance, was consistently escaping us. The male member of our team retired in the manner just described and found himself completing a fantasy along with sharp, clear imagery.

He "pictured" the client as a little boy, perhaps six or seven, and vividly imagined a sequence of experiences which revealed how the boy had felt and thought about himself at that particular time. And what was so remarkable about what the therapist imagined? Only that the little boy had come to think and feel that he was deeply and fundamentally defective. Why? Apparently about this time the youngster had lived in a series of most unsatisfactory foster homes. In none of them had he been welcome, let alone loved. So in the fashion of children he had explained the whole matter to himself by assuming that he was defective in some basic, unknown, unspecifiable way. This was the meaning, the nuance, which had been escaping us.

The therapist who had retired returned to the interaction and soon quietly said something like, "I know now that you feel you're defective and unwanted." The impact was massive. The client abreacted and was eventually able to recover the meaning of his own experiences. Therapeutic progress with the client turned the corner on this particular day. That we might have accomplished the same gain in some other way is possible, but we doubt it. It is perhaps important that the male therapist was the one who retired to have the fantasy and imagery, for this client had never known his father!

Sharing Fantasy and Imagery. Another way in which feelings, fantasy, and imagery are both useful and pleasurable in multiple therapy is for one or the other therapist to share and facilitate fantasy and imagery with a client during the therapy hour itself. We do this when it becomes apparent to us that the client has tight control on certain kinds of feelings and that fantasy and imagery are truncated or even absent as a consequence. One of us offers and may even insist on sharing a fantasy with a client. In such instances we commonly find that the therapist who offers is of the same sex as the client's parent from whom he feels most estranged. In a typical instance the dynamically most appropriate one of us will say something like, "Let's see if we can share a fantasy together. Let's both close our eyes and see what we can imagine."

Ordinarily what happens is that the therapist must initiate the process by reporting some fantasy and/or imagery of his or her own. The interaction, building, and sharing of the experience then begins, for clients almost inevitably respond by reporting first feelings, most likely anxious ones, and then fantasy and imagery of their own. As the experience grows and builds, it may remain clearly mutual, with both persons contributing, or the client may become fascinated by his own associations and largely take over the production of the fantasy. When this latter happens, as it frequently does, the therapist facilitates by making appropriate remarks, suggestions, and contributions from his own imagery, but basically he allows the client to take the lead. Usually we find that these experiences, whether they are truly mutual or led by the client, take up the balance of the therapeutic hour, for the flow of imagery and fantasy seems irresistible once it begins.

Such a happening may be repeated with the client in a later therapy hour, but more often we find that one such experience is sufficient to establish the necessary emotional bond. Further, one experience seems to be enough to enable most clients better to know and have their own feelings, fantasy, and imagery. Once the process sequence is begun, it tends to continue.

One other thing needs to be noted about the nature of the fantasies and imageries promoted in this way. The initial experience, at least, is usually benign and pleasant but is deeply meaningful in a dynamic way nonetheless. Later experience in normal multiple therapy sessions reveals that these clients are more open and available to working and interacting with both of us and to doing so in increasingly meaningful ways.

But what of the therapist's sources of pleasure in such fantasies with clients? And what of the therapist who may seem to be left out of the experience? It is evident, first of all, that we think such experiences enhance our effectiveness in the therapeutic work, and that itself is pleasing to us. But the enhancement of our therapeutic effort is not the whole of the story. Sharing fantasies and imagery with other persons, be they cotherapists or clients, is deeply rewarding and fulfilling in a very personal way, which is a separate pleasure from the enhanced effectiveness. One of us, for instance, still remembers vividly and with great pleasure forty-five minutes of imagery and fantasy about being on a beautiful Lake Michigan beach, a fantasy shared with a particularly lonely, alienated client.

The Caring Observer. The therapist who is apparently left out of the experience is not really left out. Both of us have often had a most pleasant experience in being the appreciative and "caring observer." We emphasize the importance of the caring observer, incidentally, because his is a very worthwhile function for dynamic reasons of direct concern to us, the therapists, as well as for personal reasons; also for dynamically significant reasons of concern to the client. Being a therapist team, we have many opportunities to appreciate each other, but it seems especially important to be able to observe and appreciate the sharing of a moving, emotional, fantasy experience of two other people. Particularly is this true when the "caring observer" therapist perceives the experience as something he or she has wanted to have happen.

Also, we think that the caring observer serves another important function, that of providing a potential limit or control on the experience of the other two persons. This control, although rarely if ever exercised overtly in our practice, provides the promise that the fantasy experience will not become too regressed or too threatening. Put another way, we believe that it is the caring observer who helps to make such experiences possible simply by being there and caring positively about what happens. We observe, for instance, that we do not often attempt such things in our dyadic therapy relationships and that when we do, the process is likely to be constricted or very anxious and threatening to both therapist and client so that the experience is less effective.

There is an additional dynamically significant reason of concern to the client for the presence and attention of the caring observer. The reader will remember that earlier we said many client problems originate, in part at least, from impaired relationships with parents. In the case of a male client alienated from his father, for instance, the common situation is not only that mother and son are emotionally close but that the mother is the fomenter of trouble between father and son. Thus we can see the dynamic and emotionally significant meaning of having a caring, appreciative female therapist present when a male therapist and a male client go through a deeply moving fantasy experience together. And reversing the circumstances, we see how important the presence of a caring male therapist is when a female client, alienated from her mother, and a woman therapist go through a close, emotionally moving occurrence together.

Imagery and Fantasy for the Therapists. Finally, we find fantasy and imagery to be especially pleasurable and useful to us as multiple therapists in one other primary way. These are the times when we, the therapists, fantasy and image together, perhaps excluding our client for an interval. We do this when our client is puzzling to both of us or when he pouts and withdraws or perhaps when we find that he has been trying to foment disagreement or a fight between us. When such situations occur, we often turn to each other and begin by talking and speculating about our client and what may be going on. We exchange remarks on how we feel and think. When our client tries to interfere, as is often the case, we sometimes even tell him that we need to talk to each other and that he is excluded from our interaction.

We find on some occasions that simply talking to each other and perhaps exchanging observations on how we are feeling is sufficient, and we are pleased when that is so. We can then permit the client to reenter the interaction with us, but the client is likely to have begun to learn something most important to him. What is that? Simply that an adult man and woman can be puzzled, anxious, or even in conflict and that these same adults can resolve their problem by talking to each other. Such an outcome between adults, particularly a man and woman, is likely to have been most rare in such a client's past experience. We may have to repeat this kind of interaction, of course, for some clients are slow learners, but we are willing to do so.

On other occasions, talking and exchanging how we feel are insufficient to solve our problem or puzzlement. And we add that the most meaningful criterion of when we have resolved the problem is that we both feel pleased. At such times when talking is not enough, we go further, often excluding the client from the interaction. On these occasions we fantasy and image, sometimes together, sometimes separately. In a sense what we try to do is to set our own truncated process sequence of feelings-fantasy-imagery into motion.

If we are successful in our effort, either separately or by stimulating each other, then our fantasy and imagery will tell us a story which is both useful and pleasurable. The usefulness of the story is in its content, for we are often able to imagine with considerable vividness the emotional atmosphere and the interactions in the client's home, for instance. The pleasure resides in our restored ability to fantasy and image and the realization that in so doing we are enabled to solve our problem and understand our client better.

That our clients are often helped by our ability to fantasy and image is evident. Sometimes the help to the client comes through our example. He is enabled to fantasy and image for himself or in relationship to us, for instance. At other times our own fantasies and images are useful mainly in stimulating the client to remember in a less distorted fashion how emotional matters really were in his home. In fact, on occasion we have had an excited and stimulated client break in on our imaging to assure us, adding nuances of his own, that we were recapturing "how it really was."

COLLABORATION IS ALSO SERIOUS

We take some aspects of collaboration very seriously. We are serious about them because we have wrestled with them personally. We refer primarily to the needs each person has to be both autonomous and dependent. As we observe ourselves and others, it is clear to us that in a multiple therapy team both needs must be met for both therapists; otherwise their relationship will be ineffective, continually conflictful, and unsatisfying. In fact, we think it is the presence of both needs, in some reasonably harmonious balance within each person, which enables a therapist pair to choose each other. Once the choice is made, they then have the capacities to form an effective, pleasing relationship.

The remainder of this chapter reflects our awareness and understandings of the interactions of these needs both intrapersonally and interpersonally for the therapist partners. Being autonomous, being dependent, agreeing, disagreeing, perceiving and understanding differently, enhancing sexual separateness, intervening, and accepting intervention are all ways we have found for understanding and satisfying our individual needs as we work together.

The Autonomous Need. First there is the need to be individuals, the need to be separate. We are not especially aware that being or feeling autonomous in our multiple relationship has been a particular problem. Having known and respected each other for a number of years before we actually joined our efforts in multiple therapy has helped us in this regard, we believe. We also observe that our students and colleagues seem to function better in their multiple relationships when they have known each other for a time before joining their efforts. To us this is not strange. Knowing another person certainly involves some understanding of the human needs the other person has. If this understanding does not lead to acceptance and respect, it is unlikely that the persons will choose to work closely together in multiple therapy.

We think, then, that multiple therapy partners do not often have serious, overt problems in regard to autonomy, or separateness. Most pairs seem to be well aware that they have chosen each other for mutually acceptable reasons. Each pair usually knows that respecting each other for being separate, functioning persons was one of the basic reasons for their choice. Mutually respecting partners also seem to know quite easily how to enhance each other's separateness.

It is when the partners do not know or understand each other's needs that conflicts arise. However, when the choice of partners was made for confused, unclear, or inappropriate reasons, whatever they may be, then the conflicts are usually about dependency, distrust, disagreement, as well as autonomy. Even for appropriately chosen partners, the matter of how to depend seems to be complex and problematic.

The Dependent Need. We have depended on each other in so many ways that it is difficult to remember that this was not always natural to us and that it may be a rather unnatural way of being for professional people. Most of us think readily enough of clients' dependency on therapists, and we believe that this is natural and good. Yet therapists have dependency needs also. On whom do they depend? Wives, husbands, friends, even clients, of course. But how about a cotherapist to depend on? Such a notion can be both enticing and frightening. Our own experience, as well as that of other therapists, tells us that being able to depend on each other is vital to the multiple therapeutic venture.

For example, one of us may be very puzzled, even bewildered, by an interchange of a sequence of events. One can, of course, try to keep such an "awful thing" hidden. Yet is it so awful not to understand something? Determined autonomy at such a time can result in continued bewilderment and ineffectiveness rather than the help and clarity a therapeutic partner can give. We note, however, that in our work together we grow increasingly able to ask when puzzled or to be openly bewildered when that state obtains, too. We are also able to permit our cotherapist to inquire about a concern. For example, if a cotherapist says, "Does something about that bother you?" it requires a great deal of basic trust and willingness to be helped, not to brush off the offer but instead to feel relieved by an offer of help.

It is one thing to recognize cognitively that dependency is a good and important part of the multiple therapists' relationship and quite another to respond dependently and appropriately in a spontaneous, therapeutic interaction. We have referred earlier to therapists' defenses against being dependent and to the ways in which being a helping person assures that one never asks for help himself and never has to realize that he needs it. The experience of the multiple therapeutic relationship exposes these defenses and makes us not only vulnerable to our own dependency needs but also reasonably comfortable with them.

Once having got over this hurdle, the therapist finds it very nice to have another person who shares the responsibility, who can be depended upon to have a different yet complementary under-standing, and who when the therapy is difficult provides reassur-ance and support. Take, for an example, the time when a client is angry and threatening, perhaps living out a conflict which seems very real to him in the relationship to his therapists. The fact that the therapists share the attack and rejection means that both can permit the client to live out his feelings. Either or both therapists can be rejected by the client, and yet neither will have to with-draw, strike back, or respond defensively in some way. There is not that abandoned, perhaps guilty, feeling one has when a similar thing happens in dyadic therapy.

The on-going dependency is a more subtle experience. There is dependency in the freedom to withdraw into oneself and think or to explore one's feelings or even to regress and fantasy. The one therapist may overtly signal the other therapist to take over for a while, but he may also do it with no thought other than a sense of total reliance on the other to carry on without him. Further-more, the freedom to depend is the basis on which a therapist may enter with a client into a regressive feeling experience in which both permit themselves to lose contact with emotional reality. Here the active therapist is implicitly dependent on the other for bringing both himself and the client back to emotional and inter-personal reality. In dyadic therapy such experiences are often less complete and more guarded because the therapist can depend only on himself to set the limits and maintain the sense of reality. Thus he must of necessity hold back a little.

Suppose one therapist enters into a regressive experience with the client, and after it has gone on a while, the cotherapist realizes it is time to interfere and help bring it to an end. The active thera-pist, deep in primary process (or even afterward), may feel irritated and resentful and think, "I wonder what is wrong with what I'm doing." The resentment will be short-lived only if the relationship is one which is trusting; then the question will change from a self-critical one to "Something very deep was occurring. I wonder what it was?" Or the affect may be relief, "I guess I knew I needed help to extricate myself." With this there is also a deeply reassured feeling because help was available, as well as a sense of enhancement because one was able to accept and appreciate the help.

These openly dependent experiences of the therapists have a particularly beneficial effect on the client. Being dependent is frequently an area of conflict for clients, and it can be helpful to them to see people whom they perceive as strong being dependent, too. We will have more to say about this in the following chapter when we discuss multiple therapy from the client's experience of it.

Collaboration and Lack of Agreement. We do not imply that our multiple therapists' relationship is only a dependent one or that our dependency on each other is the only therapeutic dynamic which we have recognized in the relationship. One troublesome experience in all kinds of relationships occurs when there is lack of agreement. Lack of agreement can arouse more anxiety and concern between therapists than in almost any other kind of relationship. We depend so strongly on each other's validation of our perception of intrapsychic experiences that to meet with disagreement from the other is often to lose confidence in what we have understood. It would almost seem that successful collaboration can occur only when therapists totally agree. Let us examine the problem to see whether this is true.

We prefer to call the phenomenon discussed here lack of agreement rather than disagreement for a definite reason. Suppose one of us does not agree with the other but simply notes to himself, "I don't see it that way. It seems to me. . . ." This is lack of agreement. But suppose, on the other hand, that one *has* to bring the other into agreement with him. Then he says, "But don't you see thus and so? Can't you see you are wrong?" The person attacked has to defend his position, and there is true disagreement between them. Disagreement, then, occurs when one or both persons cannot permit lack of agreement about something. We insist that lack of agreement is simply lack of agreement.

In addition, we propose that lack of agreement has value to the therapeutic process. However, we acknowledge that agreement between cotherapists is requisite when the issues have to do with fundamental human values and beliefs about what life is like. We cannot think, for instance, that two therapists can work together very well when one sees life pessimistically and as a constant struggle and the other views it optimistically and as full of delightful opportunities. The way the last sentence is written shows the disagreement the writer feels about the views of the pessimist, and indicates that for the writer to work with him would involve a struggle to change those pessimistic, depressive notions. This, then, is not a permissible area for lack of agreement.

But in the case of understandings of intrapsychic phenomena and of interpersonal experiences, lack of agreement between cotherapists can be exciting and enhancing. This is true in spite of their admitted dependency on validation by the other. For example, if one can say, "Oh, you see it that way. Isn't that interesting! I wonder why we see it differently," and then go on to discover that the differences have to do with personal uniqueness, then both persons can feel enhanced. Too, the client involved may feel truly understood and even enlarged because he has been able to affect two people differently.

Often differences in understanding come out of reactions to the two sides of a client's ambivalence. Thus one cotherapist experiences the positive and the other the negative in such a way that both are presented to the client at once, a feat which we are often able to accomplish with much greater facility in multiple therapy than in dyadic therapy. Thus we contend that simple willingness to permit the other therapist to see something differently or to hold a different opinion is frequently very useful to all concerned. One way in which cotherapists can be most effective is to expect to understand their client differently, to feel that each person has a unique way of perceiving the client and his experience, and that each way is important to the client. When a therapist has this expectation, he has no great need to force his particular understanding on the other.

On the other hand, when genuine disagreement occurs, that is, when either one of the therapists cannot permit the differences between their understanding or perception, it becomes imperative that they discuss it or in some way work toward a resolution. The suppression, or, even worse, repression, of an affectively experienced conflict between the therapists can only serve to create conflict and confusion for the client. It can make him worse instead of better.

Where should conflict be dealt with? Should therapists fight it out in the presence of the client? Should they work out differences privately? We would not want to make any arbitrary rules about this since we feel most strongly that therapists are people, too, and that they can be most effective when they are able to communicate their humanness in their own ways. All of one's therapeutic sensitivity and training go into making a decision about whether a client at a given time can cope with and learn from the experience of having the two people whom he is trusting to help him, become human beings with problems in their own relationship. Yet to be a part of living through such an experience can be one of the most therapeutic kinds of experiences for a client.

We have realized that some clients try to create dissension between us. We are now sensitized enough to this possibility that if we find ourselves in disagreement, we often assume that the client has somehow subtly set up a situation which causes us to disagree. We know that he has recreated the "old pattern at home," where he derived a sense of power and at the same time felt dismal disappointment that the adults in his life could not handle things the way "they're supposed to." We neither believe that these occurrences should always be avoided, nor do we think that conflicts should always be allowed to reach their full proportions. Here again we depend on our individual and cooperative sensitivity to the client's immediate state to guide us in how to deal with the problem.

On the other hand, we hope we do not become so sophisticated that we rationalize away all areas of disagreement. Clients are often people for whom to disagree is to be wrong in the eyes of the other, and to be wrong is to be degraded, a painful, punishing experience. We know that we need to be able to participate with our clients in real, human disagreement and to be able to offer them an opportunity to learn that disagreement can have different meanings.

In certain situations lack of agreement is inevitable. For example, when our client is a woman, sometimes the male member of the team becomes aware of the client's seductive behavior and calls attention to it in some way. The female therapist does not have the same cues and cannot have them. She may feel resentful toward her cotherapist and protective of the client; or she may be pleased that the client has been seductive; or she may vicariously enjoy the male therapist's approach to the seduction. She may even feel like punishing the client; or she may withdraw psychologically from the whole interaction; or she may be an active observer, waiting to see.

Here a therapeutic interaction arises where perceptual agreement is impossible and where tolerance for the other therapist's understanding is essential in order for the joint effort to be effective. There is no way in which the emotional experience of the two can be shared and thereby mutually understood, yet there need be no conflict if both have confidence in their differences. In fact, a lot of pleasure will be had if the therapists later discuss and share their different feelings about these interactions.

A MAN AND A WOMAN:

THE IMPORTANCE OF BOTH

The differences in perception due to sex which were pointed up in the last example bring us to a discussion of why we think it is important that multiple therapists should usually be a man and a woman. We have a small amount of experience with multiple therapy when the therapists are the same sex, almost always both men. Earlier, and to some extent it is still true, so few women were trained as therapists that the disparity in numbers between them and men meant that there were simply not enough women for cross-sexed, multiple therapy teams.

We have observed that when two men work together, they find it very difficult to maintain a noncompetitive, emotionally close, equalitarian relationship. One pair of young male interns whom we supervised found to everyone else's barely contained amusement that they were competing over who was to nurture the client, who was going to be symbolic mama. After we had thought about it, the fact that their competitiveness centered around this facet of the relationship was not at all surprising.

Sometimes two males have worked together effectively, perhaps optimally, with certain selected clients. We can even hypothesize that an all-male relationship would be useful to a male client whose developmental problems originated from deprivation of male companionship in adolescence, for instance. For the most part, however, we feel that the greatest power of multiple therapy lies in recreating primary family relationships and thus should include a therapist of each sex.

The fact that one therapist is a man and the other a woman does not guarantee that the relationship will be easy, comfortable, and without conflict. Men and women can be competitive, too. There is a peculiar way in which the graduate academic training experience sensitizes both men and women to the possibility of a destructive intent toward each other. We refer to the castration fabrication and the bases it offers for identifying and yet not coping with heterosexual problems.

Men learn or bring with them a fear of competing with their women colleagues in academic matters. They resent their bright, able, intelligent sisters. They may be half consciously convinced that the women should not be there muddling up the allegedly nice, clean competitiveness men have with each other. Sometimes they feel contemptuous that these women have chosen graduate school instead of or along with marriage. They are ambivalent about straightforward competition for academic excellence, and the women, struggling to find a place and also ambivalent about being there, feed the men's ambivalence in countless subtle, perhaps unconscious ways.

On the other hand, women faced with male rejection for being bright and able seem to have only two choices, i.e., to flaunt their ability or to hide it. Either alternative serves only to aggravate their problems with men, because the overdetermination of the flaunters somehow draws them into bitter competition, and those who hide their ability, while initially perhaps better accepted, cannot hide it forever. When the competence comes bursting out of hiding, men respond as though they have been betrayed into trusting this nice, unthreatening, relatively unable female only to discover that she, too, has the capacity to win at the academic game. When they are offered the castration notion as an explanation, both men and women grasp it almost eagerly as an explanation for their feelings and often fail to go any further to understand themselves and reach a more appropriate resolution.

We have focused our attention on the matter of women's capabilities as the source of conflict between the sexes in this particular subculture, but the academic arena is obviously not the only one. A battle between the sexes goes on for other reasons in other subcultures.

We need to examine the source of conflict a bit more. It often appears to the participants that there would be no problem if once and for all it could be settled that men are stronger, more able in all ways than women and if men would proceed, then, to function in this way. Perhaps it does work out to be true in some societies; we cannot say. But we really do not believe that this is a tenable solution in our modern world, where more and more women are professionally competitive with men, for there is more to heterosexual relationships than this.

Competition obscures the needs men and women have to be dependent on each other, and these needs increase as the dependency extends outside the home and into their professional worlds. What we have been saying sounds as though it were generally applicable—and so it may be—but it is also directly applicable to our professional therapist population. It is not hard to see that if men and women must depend on each other, what is important is not that one be stronger so that he can win over the other but that each be as strong, whole, and complete as possible. Strength in the other is what we must seek, not weakness. Capability in the other is what we must enhance and support. And so we think the multiple therapy experience can contribute to the resolution of the conflict which has often been exacerbated by previous training and living experiences.

Let us think now about some of the ways in which we accomplish this last goal—resolution of the conflicts between men and women. Perhaps the central factor in the way in which we go about this task is our emphasis on our maleness and femaleness. Emphasis is too strong a word to describe what we do that can be seen objectively because the "emphasis" occurs covertly and subtly. Perhaps it is enough to say that we attend to our differences, that while we have a way of attributing some of our lack of agreement to masculinity and femininity, we do so with respect and acceptance and not with derogation.

We also believe that enhancing and clarifying the meaning of sexual identity is therapeutically important for clients as well as for therapists. The way in which we communicate differences and/or similarities to each other and to the client are rather self-conscious at times but not necessarily contrived. We find ourselves, consciously and purposefully on occasion, behaving and responding with each other and with our clients in ways which will enhance and keep clear our own maleness and femaleness. As a man one would expect to feel and look at some aspect of the client's feelings or behavior differently than a woman. One of us may say to the other, "This is the way it appears to me. How does it seem to you?" thus emphasizing and accepting possible differences and similarities. The differences may apply to perceptions and the meaning of feelings as well as to the meaning of other experiences or behavior. We frequently find ourselves in agreement, but the subtle significance of asking rather than taking for granted is that we recognize there may be differences.

At other times as we look back over a span of therapeutic interaction, we are pleased and astonished at the clarity and preciseness of our behavior as male and female that was not deliberately conceived or intended. There is a naturalness in the way that we respond to different things at different times which seems to us to express in an appropriate manner the ways a man's point of view differs from a woman's.

While we wish to make clear our conscious, purposeful awareness of our sexual separateness, at the same time we recognize that what may be most therapeutic is an unconscious, uncontrived reaction to a client's problem. The following interaction from a case will help us to present our conscious understanding and its unconscious implementations in interaction with the client.

In the case of Paul, we came to understand over time that he had been emotionally estranged from his father for a long period and that he had uncomfortably enjoyed a much closer relationship with his mother. We felt strongly that Paul needed to establish a better and different kind of relationship with men and with his father, and we worked consistently toward this.

Yet perhaps the most powerful therapeutic moment came in an uncontrived, unconscious way for all of us. Our client's father had a heart attack, which precipitated a necessity for the client to do something about the conflict he felt. Both therapists perceived him as trying to avoid dealing with his feelings by maintaining his attitude of distance and alienation from his father. The two therapists, however, each had different feelings about his behavior and talked to him differently about it.

The male member of the team rather matter-of-factly pointed out that both he and his father were behaving in an immature way toward each other. The female member of the team in an emotionally involved way expressed concern over his welfare if he did not make the appropriate overture to his father. The male therapist felt sure that when the client knew the alternatives, he would choose appropriately. The female therapist was involved in the consequences to the client if he did not establish emotional contact with his father and felt less assurance that he would actually make the effort. As a consequence, the client received (1) an emotionally directed message for acting appropriately, and (2) a message which offered both emotional support and at the same time a matter-of-fact set of alternatives through which he could make an appropriate choice and still maintain his autonomy.

At the time, the client's own mother was highly anxious and unable to communicate emotionally with the client at all, either to give or to ask for support. We have thought that our reactions were very closely related to the cultural expectation that women and mothers are affectively concerned and that men and fathers, though concerned, are controlled and more preoccupied with considering the alternatives.

From a diagnostic point of view we perceive that we were dealing with repression but did so in terms of our own sex roles, i.e., the male offered a way in which the repressed emotional components could be experienced yet controlled; and the female, a way to exacerbate the repressed or denied emotions. We see such separation of function as one of the powerful therapeutic aspects of multiple therapy. The therapists can behave in accord with their appropriate sexual identities and are not confronted with the somewhat incompatible tasks of simultaneous control and stimulation of emotions.

In thinking about the "battle of the sexes," we have come to realize that in the traditional, or shall we say more natural, older relationships between men and women, the conflicts are ameliorated or perhaps sometimes obscured by sexual relationships. And we have been asked by sophisticated people, whether cotherapists experience a problem about sex. When we say that this has not been of any concern to us, we are sometimes met almost with disbelief—we assume because our descriptions of our emotional experiences with each other and with our clients are so graphic and suggestive of emotional closeness. With very rare exceptions, the problem has not occurred either in our experiences as multiple therapists or in that of our colleagues and graduate students.

One of us has had the experience of working with a spouse as cotherapist. The problems which husband-and-wife teams have seem to be no different in kind and no fewer in number because the cotherapists also have a sexual relationship. We must assume, then, that mutual respect, awareness and acceptance of differences, owning of one's own competency, freedom to feel and to express feelings, both affectionate ones and those which are less positive, are the primary elements which make up a good multiple therapeutic relationship.

And We Work with Others. Thus far in this book and in this chapter, we have concentrated largely on the present authors' collaborative relationship. We have referred to the fact that our students often work collaboratively together as do some of our colleagues. Also, each of us, the authors, has worked with a number of therapeutic partners, and we have learned a number of interesting things from these varied experiences. We have learned, for instance, that success as collaborators is not a peculiar matter which means that only one—or at best a very few relationships— can be enhancing and successful. We have found, rather, that any two reasonably open persons can probably create a relationship which is enhancing for them and helpful to their clients as well.

We do not mean that problems, sometimes serious ones, do not occur along the way to developing the working, collaboratively effective relationships. There are real problems nearly always, but a combination of persistence, openness, talking and working together, and sometimes outside supervisory or consultative help usually enables the relationship to become collaborative, enhancing to the participants, and effective with clients. Our students probably find that their experiences together in multiple therapy are the most rewarding and useful aspect of their training and learning.

In this chapter we have delved deeply into our own collaborative relationship to tell how doing multiple therapy is rewarding, enhancing, and pleasurable to us. But problems occur, too, in learning to collaborate, and we have written about them—our own and those of others. We have suggested that clients can join in fomenting problems between multiple therapists. And we have suggested, too, that resolution of therapists' conflicts can be therapeutic for a client as well as enhancing for the therapists. We have attended to the pleasures and uses of humor, fantasy, and imagery, and we hope we have been intriguing and stimulating in these regards. We have also attended a bit to our clients in this chapter, and we have added something more about our conviction that multiple therapy is powerfully effective in helping them.

Finally, we have a hope to express. It is that those who read us will be stimulated to find out for themselves the pleasures, tribulations, and rewards of collaboration in therapy.

what has transpired. Whether we tell the client that we have conferred about the contact usually depends upon the awareness we may have of dynamic reasons for doing so.

For instance, it is not uncommon for a female client to telephone the male therapist. When this happens, the female collaborator is usually quickly informed of the contact. The client is then usually disappointed, angered, and ultimately relieved in that feeling sequence when she learns—whether we tell her voluntarily or she asks—that we have conferred. We see significant conflicts being generated and resolved in such ways. The way to generate conflicts is to let the phone call happen. Unless the conflict generates, it is not usually resolved.

SPONTANEITY AND PURPOSE: ASPECTS OF COLLABORATION

Another aspect of the power of multiple therapy lies in the degree to which we plan our behavior and the degree to which we are spontaneous in responding to a given client. Ordinarily we think it is important to do both with most clients, and so we do. Planning and being obviously purposeful help us as therapists and also convey to our client, sometimes to his dismay and conflict, that we intend to do the best we can to help him with his problems. That our clients are usually ambivalent and conflicted about our purposefulness is generally true, but most clients are also ultimately able to be most appreciative that we have cared that much.

What does the fact that we are often quite spontaneous in how we behave with a client—whether our individual behavior is similar or different—add to the power of multiple therapy? We think, for one thing, that being spontaneous is in and of itself a most important thing for many clients first to witness and later to become very much involved in. What we want our clients to feel and learn is that living in the world and interacting with others can be free, even impulsive, at times, as well as purposeful, rational, and directed toward the achievement of specific, defined goals at other times.

But there is another reason why we are spontaneous in our similar and different behaviors with clients. When we are purpose-

Chapter 11

The Power of Multiple Therapy

In the last chapter we attended to the multiple therapists—their joys, rewards, pleasures, and problems. Only incidentally did we deal with clients and the fact that multiple therapy is a powerful instrument in their behalf. In this chapter we will turn to some of the ways in which multiple therapy is tremendously effective in helping clients.

RECIPROCITY AMONG THE PROCESS FUNCTIONS: A BASIC PRINCIPLE AGAIN

In order to begin, we turn to our three process constructs—phenomenological, interpersonal, and rational—and to the desired reciprocal effects among them. We have said that human beings may be more or less differentiated in one, two, or all three of the areas of functioning. Further, we have said that ideally a person is differentiated in all three ways, and when that is so, there is constant ebb and flow and modification, which we have called reciprocity among the functions. We have written of how in dyadic therapy we work to promote

235

differentiation in a client in one or more of the areas and how the reciprocal effects occur as the differentiations develop. But we think that oftentimes practicing dyadic therapy is doing therapy "the hard way," and we are not so devoted to the effort syndrome that we must always work that hard. Multiple therapy is often more effective as well as more pleasurable for the therapists. Its probable greater effectiveness in many instances is due to its greater efficacy in promoting differentiation and reciprocity, and we will show how this may be so.

How is it that two therapists complement each other in this important work? Our use of the word "complement" suggests both a key concept and a way to begin. For example, while we may both respond to a client in similar ways, we are also likely to respond over a period of time in different but usually complementary and collaborative ways. We think not only that our different ways of responding are appropriate in helping us, the therapists, to be differentiated individually and from each other, but also that such different responses promote differentiation in a client.

For instance, with respect to the process constructs, commonly one of us responds in a phenomenological way with the intent of encouraging and rewarding phenomenological differentiation in the client. The other of us may respond rather consistently in a way which is intended to have more interpersonal impact, thus promoting the fact that interpersonal relationships should also be varied and differentiated.

Don't our different ways of responding to a client confuse him and simply add to his conflicts rather than help him? some may ask. Sometimes confusion does result, and our client may powerfully try to convince us that we are wrong, that we don't understand him very well, or that we should not behave as we do. If such happens, we listen to our client. We may act to lessen his confusion a bit, but we are also likely to persist in our different ways of responding and behaving. We are particularly likely to persist if we are able to assure ourselves and each other that a conflict is generating appropriately.

Therapists Confer. At such a time we may need to co order to assure ourselves that we are doing what we want to are not committing an error. We observe, too, that the com of a client about our different ways of behaving and respo are frequently an effort to foment anxiety in us and to ca to be concerned about disagreeing with each other. Thus w need to confer with each other in order to maintain our relationship in the way we wish.

Do we have rules for conferring? We have only one w aware of: to confer when either or both of us has some need t so. We consult when the need is present, which means we sometimes confer while the client is with us and at o times after he has gone in order to understand, say, the mear of a complaint he has or a possible difference between us. Bu any case we value the opportunity to consult each other whene we wish both for ourselves and because open, spontaneous c sultation can be powerfully therapeutic for the client. Clie react variously to our open conferring, but we note that th usually feel both privileged and embarrassed. Whatever a clien reaction may be, however, we are likely to be interested in it an to discuss its meaning if that seems appropriate.

Clients are also likely to be curious, sometimes suspicious o hostile, about the probability that we talk about them in thei absence. If a client becomes in any way concerned about whethei we do confer, we are careful to tell him that we do so. Whether we report the nature of our discussion to him depends upon what we think he ought to know. Usually the decision of whether to report our private conversations to a client is based upon the dynamic considerations we are aware of at the time.

One further matter of dynamic significance in the conferring of multiple partners is the way in which multiply-seen clients will test us to see whether and in what way we do confer. Often a client will seek one of us out to talk about something. The subject matter may or may not have special dynamic meaning, but the act of singling one of us out does usually have particular significance. We do talk to each other about such contacts and tell the other

ful and goal-directed in our behavior, we may not be the only ones who know what we are doing. Clients are very observant. At such times they can be either astonishingly resistant to our efforts or amazingly able to discern and then produce what is desired. In neither instance are we pleased with the progress. Some spontaneous change in the behavior of either one or both of us is often a powerful factor in restoring life and movement to our effort.

A reference to dyadic therapy will make our meaning more clear and also show that multiple therapy may have a special advantage in such matters. Commonly in dyadic therapy a conflict generates to impasse rather than resolution, or the client carefully conforms to what he perceives his therapist wants. While it is possible for the therapist in a dyadic relationship to resolve an impasse or change his behavior, we think such changes are inherently more difficult to accomplish than in multiple therapy.

Why should this be? There is at least one significant reason, we believe. Interpersonal, affectively powerful relationships are essentially participant in nature, and affectively involved participants typically have lowered capacity to be observant or objective about their relationship. Many psychological experiments indicate the low reliability of witnesses who are affectively involved in the situation they report on. Being observant and/or detaching to observe is possible to achieve in a dyadic relationship, and we have earlier written of some ways of doing so. But we are convinced that the task is more difficult in one-to-one therapy and that multiple therapy offers more ready means for accomplishing what needs to be done. Seldom are both multiple therapists involved in the same affective way with a given client. Their differing involvements ordinarily enable one of them to observe, to change in some way, or even to intervene in the relationship between the other therapist and the client.

Intervention: Breaking the Chains That Bind. Intervention has come to have increasing significance to us as a means of promoting the power, the effectiveness, of the therapists' collaborative relationship. What do we mean by intervention? We mean simply that one therapist, the more observant one usually, interferes in an ongoing interaction between the other therapist and the client to change the nature of the interaction. Both the ability to intervene and the ability to accept intervention are most important. Both capacities reflect a high level of trust that the intervener has a good reason for what he does. We feel that the ability to intervene and to accept intervention embody the highest order of collaboration we know. Our students are intellectually able to understand the concept rather quickly, but their ability to perform intervention well comes only with time, experience, and development of trust in their collaborative relationships.

Two examples of intervention will help to clarify its nature and meaning. Several years ago the male member of our team was working with a woman who could be best described as hysterical. He had worked long and hard to help this woman, and some progress had been made, but it finally became evident that help was needed. Accordingly, the female member of the team was invited into the relationship. We discussed ahead of time something of what might need to be done. It was clear that the male therapist was well caught up in the effort syndrome and that it would be most appropriate for him to be released from the affective bondage. We even agreed that accomplishing this affective release would be part of the female therapist's function. Yet the affective power of the relationship was such that in the first multiple interview, the male therapist and the client continued to behave as though the female therapist was not there.

After some twenty minutes of being essentially an observer, the female therapist intervened very effectively. She said something like, "What in hell are you working so hard for? That's what I'm here to help with!" The male therapist still vividly remembers first the sense of shock and then the relief which occurred. After some momentary feelings of confusion about what to do, he leaned back, propped his feet up, deeply enjoyed being relieved, and observed with interest as the female therapist and the client went about the conflict-filled matter of establishing the relationship they needed to have. The male therapist was able to return to the multiple relationship in later interviews to be effective in different ways than he had been.

We thought later as we discussed the situation that the male therapist and the client had recreated a very similar relationship to that which she and her father had had. Thus the conflicts had been well generated, but impasse had occurred. The client's mother had been a sick, ineffective woman who had been able to do little for either her husband or her daughter. The female therapist provided a different example, and the collaboration between the therapists eventually enabled them and the client to move along to a successful conclusion in about fifteen more interviews.

Effective intervention can also function in a different way. We refer to participation by one therapist in an abreactive, regressive experience with a client and intervention by the second therapist to set a needed limit on the experience.

Our example is an affectively powerful experience which occurred between a young woman client and the female therapist. The client had not respected nor been close to her mother. She had talked in earlier interviews of having missed a warmly meaningful relationship with her mother, but she had not felt nor known in any significant way the depth of her deprivation. In a later interview with us she was precipitated into the abreactive experience of how deprived she had been. The female therapist found herself holding and comforting the client, who was sobbing and clinging to her. The female therapist's efforts to set a limit on the experience were ineffective, and the client was unable to accept the comfort and to recover from the abreaction.

The male therapist eventually intervened in the experience. He did so by moving his chair close and speaking quietly but firmly to the client and his female partner. After a short time the client recovered and was eventually both relieved and strengthened by the experience. The cotherapist was so involved in the interaction that she did not understand what had occurred even though she had accepted the intervention. The interview closed with the female therapist still not recovered from the depths of her involvement in the primary process interaction.

Some two hours later, still caught up in the experience and being unable to understand and rationalize it, the female therapist sought out her cotherapist to ask him what had happened and why he had intervened. He answered that he had felt the participants could not break off the abreaction and that the interaction as it was continuing was going to be ineffective, that the emotional meaning would not be successfully placed in the past. It took some thirty or forty minutes of talking with the female therapist to enable her to recover and understand the nature and meaning of the experience.

We have some observations to make about such deeply moving and involving emotional experiences as regression, abreaction, and primary process. The immediately preceding example illustrates how we think and act in regard to such matters. We note, first of all, that some experiences of regression, abreaction, and what we have called primary process must often occur even in our functioning population in order for effective therapy to occur. Yet we observe that such experiences often do not occur or occur inappropriately, perhaps resulting in impasse or failure, or lack needed limits with the result that the experience, which may ultimately be effective, is unnecessarily prolonged.

Multiple therapy has provided us with a way to ensure that the necessary experiences occur and are accomplished in such a way that they are therapeutically effective. Also, multiple therapy has provided us with a way to observe and to understand better the probable meaning of such experiences. In addition, we have been able to understand better, we think, the meaning of such interaction in dyadic relationships.

One observation that we made early in our multiple therapy experience was that abreactive, powerfully moving emotional occurrences happened frequently. And we observed that what happened was therapeutically effective and that the experiences, although deep, seemed to have inherent limits. These limits made a significant contribution to controlling prolonged duration of regression.

At first, we were satisfied with our observation and simply accepted the therapeutic benefits. But we are curious individuals and usually need to develop some notions about why something turns out to be effective. So we thought, observed, and theorized further. We now think that needlessly prolonged regression may be most characteristic of dyadic, one-to-one relationships. If this is so, it may explain why dyadic therapy can be effective, as it often is, and yet seem to be unending. In fact, we have come to think that appropriate regression is often avoided in dyadic therapy. Another probability is that regression may occur but take place in at least two ways that are not very effective. One instance is when the client regresses while the therapist remains relatively distant and uninvolved. Such a client will have a lonely, abandoned, most frightening experience, and he may or may not get better. The other instance is when the therapist is emotionally close but so involved that uncontrolled, apparently unending, regression occurs.

Actually, we think that what happens in the second instance instance is that the primary, abreactive experiences which are emotionally correcting are avoided and that what develops instead is a symbiotic, ineffective relationship. This relationship may recapitulate a past relationship, but if it is symbiotic, it will be therapeutically ineffective. Said another way, the relationship is emotionally important and may have in it the seeds of conflict resolution, but it may also have in it a rather endless number of "undoing" seeds which slow resolution and perhaps prevent it. In another sense, what has been created is a shared feeling state rather than the ebb, flow, change, and modifying effects of thoughts, feelings, and experiences which characterize the reciprocity among the process functions.

We return now to our examples of intervention. In both instances we think regression is involved. In the first example, the relationship between the male therapist and female client was undoubtedly satisfying and certainly unresolving as we now look at it. The intervention by the female therapist was effective in breaking up the prolonged, unresolving relationship and setting the course of therapy on new paths which led to resolution of many problems for the client. The therapists learned something, too, and we are grateful for that.

In the second example we think at least two matters of therapeutic import are involved. First of all, we doubt that the female therapist and the client could have precipitated themselves into such a powerful, abreactive, primary process experience as they did without the presence of the male cotherapist. Both female participants, particularly the female therapist, trusted the male therapist to help them to have the necessary experience and to intervene in order to limit and resolve the experience. As evidence of the probable truth of the last statement, we offer the fact that neither of us has ever had such a limitless, uncontrolled experience in dyadic therapy, but that both of us have had a number of such experiences in multiple therapy.

AND NOW TO SOME EVIDENCE

Thus we have written of the power of multiple therapy, intervention, differentiation, and reciprocity. In the following pages we will turn to a former client, who will tell us more of what multiple therapy can do and mean.

Once as we worked to clarify our ideas about multiple therapy, we asked a colleague who had been our client several years before to come in and talk with us about some of the ways we were finding to conceptualize the process. We recorded our conversation and had a typescript made of it, which we laid aside. Now two years later, we have reread the typescript and are intrigued by what he told us about his therapy experience. We find in it examples of the more sophisticated conceptualizations we have since been able to develop. We have edited the typescript and will present portions to illustrate some of the theories we want to explicate.

Our client was thinking back on an experience which had ended some two years earlier and had begun two years before that. He was seen first by one of us, in this case the female therapist, and then by both of us. As he tells it, the introduction of the male therapist was purposeful and a dynamic experience for him. His description of himself when he began therapy is rather accurate, except that he does not mention that he is a very bright, intellectually able young man whose interpersonal experiences were far from satisfying.

We asked him how he saw us as different from each other in our therapeutic efforts, and he answered as follows:

cl.:* One of the first things that really tends to distinguish you is the extent to which you focused on internal versus external processes. What I was trying to do when I started therapy was make sense out of myself in relation to the world. And I had very little feeling to go on in the way of helping the order of things. And we spent most of the time exploring the inner world. And even after I had begun to get some feel for what I was about, we still seemed to spend more time on that.

On the other hand, Bill seemed always, or generally, to be more concerned about what I was doing in relation to other people and to the world. He tended to be not too interested in what I was thinking about or feeling about it, but emphasized more what I was doing about it. Often he would set tasks or goals, making it anxious as hell. I guess that's the essence.

k.: Do you see this difference between us as something that is characteristic of us generally speaking?

cl.: The distinction holds to some extent, but it gets more subtle when you generalize beyond this. I think Jo has often set goals or tasks or specified certain behaviors that might work out better for me, but it's been a matter of reference to the outcome, with no kind of, without very much push behind it. It's just kind of out there, and if I had any sense about me, that would be the way to do it. And I think sometimes Bill, or generally Bill, was somewhat firmer. At least he has been with me.

———————

Having mentioned that one of the differences between us had to do with the clarity and specificity with which we expressed our expectations of him, he goes on to tell the meaning which this difference had for him.

———————

cl.:[*Regarding the nonspecific expectations of* B.] You have more range or scope to range over in terms of alternatives. It's a

*cl. = Client.
 k. = Kell.
 b. = Burow.

broadening of options, but you don't really say where I'm going to find them particularly.

B.: That's right. And Bill was more specific in things.

CL.: I think you need different things at different times from different people. I don't know how characteristic this is of clients, but in my case I certainly needed more direction as the treatment continued because in a sense I was freed up to do a lot of things that I couldn't do before. But because of being closed up for so long, I really didn't have too much awareness of what some of the more fruitful behaviors were that I could engage in.

This last illustrates the complementary nature of the differences in the therapists. As a result of their different approaches, the client was able both to expand his world and also to learn to control it, which are usually dynamically contradictory processes especially for very compulsive people. Yet because the two proc-esses—that of loosening and expanding and that of controlling—were experienced in relationship to two different people, both could occur.

The following passage suggests that the introduction of the male therapist after the client had worked with the female therapist for a period of time had a number of different meanings. We do not have a clear recollection of our reasons for shifting from dyadic to multiple therapy. The decision had been thought about, but the cues which prompted it are no longer available. Our client tells us what it meant to him:

CL.: That was a curious thing though, because when I went in with you [B.], I really felt like my dad was a real bastard. Had it not been for him I wouldn't have been the way I was. And it was only my mother that pulled me through. And we changed at about the time that I had begun to realize that it was my mother that used to come in and hold me and comfort me after my dad kicked shit out of me. In a sense I learned all kinds of ways that my dad was a bad guy, and I was beginning to have some real thoughts about what kind of a person she was, and how much I had really missed in not knowing my dad. And that's when we shifted [from dyadic to multiple therapy], and I remember the first time Bill came in. God, I was just scared to death. I'm sure you had some real reasons for shifting when you did.

K.: Do you remember what I did?

CL.: Yes, Jo was sitting on the left as you go in your door and I was over in the right-hand corner and you were at the desk, and we all came in and sat down, and Jo said . . . oh, I guess she made some kind of remark, introductory remark. And then it was just about two minutes, and you had pulled your chair over toward me and I was starting to, you know, kind of pull back and get pretty shaken. And then Jo said, "It's all right; you can trust Bill." And I remember how much that meant to me, because I was very scared. When you said that, it was like I opened up enough to know he was there.

And the thing that kind of always struck me was that you [K.] insisted that you stay in focus, whereas you [B.] got so blurry sometimes that I wasn't sure I was in the room, and we just kind of drifted back and forth wherever I went. But there were very few times that you [K.] got that out of focus. You got out of focus but not that much.

We wish to point out some of the theoretical notions which the preceding passage illustrates. We can, for instance, infer at least two reasons for introducing the male therapist at that particular point in therapy. First, there is a suggestion that the oedipal conflict was beginning to generate, and, second, the client was beginning to be aware of needing a father for other reasons.

We note, too, that he talks about how B. intervened to facilitate his relationship to K. and that this had meaning to him. We also observe that he was well aware of conflict in relating to K. His remarks about differences in "focus" of the two therapists are intriguing, but there is no other reference to it in the tape. We suppose he was referring to the reality orientation K. gave him as contrasted to the phenomenological experiences with B. in dyadic therapy. By being clear and specific, K. interpersonally reversed the client's experience with his own father, about whom he was quite unclear.

The way in which the therapy parallels the client's developmental process and has in it an opportunity for dynamic reversal is further illustrated in the following. Here the client describes how and why he chose to work with a woman in the beginning:

———

CL.: At that same time I felt safer just because you were a woman; that was very significant. I remember being quite torn between the unknown which you represented, yet you were a woman, and Jackson, whom I knew, but somehow he wasn't right for me. And so I really don't know if I could have done it any other way.

K.: I see what you mean. The thing that interests me, I guess, is that it seems like it fits you developmentally.

CL.: Yes, that's the thing that I was trying to get at here. I kind of got stuck with my mother and never did get to know my dad, and that's just where I stayed.

K.: But it seems it was important that really your first therapy relationship was with a woman and that in a certain sense you picked up at the point where your relationship with your mother was. And then I was introduced into the situation after that relationship had been well established. But I was introduced so that you'd get to know if not your own father at least somebody who met some specifications of a male significant person.

———

Then at another point the client ties together, both with us and for us, the way in which he had conceptualized his problem developmentally and the way in which therapy functioned to accomplish otherwise incomplete developmental tasks. He speaks here of the therapy experience.

———

CL.: Yes, you know being so small, I was reacting to the anxiety and had no notion what it was about.

K.: Your father had his first heart attack when you were about three?

CL.: He had his first heart attack when I was about three, but he had that gall bladder attack when I was around one, between nine months and a year old. He was hospitalized for quite a while —I guess a couple of months—and they really weren't sure he was going to live. And then, you know, I suppose I got to feel comfortable once again, and then he had a heart attack, and they didn't know if he was going to get through that one.

B.: Well, your mother didn't tell you about it because you really were too little. But that explains her anxiety. And you stayed unclear, and perhaps that was in part your need to not understand. But that wasn't all, it was at least partly determined by my ignorance of the facts. That was something we needed to send you to ask your mother about.

CL.: Yes, I had a thought about that this morning. The only way that I ever could have anything that resembled a feeling was through imagery. And very often with the images, as they got more and more full-blown, I would have some violent emotions, really powerful feelings.

And as we went along, it was possible for me to have a few emotions between visits. But as you recall when we stopped our last session, you kind of left an assignment with me in a sense because you were still a little puzzled about the fact that I was still experiencing emotions as pictures. And it was about a year after that, really, that I started to have ongoing kinds of feelings without the intervening images. So that the task you had when I came to see you was, you know, quite an enormous one. And to specify any kind of behavior wouldn't have done a damn thing in terms of helping me to become a human being.

B.: Well, I think it's . . . .

CL.: I remember times when just talking about some of the imagery, I would walk out and I'd be disorganized as hell. I remember after one of the first times I came in, I was walking along and wanting to run up and touch a tree.

B.: Like that would make it real, or you real?

CL.: I'm not sure which. It was just that things usually were just what they were: a tree was a tree, and in the same way a car was a car. And you just kind of walk among them, but somehow things had taken on this quality of life, and that was what made that tree somehow new to me and different from other things that I passed.

Then, in answer to a question about the primary process type of interactions in therapy, the client goes on to give his own theoretical assessment of the meaning. One interesting thing is he seems to know that the therapists' regression had an effect on him. The fact that he doesn't explain it seems appropriate to our hypothesis that when one explains primary process, it loses primitive impact. Thus his rather roundabout way of talking about it seems suitable.

CL.: Well, I've come to think about that a little bit differently. I think about it in terms of beginning with undifferentiated feelings. Feelings are so gross and global in an infant, and it's only through an interaction with significant others that the feelings get differentiated, and certain kinds of responses bring responses in the people around him. A kid pretty early learns to differentiate crying from noncrying and then different kinds of crying and different kinds of gestures, and as these different responses become available he can more effectively satisfy his needs.

B.: This is while he teaches his parents what his feelings are.

CL.: Yes, but you know ideally this is an ongoing, continuous process. But you take some global gross area like my feelings about my father, and if you don't allow for exploration of what those are, they stay. You have to assume they stay in their same undifferentiated way, and as time goes by any response is more and more maladaptive and inappropriate because you're getting a bigger body and your peers have become more socialized and so on, so the option becomes more and more one of not responding. So that the—any awareness you have of making responses—say, particularly if you're angry with your father, and you have this kind of infantile rage, you've never been permitted to express it, and then your dad says, "You sound like you're pretty mad at me," or some such thing, so that the next time it becomes a little more refined. Gradually there is this kind of anger and that kind and this kind and that kind, and they all have to do with very discriminable features of the environment.

Now, that's what I think about this primary process. And that puts you back into a developmental framework so that when we get up to therapy we're talking about me having never had much opportunity to express certain classes of feelings in relation to certain kinds of situations and people. I just never had a hold of or knew what these were all about. And, of course, not having any feelings, I couldn't begin to separate some of these things out until we did what we did. So then I could say, "Ah." In fact, you did this all the time. You used to cry for me or hurt for me or be mad for me, and not only could I see it in you, but you would point to me and say you must feel very, very, lonely. And I would think what are you talking about? I see you are.

And the first time we really got talking about our relationship and talking about my mother, this was really one of the first negative feelings I started to have toward my mother. And I was talking about these, and you got all torn up and said, "God, it feels like you're tearing my breast off." You know it was apparent to me that you were torn up all right, and then you said something about feeling like, "I was just gouging at you with a knife," and I had just had a few flickers of the possibility that maybe there was something in me that was angry, and I think this was the first time that I really knew what my anger could be or that I had any. We worked on that a little bit, and then we made the shift. I don't know if I did answer your question about primary process because I went the long way around there. Isn't that in a way what you were asking?

B.: Well, yes, that is what I'm asking.

K.: Well, let me try something out on you and see if it seems to fit any way. I think one of the things that I pick up here is that once you began to have feelings—and I gather there was a considerable length of time when you really didn't experience very many except for some kind of images and this kind of thing. But then you did begin to experience feelings which I would think were pretty primary.

Now they were without a sense of your having any kind of control on them or of being manageable. And I think that one of the things I was pretty important for was not to teach you that the feelings were bad but that they were controllable and even usable. I suppose in a certain sense one of the things I may have done with you was to help you know that you can actually have these feelings and yet at the same time have some control on them, which is really a kind of regression, I suppose, in the service of the ego.

Now I think one of the ways I did it was by setting tasks for you: "In spite of the fact that you're confused or that you're feeling this way or that way, you can do so and so." I don't know if I ever said it quite that expectantly, used words just exactly like that. "I don't care how confused you are, I think you can do something."

The client also tells us the meaning to him of a particular episode in therapy when we had tried to reenact for him what we understood about a primary relationship he had had.

CL.: I've thought a few times about the session when I came in and you two kind of acted out some things that we'd been talking about. I've thought about that a few times and that if I only could have told you to do it just a little different, we could have resolved it. But, of course, I couldn't do that.

B.: Well, Bill was trying to tell me how to do it because I didn't know.

CL.: Because you were so close and yet not quite close enough. And all I could do was be very reactive, but I couldn't tell you what to do to make me react. It was like if you had just said it a little different or done this or that, then I could have resolved it, but I really felt like that was a tremendously profound experience.

B.: [to K.] Do you remember it? I do, too. That one really stands out for me. I think that's the kind of thing it's good to get feedback on.

[*Comment: Perhaps because this was primary process there is no way to make it rational.*]

————

The client then told us the meaning of several incidents in therapy in which earlier primary relationships had been reenacted with the therapists.

————

CL.: One example that comes to mind is the time that I came in and I'd had a few drinks and I was pretty bent on going out and carrying on, you know. And you [K.] made a comment, "I don't want you to do that." Well, I just started to, oh, man, the anger just welled! And I felt like I was ready to murder you for telling me that, and then you obviously were watching me, and you said, "But I can't really say that to you because I'm not really your father," or "I'm not your father." And then it was just like whew, coming back down!

It was at that time that there was this real precarious balance that had to do with the relationship and having some feeling about how much you meant to me. But the relationship wasn't that cemented, and I didn't have enough strength that I could really do that because you wanted me to. It was like, well, the relationship just didn't have the ingredients. But as time went by, it seemed like you could be clearer about what it was you wanted without raising my hackles. And there was more in me that wanted to do what you wanted me to do. It was kind of like really knowing how important you were and feeling that this was the way that we kept things going.

————

In a very real sense he is telling us that the development process was reentered by K.'s setting a limit for him and then that through the ongoing, developing relationship he was able to develop maturity in his own behavior and to learn to control it very much as a child learns—but in a remarkably short period of time. One other aspect is notable, i.e., the fact that he recalled the statement, "I am not your father," and the relief it afforded him. We understand this last theoretically as an instance of conflict generation and resolution by interrupting the parataxic distortion.

One final incident will illustrate how a very primary problem was at least partially resolved by changing the outcome.

CL.: But one of the outstanding features of my relationship with my dad was that, you know, I just busted my ass to please him. I just was all over the map doing everything that was a challenge —you know, picking up challenges here and there. I'd be climbing up that ladder, and I'd get out so I was doing the task better than most people, and somehow expecting that this would do it, this would get a response, but it wouldn't. And I remember we puzzled about that quite a bit when I first came in. I didn't know quite what it meant. But I just kept going up all these alleys, and I never could get any clear, direct feedback from him about what it was that he expected of me.

K.: So, then, one of the things that I did was to make it clear what my expectation was and then say when you had done it, "That's good."

CL.: That's right.

K.: That's good enough.

CL.: In fact, one of these times in there when I was cavorting around the countryside, I came in and I had essentially bound my impulses and come out pretty well. And you went snorting down the hall to get Josephine to bring her down and just made an awful big to-do about what I had accomplished. And it was just, you know, that the reinforcement was so overwhelming. There was not a lingering doubt in my mind that I'd done a good thing.

The foregoing interpolation of our experience of looking back at therapy with a client, now a colleague, has, we hope, satisfied the needs of some who would like to get a flavor of therapy from case material. It also satisfied some needs we had to try out our theoretical constructs on others, particularly sophisticated others who know what the experience of therapy as we know it, is like.

We have another need, too, and that is to be effective in what we do. As individuals we share a discontent with a job half done, a person improved but still crippled, a less than good outcome in our therapeutic efforts. Thus we have both been experimenters and risk takers. We have chosen to take such risks—well aware of our fears about doing so—rather than draw back and refuse to try. We have tried, and we have controlled our fears and made them bearable by sharing them. It was our mutual risk taking which led us to join our efforts, to experiment as multiple therapists.

Chapter 12

Helping Others to Collaborate

Collaboration between multiple therapy partners is a pleasure when it occurs. It is also deeply enhancing to both of them when the interaction is effective. But collaboration is more than simply deciding to do multiple therapy or choosing a partner, although both decisions are important. We suspect sometimes that our students, for instance, are both encouraged and misled by our enthusiasm. The fact that they are eager to approach both the risks and the pleasures of working together is most rewarding to us. In fact, we might not have persisted as we have if some of our colleagues and our students had not enhanced the importance of what we were doing by joining with us in the development of the multiple approach as we know it. We are grateful to them for sharing their efforts, troubles, pleasures, thinking, and feelings with us. Without them not only would we have been unable to persist in practicing multiple therapy, but we would not have known enough to write this book. And so we acknowledge our debt.

But our own experiences together and with other collaborators, as well as the experiences of our colleagues and students which we have been privileged to observe and participate in, have taught us that troubles and ineffectiveness, as well as enhancement and therapeutic effectiveness, may ensue from working together. We will write further about both in this chapter. What we write will not enable others to avoid the troubles and errors but may help by engendering a set which accepts the fact that problems as well as therapeutic effectiveness are inherent in the multiple approach. Further, we suggest that a collaborative relationship which is easily arrived at is usually pleasant but may not be truly collaborative. A relationship which survives and grows through difficulties is likely to be more prized and meaningful to the participants.

Choosing a Partner. While we cannot claim to know about all the complexities, attitudes, and feelings which go into choosing a collaborator, we do have some observations to make. We note, first of all, that if prospective collaborators have a genuine desire to work with the other, the prospective relationship is likely to be enhanced ultimately by the mutual wish. Such mutual choosing and valuing may be in considerable contrast to what sometimes occurs.

What is a less favorable sort of choosing, then? Sometimes it happens that a student decides that he or she wants to do multiple therapy out of a genuine interest in the method. But the interest is the dominant desire, and the partner is chosen simply because he or she is available. While such relationships can become truly collaborative and effective, the way the choice was made is likely to remain as a problem for a time, consciously and otherwise, to plague the would-be collaborators. The partner so chosen commonly feels disvalued and exploited by the way the choice was made and the way the relationship develops, while the "choosing" partner may be both dismayed and disillusioned by the poor progress the collaborative relationship makes.

But none of the less than totally desirable reasons for doing multiple therapy or choosing partners means that collaborative disaster is the inevitable outcome. Ordinarily what is needed is that the less than joyful partners face and know the pain their initial motives have generated. Such is not easy, but it is often possible. The personal relief and the enhancement of collaboration which occur as a consequence of facing and "owning" less than totally desirable motives are often large indeed.

Frequently, troubled partners are able to work out their difficulties by themselves, and to be able to do so is most satisfying. At other times they may need help and seek it from one or both of us. When that happens, particularly with partners in their first collaboration, we are most likely to explore with them both their reasons for doing multiple therapy and their reasons for choosing each other. We add, incidentally, that the "cry for help" is often couched in terms of a problem with the client or of a problem of some vague, ill-defined discomfort in their relationship.

In such a situation commonly we find that some discussion of the client is necessary but that discussion of the partners' reasons for doing multiple therapy and for choosing each other is even more imperative. While other reasons for the troubles may be found, the initial motives are often powerfully involved. Partners in trouble are not always eager to discuss their relationship, incidentally, and they are likely to offer their client as the source of their difficulty. We accept this, for clients often have an extraordinary ability to foment difficulties between collaborators who are already in conflict. However, we wish to emphasize the fact that discussing the client and how he may be contributing to collaborative conflict is often insufficient. Usually the collaborators with supervisory help (sometimes insistence is needed) must face the fact that their relationship had in it the seeds of conflict before the client was ever seen.

As we see it then, if outside supervisory or consultative help is useful for therapeutic collaborators, the most effective direction of attention is often the collaborators' relationship. We think this is likely to be true for both experienced and inexperienced collaborators. To put it another way, as in supervision of dyadic therapy, supervision of multiple therapy turns often to the persons of the therapists and their relationship, although clients may be profitably discussed when the therapists' relationship is collaborative and functioning. Something more of how we as supervisors may enhance and facilitate the relationship of therapist collaborators is the subject matter of the next section.

Supervision: Facilitating Multiple Therapists' Collaboration.

Since we view the collaborative, partnership relationship of multiple therapists as being very basic as well as unusually open to supervisory or consultative help, we are rarely willing to see only one of a therapeutic team. If one partner is unavailable for some reason and we must talk with only one member, we still endeavor to concentrate our attention on the problems the partners are having in their relationship.

Our reasons may be evident, but we wish to state them. First of all, when collaborators are in need of help, whether they perceive their troubles to reside in the client or in their relationship to each other, usually each partner is in rather desperate need of support for his or her view. Since collaboration, appropriate dependency, and support are not found within the therapists' relationship, each partner is prone to seek support or agreement wherever it can be found. Frequently supervisors are exploited as a result. In fact, when the two members of a team are assigned to different supervisors, it is not uncommon in our experience for each person to seek the help and support of his or her own supervisor.

If the supervisors too readily accede to the wishes and needs of their supervisees, a dynamic situation is created which reminds us all too much of small boys shouting at each other. "My dad can lick your dad." When such occurs, each partner and each supervisor may have enhanced himself and each other, but the collaborative relationship of the multiple therapists may be further damaged. For such reasons as these, we try to see therapist collaborators together—as a team in trouble—rather than as separate individuals when they need help.

Even when we see therapists together, however, there is no guarantee that a better relationship will result. But we are optimistic, and our experience confirms that we should be, for seldom do the members of a team remain bitter and unrelenting to each other. If we are as persistent and sensitive as we should be as supervisors, then it is a rare team which will not be able to achieve more personal ease with each other as well as improved collaborative capacities, which will benefit their client or clients. It is true that resistance to help can sometimes be strong and feelings bitter, but if the conflicts can be resolved, the relationship will be better for having survived and grown through difficulty. Some of the best collaborative relationships we know have developed from inauspicious, conflicted beginnings.

Enhancing May Need to Be Learned.   Many multiple therapist teams seem naturally to know how to enhance and appreciate each other and how to make their relationship develop and become beneficial to themselves and to their clients. But at times multiple partners need to learn how to appreciate each other. What do we mean? Appreciation is simple enough, isn't it? Perhaps appreciation is a simple matter, but we are interested in the fact that multiple partners are sometimes unduly inhibited in their relationship to each other. We are not concerned here with expressions of appreciation which are not felt, for these are artificial and unreal. We are concerned rather with why therapists inhibit genuinely appreciative feelings, which would be enhancing if expressed.

An example will help to clarify our meaning. Some time ago a young therapist pair came to one of us seeking help. They were mildly dissatisfied with the progress of their client but not much, for when they assessed his progress, it was evident that he had moved rather rapidly. They were left, then, with the recognition that there was something unsatisfactory in their relationship to each other even though their collaboration was sufficient to help their client.

What could be the matter? They seemed not to have a clue. The one of us who had been consulted was observant as the session went along. Also, he knew certain facts about the therapist pair. To begin with, they were both attractive, personally engaging young people each of whom had been recently married to someone else. Further, as the session went along, the consultant noted that although they were polite and attentive to each other, they were formal, very serious, and quite task-oriented about their client and their relationship with each other. Evidently the "effort syndrome" was operating, but there was something else. What was it? A comment or two by the consultant about their formality and seriousness was sufficient to help them to relax a bit, to laugh a little, and to begin looking at their relationship somewhat differently.

Yet something else seemed to be needed, and the consultant finally said something like, "Could it be that appreciating and enjoying each other would mean that you were both being disloyal to your spouses?" That did it! They were startled at their realizations at first, but as they talked to each other, they grew more and more relaxed and spontaneous with each other. The humor and ability to laugh together grew greater, too. Also, they were able to conclude that each had been concerned unduly and that they could enjoy their relationship together and their spouses would not be cheated. A later brief report from them, for they needed no further consultation, confirmed that all had continued to go well. Their client had terminated successfully, and they were most pleased with their collaborative relationship.

It is true, of course, that spouses may grow concerned, jealous, even suspicious about what their therapist husbands or wives may be doing with their clients. It is even true that sometimes the concerns are justified. Too, husbands or wives may be distressed when their therapist spouses collaborate in multiple therapy. Again the distress may be justified, but seldom is this so in our experience. In fact, we are inclined to think that more problems arise from inhibition of feelings, especially feelings which are appreciative or enhancing in nature, than from open recognition and expression of such feelings.

For example, resentment may well grow toward the husband or wife who is seen as interfering in a personally important professional effort to learn and grow such as multiple therapy affords. We are inclined to think that unprofessional "acting out," such as sexual misbehavior, is more likely to occur when resentment about interference, whether real, imagined, or projected, occurs too long and intensely. Further, we believe that good interpersonal relationships enhance persons rather than harm them in any way. But this is a lesson which people must learn or relearn, rather than be deterred from learning by either their own or others' fears. The therapist can largely avoid such troublesome matters, incidentally, by having as many significant and meaningful relationships as possible. We, the writers, for instance, collaborate with each other and with a number of others. And we encourage our students to have more than one collaborative relationship and thus learn that closeness, sharing, appreciation, as well as separateness, can occur in more than one relationship.

Enhancing Sexual Separateness. The use of the word "separateness" in the last sentence of the previous section suggests another way in which multiple therapists sometimes need consultative or supervisory help, that is, in recognizing and enhancing sexual separateness. We recognize that for ourselves sexual separateness is important for personal as well as professional reasons. We have said earlier that we believe there are significant differences in how a man and a woman may feel and react to a situation or another person. Our experiences in multiple therapy have taught us that these differences are often complementary and very useful rather than conflicting. We have seen our sexual separateness and different reactions as not only contributing to our individual sense of identity, but also as greatly helping our clients. Sexual confusion and uncertainty seem to be a basic and increasing problem in our present society. As psychologists, therapists, and persons who live in this society we are concerned about the problem and wish not to add to it but to help solve it.

When our students first come to know us, they are usually intrigued by some of our ideas and attitudes about the importance of recognizing sexual identity and separateness. But even though intrigued, they sometimes think that we are unduly concerned, even old-fashioned. However, the eventual relieved reactions of many of our multiple clients to our separateness and our differences suggests that our ideas are therapeutic at least.

One argument which confused clients often offer in support of the view that sexual confusion and identity problems are a way of life is that society is confused and that they cannot do better if society doesn't. Further, they often say or imply, as do our students sometimes, that society makes fewer and fewer distinctions between men and women, particularly as opportunities for women grow more and more equal with those of men. Some have even said that women are dominant and more than equal. We think that all these arguments have truth, but we also think that some erroneous further conclusions are often reached.

A simple analogy will help to make our meaning clear. A dozen apples and a dozen bananas both add up to the same number; but equal numbers do not mean that bananas and apples are the same, although they are both fruits. It seems to us that equality of men and women means only that both sexes belong to the human race and that the sexual differences are just as important and necessary as ever, although perhaps harder to feel and maintain.

Thus, as we have said, our students, our clients, and sometimes our colleagues are variously intrigued, puzzled, argumentative, and rejecting of our attitudes on sexual separateness and differences.

Usually, however, our students and our colleagues, too, become increasingly interested in these ideas in much the same way we are, particularly as they may become more involved in doing multiple therapy. As we have already said, when troubles arise between the multiple partners, as they nearly always do, and they seek supervisory or consultative help, we are intrigued by how often the conflicts seem to have been generated, in part at least, by sexual differences in attitudes, understandings, and reactions which have been unrecognized, suppressed, or denied. Moreover, if the differences have been recognized, they have usually been seen as conflicts rather than as complementary, useful and necessary differences. But commonly the problem is not recognized and presented as one pertaining to sexual differences. This is true even though the male therapist may be more or less overt in saying or feeling that his female partner is stupid for not agreeing with him, thus implying a sexual difference, although a negative one.

Similarly, the female therapist may be overt in saying that her partner is blockheaded or stubborn, implying another negative difference. It is true, of course, that we all may be stubborn, even stupid at times, and we think that when we are so, it is important to recognize and accept these ways of being as best we can. But some important distinctions in regard to reality and the usefulness of sexual differences in perceptions and reactions may be lost if these are the only conclusions we arrive at and we fail to explore further possible meanings.

Thus as consultants or supervisors to multiple therapists having troubles, we accept that the feelings the partners have are real. We even accept that the client may have helped to foment the conflict. But we are usually insistent that such feelings have reasons for being other than the self-evident ones. What our troubled partners may have to recognize—painful though the recognition may be—is that even though their feelings are real and their perceptions about each other and themselves have truth, each one does not like or trust the opposite sex very much. A confrontation of such attitudes in oneself is painful, as we have said. And, to change such attitudes means that historical "truths" learned long ago about the nature of the opposite sex must be modified or given up. But if we as supervisors or consultants are sufficiently persistent and sensitive, the troubled partners may be enabled to respect each other. After mutual respect has been established, then trust, dependency, reliance upon the usefulness and significance of differences, and genuine collaboration can develop, and the therapeutic power of multiple therapy comes to be for the partnership.

As multiple therapists become increasingly convinced that their differences, whether they are associated with sexuality or not, can be enhancing and complementary, the two partners become increasingly able to respond to each other in ways which enhance. And we believe that these ways of enhancing each other are usually beneficial to clients. Simple, direct behaviors are ordinarily involved in such exchanges. A male therapist may say, "What you did with him was great. Only a woman could do it." Or a female therapist may say, "It's wonderful you were here. That boy couldn't have done that without you." We add that often such interactions occur spontaneously and while the client is present. And so it is that collaboration grows, changes, and is therapeutically good for both therapists and clients.

Case Conference: Another Way to Learn.   We have successfully used the case conference method for providing supervision and consultation to multiple therapists. This has many advantages since both of us can not only participate but also function as collaborators, which has been a significant part of the experience for us. The groups at first were made up of pairs of cotherapists, each pair having perhaps one case. Usually the members have recombined several times to gain experience in working with more than one person. If this was a source of conflict or hurt feelings, it was not apparent because the concern to keep the group intact was great enough to prevent anything from damaging the relationships.

The pairs of cotherapists struggled with their client, and they were often able to report success and share their pleasure with the rest of the group. There were also instances of failure in which the group gave support for the cotherapists' ability to terminate what had become a fruitless venture. Although suggestions worked out in the group often played a part in what the multiple therapists decided to do, not infrequently decisions were made and carried out independently of the group, and the results were shared.

Multiple Therapists Need Not Be Aged.   We have speculated about the meaning of young cotherapists to their clients. We have indicated earlier that in our relationship to our clients we seem to them to be parentlike because for the most part we approximate the age of their parents. Thus no great distortion is needed for them to perceive and react to us in the same ways they did with their parents. Thus the parental conflicts are regenerated, reenacted, and resolved.

But how do clients perceive and react to young therapists, who are only a few years older than they are or in some cases younger?

It appears to us that the same conflicts are generated, perhaps more subtly, but nonetheless with enough clarity so that they can be resolved. Certainly the across-sex type problems develop rapidly and clearly and are perceived as real rather than fantasy. The introduction of a multiple partner into cross-sex dyadic relationships has been very useful in bringing about a resolution without the sometimes painful acting out of conflicts outside of the therapy.

The impact which youthful therapists may have is clearly evidenced in an example in which the client was a considerably older male who was used to being responsible and unchallenged in his ways of behaving but who was extremely unhappy with himself and his interpersonal relationships. He had previously had a great deal of therapy and could interpret and bewail his behavior ad nauseum. The therapist, an attractive young woman, described him with all the appropriate affective expression which the client would be expected to elicit from others. Because he was able to control the way in which others reacted to him, except their usual final reaction of giving up and withdrawing, he probably never got clear reactive feedback.

The therapist was contemptuous, amused, sorry, and nonplussed. We suggested to her that she give up interpreting and withholding her feelings and instead react out of them. She invited a young man into the therapy relationship about the time we made the suggestion, and they proceeded to carry out their variant of it. They worked together with him for a period of time, and then she reported that the client had terminated feeling much better. He said that he didn't know exactly why because he had not learned anything that he didn't already know but that he understood things much better than he ever had before.

We do not know all that went into the therapy, but we suspect that with the support of her cotherapist the young woman was able to offer him the first honest interaction he had ever experienced and that it was enhancing and freeing to him in a way which intellectual understanding had not been. We believe that such confrontation is very difficult without the support of a cotherapist and that the support extends to the client.

A Worry, a Wish, and Some Final Words. We come to the end of this chapter and to the end of our book, and we ask ourselves what more can we say? We began by saying who we are. We expect we are better known now. We have offered ourselves, our ideas, our beliefs, our sets and attitudes, for the reader's understanding, comparison, elaboration and expansion, even rejection. We will not often know what effects our words and ideas have. That is a worry, but it is manageable just as we manage our worries about our effects on our clients, colleagues, and friends.

We have thought about the process constructs that we have utilized and why we have needed them. What has the fact that we have now hypothesized some ways of ordering therapy meant to our own therapy? Does it change our behavior to be able to name it? We expect that it does. We are, for instance, perhaps a bit more self-conscious. Does that mean we are less free and spontaneous, less able to react with real feeling and meaning? We don't think so, for the feedback from our clients and others is probably better than ever. Apparently our self-consciousness keeps us changing and modifying, instead of letting us grow complacent and unchanging. If this is so, we are gratified rather than distressed. We have not violated our most dearly held premise about the nature of therapeutic change.

But why try so hard to think out a theory of process, to develop constructs, and then to describe and explicate them? Because we have needed to communicate about our experiences, and this is the way we have chosen. We might have been able to tell a series of stories about working with different clients and thereby accomplish the same thing, but we doubt it. We would then have surrendered to the reader the right to generalize from our experience with less data than we have. No, we had to find some way to generalize out of the intimacy of our therapy sessions in order for us to be satisfied that the generalizations approached our subjective experience. So the basic purpose of our theory building has been better communication.

We have had another motivation. We are curious individuals, and we need intellectual understanding of what we do. No doubt our need for understanding has to do with a desire for mastery and control—for that is part of our theory, and we could not have known about it if it had not belonged to us as people. We have some feeling that now, having understood better, we have more control. But as long as our ideas remain hypotheses, we leave them open to the same kind of exploration and change we reserve for ourselves and our behavior. And we think it is significant that our intent, at least for the present, is not to test our theory further nor to collect "hard" data to support it. We do believe, though, that some of the theoretical constructs objectify processes more clearly than has been done before. But we also believe that much research on therapy processes and outcomes has been premature, that it has been undertaken before the constructs were clearly enough formulated to do definitive research. We invite attempts to test our theoretical notions.

We return once more to the question of whether the theory we have developed has affected our therapy behavior. Our perception is that now as we wrestle with ideas and try to clarify them in our experience, we are self-conscious, and aware in ways we haven't been before of our feelings and behavior and the sequences involved. We are observers, and to the extent to which we devote ourselves to making observations, we are temporarily less interactive with our clients—not less sensitive, perhaps, but somewhat diverted from the necessary phenomenological and interpersonal involvement. Then after we have observed, and have formulated the ideas, talked them over perhaps, and written them down, they sink back out of our awareness and influence our behavior in ways unconscious to us. Thus we think our theory building has affected our behavior, and we welcome such influence.

General Bibliography

Allen, F. H. *Psychotherapy with Children*. New York: W. W. Norton & Co., 1942.

Angyal, A. *Foundations for a Science of Personality*. New York: The Commonwealth Fund, 1941.

Axline, Virginia M. *Dibs: In Search of Self*. Boston: Houghton Mifflin Co., 1964.

———— *Play Therapy: The Inner Dynamics of Childhood*. Boston: Houghton Mifflin Co., 1947.

Bandura, A.; Lipsher, D.; and Miller, Paula. "Psychotherapists' Approach-Avoidance Reactions to Patients' Expressions of Hostility." *J. Consult. Psychol.*, 1960, 24, 1–8.

Bettelheim, B. *Truants from Life*. Glencoe, Ill.: Free Press, 1955.

Bixler, R. H. "Limits Are Therapy." *J. Consult. Psychol.*, 1949, 13, 1–11.

Bordin, E. S. *Psychological Counseling*, 2d ed. New York: Appleton-Century-Crofts, 1968.

Buber, Martin. *I and Thou*, 2d ed. New York: Charles Scribner's Sons, 1958.

Bugental, J. F. T. "The Person Who Is the Therapist." *J. Consult. Psychol.*, 1964, 28, 272–277.

———— *The Search for Authenticity: An Existential-Analytic Approach to Psychotherapy*. New York: Holt, Rinehart and Winston, 1965.

Burton, Arthur, (ed.). *Case Studies in Counseling and Psychotherapy*. New York: Prentice-Hall, 1959.

Carkhuff, R. R., and Berenson, B. G. *Beyond Counseling and Therapy*. New York: Holt, Rinehart & Winston, 1967.

Colby. K. M. *A Primer for Psychotherapists*. New York: Ronald Press Co., 1951.

Combs, A. W. *Individual Behavior: A Perceptual Approach to Behavior*, rev. ed. New York: Harper & Row Publishers, 1959.

Cutler, R. L. "Countertransference Effects in Psychotherapy." *J. Consult. Psychol.*, 1958, 22, 349–356.

Davis, A. W., and Havighurst, R. J. *Father of the Man*. Boston: Houghton Mifflin Co., 1947.

Dollard, J., and Miller, N. *Personality and Psychotherapy*. New York: McGraw-Hill Book Co., 1950.

Ekstein, R., and Wallerstein, R. S. *The Teaching and Learning of Psychotherapy*. New York: Basic Books: 1958.

Ellis, A. *Reason and Emotion in Psychotherapy*. New York: Lyle Stuart, 1962.

Ewald, Carl. "My Little Boy." In *The Woollcott Reader*, edited by Alexander Woollcott, pp. 275–317. Garden City, N.Y.: Garden City Publishing Co., 1938.

Frank, J. D. *Persuasion and Healing: A Comparative Study of Psychotherapy*. Baltimore: Johns Hopkins Press, 1961.

Fromm-Reichmann, Freda. *Principles of Intensive Psychotherapy*. Chicago: University of Chicago Press, 1950.

Ginott, H. G. *Between Parent and Child: New Solutions to Old Problems*. New York: Macmillan Co., 1965.

Grater, H. A.; Kell, B. L.; and Morse, Josephine. "The Social Service Interest: Roadblock and Road to Creativity." *J. Counsel. Psychol.*, 1961, 8, 9–13.

Haigh, G. "Learning Theory and Alienation." *Psychotherapy: Theory Research and Practice*, 1965, 12, 147–150.

Hartmann, H. *Essays on Ego Psychology*. New York: International Universities Press, 1964.

Havighurst, R. J. *Developmental Tasks and Education*, 2d ed. New York: Longmans, Green & Co., 1952.

———— *Human Development and Education*. New York: Longmans, Green & Co., 1953.

Hobbs, N. "Sources of Gain in Psychotherapy." *Amer. Psychol.*, 1962, 17, 741–748.

Jones, E. *The Life and Work of Sigmund Freud.* 3 vols. New York: Basic Books, 1953.

Kell, B. L., and Mueller, W. J. *Impact and Change: A Study of Counseling Relationships.* New York: Appleton-Century-Crofts, 1966.

Kelly, G. A. *The Psychology of Personal Constructs.* 2 vols. New York: W. W. Norton & Co., 1955.

Kierkegaard, S. A. *Either/Or.* Garden City, N.Y.: Doubleday & Co., 1959.

Kirtner, W. L., and Cartwright, D. S. "Success and Failure in Client-Centered Therapy as a Function of Initial In-Therapy Behavior." *J. Consult. Psychol.*, 1958, 22, 329–333.

Kris, E. *Psychoanalytic Explorations in Art.* New York: International Universities Press, 1952.

Leary, T. *Interpersonal Diagnosis of Personality.* New York: Ronald Press Co., 1957.

Lecky, P. *Self-Consistency: A Theory of Personality.* New York: Island Press, 1951.

May, Rollo. *The Meaning of Anxiety.* New York: Ronald Press Co., 1950.

May, Rollo; Angel, E.; and Ellenberger, H. F. (eds.). *Existence: A New Dimension in Psychiatry and Psychology.* New York: Basic Books, 1958.

Menninger, K. A. *Theory of Psychoanalytic Technique.* New York: Basic Books, 1958.

Piaget, J. *The Construction of Reality in the Child.* New York: Basic Books, 1954.

Porter, E. H., Jr. *An Introduction to Therapeutic Counseling.* Boston: Houghton Mifflin Co., 1950.

Reik, T. *Listening with the Third Ear.* New York: Farrar, Straus & Giroux, 1949.

Rogers, C. R. *Client-Centered Therapy.* Houghton Mifflin Co., 1951.

——— *Counseling and Psychotherapy: Newer Concepts in Practice.* Boston: Houghton Mifflin Co., 1942.

———— "The Necessary and Sufficient Conditions of Therapeutic Personality Change." *J. Consult Psychol.*, 1957, *21*, 95–102.

———— *On Becoming a Person: A Therapist's View of Psychotherapy.* Boston: Houghton Mifflin Co., 1961.

———— "A Process Conception of Psychotherapy." *Amer. Psychol.*, 1958, *13*, 142–149.

Rogers, C. R., and Dymond, R. (eds.). *Psychotherapy and Personality Change.* Chicago: University of Chicago Press, 1954.

Rothlisberger, F. J., and Dickson, W. J. *Management and the Worker.* Cambridge: Harvard University Press, 1939.

Salter, A. *Conditioned Reflex Therapy: The Direct Approach to the Reconstruction of Personality.* New York: Creative Age Press, 1949.

Snyder, W. U. *The Psychotherapy Relationship.* New York: Macmillan Co., 1961.

Stoler, N. "Client Likability: A Variable in the Study of Psychotherapy." *J. Consult. Psychol.*, 1963, *27*, 175–179.

Sullivan, H. S. *The Interpersonal Theory of Psychiatry.* New York: W. W. Norton & Co., 1953.

———— *The Psychiatric Interview.* edited by Helen S. Perry and Mary L. Garvel. New York: W. W. Norton & Co., 1954.

Taft, Jessie. *The Dynamics of Therapy in a Controlled Relationship.* New York: Macmillan Co., 1933.

Truax, C. B., and Carkhuff, R. R. "Client and Therapist Transparency in the Psychotherapeutic Encounter." *J. Counsel. Psychol.*, 1965, *12*, 3–9.

———— *Toward Effective Counseling and Psychotherapy: Training and Practice.* Chicago: Aldine Publishing Co., 1967.

Tyler, Leona E. "Minimum Change Therapy." *Pers. Guid. J.*, 1960, *38*, 475–479.

———— *The Work of the Counselor.* New York: Appleton-Century-Crofts, 1961.

Whitaker, C. A., and Malone, T. P. *The Roots of Psychotherapy.* New York: Blakiston Co., 1953.

Winder, C. L.; Ahmad, F. Z.; Bandura, A.; and Rau, Lucy C. "Dependency of Patients, Psychotherapists' Responses, and Aspects of Psychotherapy." *J. Consult. Psychol.*, 1962, *26*, 129–134.

Wolpe, J. *Psychotherapy by Reciprocal Inhibition.* Stanford, Calif.: Stanford University Press, 1958.

Wolpe, J., and Lazarus, A. A. *Behavior Therapy Techniques: A Guide to the Treatment of Neuroses.* Oxford, N.Y.: Pergamon Press, 1966.

Wolstein, B. *Countertransference.* New York: Grune & Stratton, 1959.

—— *Transference, Its Structure and Function in Psychoanalytic Therapy.* New York: Grune & Stratton, 1964.

Wrenn, C. G. *The Counselor in a Changing World.* Washington, D.C.: American Personnel and Guidance Association, 1962.

Wyatt, F. "The Self-Experience of the Therapist." *J. Consult. Psychol.,* 1948, *12,* 82–87.

Multiple Therapy Bibliography

Adler, Alfred, et al. *Guiding the Child*. New York: Greenberg, 1930.

Adler, J., and Berman, L. R. "Multiple Leadership in Group Treatment of Delinquent Adolescents." *Int. J. Group Psychother.*, 1960, *10*, 213–225.

Alexander, L., and Moore, M. "Multiple Therapy in Private Psychiatric Practice." *Amer. J. Psychiatry*, 1957, *113*, 815–823.

Bardon, E. J. "Transference Reactions to the Relationship Between Male and Female Co-therapists in Group Therapy." *J. Amer. College Health Association*, 1966, *14*, 287–289.

Belmost, L. P., and Jasnow, A. "The Utilization of Co-therapists and of Group Therapy Techniques in a Family-Oriented Approach to a Disturbed Child." *Int. J. Group Psychother.*, 1961, *11*, 319–328.

Bird, B., and Schiffrin, M. "An ANC Mothers Club as Locale for Group Counseling." In *Group Methods in the Public Welfare Program*, edited by N. Fenton and K. T. Wiltse, pp. 134–142. Palo Alto: Pacific Books Publishers, 1963.

Block, S. L. "Multi-leadership as a Teaching and Therapeutic Tool in Group Psychotherapy." *Comprehensive Psychiatry*, 1961, *2*, 211–218.

Boenheim, C. "Dynamic Doctor Groups as a Training Method for Group Psychotherapy." *Mental Hygiene*, 1963, *47*, 84–88.

Boszormenyi-Nagy, Ivan. "Intensive Family Therapy as Process." In *Intensive Family Therapy: Theoretical and Practical Aspects*, by I. Boszormenyi-Nagy and J. L. Framo, pp. 87–142. New York: Harper & Row, Publishers, 1965.

Brayboy, T., and Marx, M. J. "Transference Variations Evoked by Racial Differences in Co-therapists." *Amer. J. Psychother.*, 1968, 22, 474–481.

Brodey, W. M., and Hayden, M. "Intrateam Reactions: Their Relation to the Conflicts of the Family in Treatment." *American J. Orthopsychiatry*, 1957, 27, 349–355.

Buck, A. E., and Grygier, T. "A New Attempt in Psychotherapy with Juvenile Delinquents." *Amer. J. Psychother.*, 1952, 6, 711–724.

Cameron, J. L., and Steward, R. A. Y. "Observations on Group Psychotherapy with Chronic Psychoneurotic Patients in Mental Hospitals." *Int. J. Group Psychother.*, 1955, 5, 346–360.

Corrigan, S. M. "Coeducational, Co-therapist Group Therapy" *Amer. College Health Association*, 1967, 15, 248–250.

Crutcher, R. "The Usefulness of Group Therapy with Character Disorders." *Int. J. Group Psychother.*, 1961, 11, 431–439.

Daniels, M. "The Influence of the Sex of the Therapist and of the Co-therapist Technique in Group Psychotherapy with Boys: An Investigation of the Effectiveness of Group Psychotherapy with Eighth-Grade, Behavior-Problem Boys, Comparing Results Achieved by a Male Therapist, by a Female Therapist, and by the Two Therapists in Combination." Doctoral dissertation, New York University. Ann Arbor, Michigan: University Microfilms, 1958. No. 58–660.

Demarest, E., and Teicher, A. "Transference in Group Therapy: Relationship: I. Its Advantages to the Therapist." *Psychiatry*, 1954, 17, 187–202.

Dreikurs, R. "Techniques and Dynamics of Multiple Psychotherapy." *Psychiat. Quart.*, 1950, 24, 788–799.

Dreikurs, R.; Schulman, B. H., and Mosak, H. "Patient-Therapist Relationship: I. Its Advantages to the Therapist." *Psychiat. Quart.*, 1952, 26, 219–227. (a)

———— "Patient-Therapist Relationship in Multiple Psychotherapy. II: Its Advantages for the Patient." *Psychiat. Quart.*, 1952, 26, 590–596. (b)

Dyrud, J. E., and Rioch, M. "Multiple Therapy in the Treatment Program of a Mental Hospital." *Psychiatry*, 1953, 16, 21–26.

Everett, H. C. "The 'Adversary' System in Married Couples' Group Therapy." *Int. J. Group Psychother.*, 1968, 18, 70–74.

Fagan, J.; Smith, R. D.; and Timms, R. J. "Three Views of an Incident at a Marathon." *Voices: The Art And Science of Psychotherapy,* 1968, *4,* 33–36.

Feldman, F. "The Tripartite Session: A New Approach in Psychiatric Social Work Consultations." *Psychiat. Quart.,* 1968, *42,* 48–61.

Fink, H. K. "Adaptations of the Family Constellation in Group Psychotherapy." *Acta Psychotherapeutica et Psychosomatica,* 1958, *6,* 43–56.

Finney, B. C., and Crockett, N. D. "Partnership Therapy: A New Technique." *Psychotherapy: Theory, Research and Practice,* 1955, *2,* 136–138.

Flescher, J. "Dual Therapy and Genetic Psychoanalysis." Reviewed in *Amer. J. Psychother.,* 1967, *21,* 698–699.

Framo, J. L. "Rationale and Techniques of Intensive Family Therapy." In *Intensive Family Therapy,* edited by I. Boszormenyi-Nagy and J. L. Framo, pp. 143–212. New York: Harper & Row Publishers, 1965.

Gans, R. W. "The Use of Group Co-therapists in the Teaching of Psychotherapy." *Amer. J. Psychother.,* 1957, *11,* 618–625.

———— "Group Co-therapists in the Therapeutic Situation: A Critical Evaluation." *Int. J. Group Psychother.,* 1962, *12,* 82–88.

Godenne, G. D. "Outpatient Adolescent Group Psychotherapy: I. Review of the Literature on Use of Co-therapists, Psychodrama, and Parent Group Therapy." *Amer. J. Psychother.,* 1964, *18,* 584–593.

———— "Outpatient Adolescent Group Psychotherapy: II. Use of Co-therapists, Psychodrama, and Parent Group Therapy." *Amer. J. Psychother.,* 1965, *19,* 40–53.

Goldstein, S. G. "The Effects of 'Doubling' on Involvement in Group Psychotherapy as Measured by Number and Duration of Patient Utterances." *Psychotherapy: Theory, Research and Practice,* 1967, *4,* 57–60.

Goldstein, A. P.; Heller, K.; and Sechrest, L. B. *Psychotherapy and the Psychology of Behavior Change.* New York: John Wiley & Sons, 1966. Pp. 233–234.

Gottlieb, A., and Pattison, E. M. "Married Couples Group Psychotherapy." *Arch. Gen. Psychiat.,* 1966, *14,* 143–152.

Greenback, R. K. "Psychotherapy Using Two Therapists." *Amer. J. Psychother.*, 1964, *18*, 488–499.

Grunwald, H., and Casella, B. "Group Counseling with Parents." *Child Welfare*, 1958, *37*, 11–17.

Gullerud, E. N., and Harlan, V. L. "Four-Way Joint Interviewing in Marital Counseling." *Social Casework*, 1962, *43*, 532–537.

Hadden, S. B. "The Utilization of a Therapy Group in Teaching Psychotherapy." *Amer. J. Psychiat.*, 1947, *103*, 644–648.

Haigh, G., and Kell, B. L. "Multiple Therapy as a Method for Training and Research in Psychotherapy." *J. Abnorm. Soc. Psychol.*, 1950, *45*, 659–666.

Hayward, M. L.; Peters, J. J.; and Taylor, J. E. "Some Values of the Use of Multiple Therapists in the Treatment of Psychoses." *Psychiat. Quart.*, 1952, *26*, 244–249.

Heckel, R. V. "The Nurse as Co-therapist in Group Psychotherapy." *Perspectives in Psychiatric Care*, 1964, *2*, 18–22.

Hill, F., and Strahl, G. "Two Against an Impasse." *Voices: The Art and Science of Psychotherapy*, 1968, *4*, 96–102.

Hulse, W. C.; Lulow, W. V.; Rindsberg, B. K.; and Epstein, N. B. "Transference Reactions in a Group of Female Patients to Male and Female Co-leaders." *Int. J. Group Psychother.*, 1956, *6*, 430–435.

Isaccs, G. "Team Conflict, a Recapitulation of Conflict in the Home: A Descriptive Clinical Case Study in Nursing Therapy." *Dissert. Abstr.*, 1965, *25* (4), 6545.

Kadis, A. L., and Markowitz, M. "The Therapeutic Impact of Co-therapist Interaction in a Couples Group." In *International Handbook of Group Psychotherapy*, edited by J. L. Moreno, pp. 446–455. New York: Philosophical Library, 1966.

Kamerschen, K. S. "Multiple Therapy: Variables Relating to Co-therapist Satisfaction." Unpublished doctoral dissertation, Michigan State University, 1969.

Kassoff, A. "Advantages of Multiple Therapists in a Group of Severely Acting-out Adolescent Boys." *Int. J. Group Psychother.*, 1958, *8*, 70–75.

Klapman, J. W. *Group Psychotherapy: Theory and Practice.* New York: Grune & Stratton, 1959. Pp. 119–123.

Klapman, J. W., and Meyer, R. E. "The Team Approach in Group Psychotherapy." *Diseases of the Nervous System*, 1957, *18*, 95–99.

Kritzer, H., and Phillips, C. A. "Observing Group Psychotherapy: An Affective Learning Experience." *Am. J. Psychother.*, 1966, *20*, 471–476.

Linden, M. E. "The Significance of Dual Leadership in Gerontolic Human Relations, III." *Int. J. Group Psychother.*, 1954, *4*, 262–273.

Linden, M. E.; Goodwin, H. M.; and Resnik, H. "Group Psychotherapy of Couples in Marriage Counseling." *Int. J. Group Psychother.*, 1968, *18*, 313–324.

Littlewood, W. "The Yin and Yang of Group Therapy: Therapy for the Therapist." *Voices: The Art and Science of Psychotherapy*, 1967, *3*, 98–103.

Loeffler, F., and Weinstein, H. M. "The Co-therapist Method: Special Problems and Advantages." *Group Psychother.*, 1954, *6*, 189–192.

Lott, G. M. "Multiple Psychotherapy: The Efficient Use of Psychiatric Treatment and Training Time." *Psychiatric Quarterly Supplement*, 1957, *31*, 277–294. Cited by B. Lubin and A. W. Lubin, "Bibliography of Group Psychotherapy, 1956–1963." *Group Psychother.*, 1964, *17*, 188.

———— "The Training of Nonmedical, Cooperative Psychotherapists by Multiple Psychotherapy." *Amer. J. Psychother.*, 1952, *6*, 440–448.

Lundin, W. H., and Aronov, M. "The Use of Co-therapists in Group Psychotherapy." *J. Consult. Psychol.*, 1952, *16*, 76–80.

MacGregor, R.; Ritchie, A. M.; Serrano, A. C.; and Schuster, F. P. *Multiple Impact Therapy with Families.* New York: McGraw-Hill Book Co., 1964.

MacLennan, B. W. "Co-therapy." *Int. J. Group Psychother.*, 1965, *15*, 154–166.

Maldonado-Sierra, E. D.; Trent, R. D.; Fernandez-Marina, R.; Flores-Gallardo, A.; Vigoreaux-Rivera, J.; and De Colon, L. S. "Cultural Factors in the Group Psychotherapeutic Process for Puerto Rican Schizophrenics." *Int. J. Group Psychother.*, 1960, *10*, 373–382.

Mallars, P. B. "Team Counseling in Counselor Education." *Personnel and Guidance Journal*, 1968, 46, 981–983.

Malone, T. P., and Whitaker, C. A. "A Community of Psychotherapists." *Int. J. Group Psychother.*, 1965, 15, 23–36.

Matarazzo, R. G., and Small, I. F. "An Experiment in Teaching Group Psychotherapy." *J. of Nervous and Mental Dis.*, 1963, 136, 252–262.

McGee, T. F. "Supervision in Group Psychotherapy: A Comparison of Four Approaches." *Int. J. Group Psychother.*, 1968, 18 165–176.

Miller, R. L., and Bloomberg, L. I. "Breaking Through the Process Impasse." *Voices: The Art and Science of Psychotherapy*, 1968, 4, 33–36.

Mintz, E. A. "Male-Female Co-therapists: Some Values and Some Problems." *Amer. J. Psychother.*, 1965, 19, 293–301.

———— "Special Values of Co-therapists in Group Psychotherapy." *Int. J. Group Psychother.*, 1963, 13, 127–132.

———— "Transference in Co-therapy Groups." *J. Consult. Psychol.*, 1963, 27, 34–49. (b)

Mullan, H. "Discussion." *Voices: The Art and Science of Psychotherapy.* 1967, 3, 12–13.

———— "Transference and Counter-Transference: New Horizons." *Int. J. Group Psychother.*, 1955, 5, 169–180.

Mullan, H., and Rosenbaum, M. *Group Psychotherapy: Theory and Practice.* New York: Free Press of Glencoe, 1962.

Mullan, H., and Sanguiliano, I. "Multiple Psychotherapeutic Practice: Prelim. Report." *Amer. J. Psychother.*, 1960, 14, 550–565.

———— *The Therapist's Contribution to the Treatment Process.* Springfield, Ill.: Charles C. Thomas, Publisher, 1964.

Nash, H. T., and Stone, A. R. "Collaboration of Therapist Observers in Guiding Group Therapy." *Group Psychother.*, 1951, 4, 85–93.

Nichols, F. L. "Psychiatrist and Nurse as Co-therapists in a Psychodrama Group." *Group Psychother.*, 1962, 15, 197–199.

Nunnelly, K. "The Use of Multiple Therapy in Group Counseling and Psychotherapy." Unpublished doctoral dissertation, Michigan State University, 1968.

Orange, A. J. "A Note on Brief Group Psychotherapy with Psychotic Patients." *Int. J. Group Psychother.*, 1955, 5, 80–83.

Perry, E. "The Treatment of Aggressive Juvenile Delinquents in Family Group Therapy." *Int. J. Group Psychother.*, 1955, 5, 131–149.

Pine, I.; Todd, W. E.; and Boenheim, C. "Signs of Counter-Transference Problems in Co-therapy Groups." *Psychosomatics*, 1965, 6, 79–83.

——— "Special Problems of Resistance in Co-therapy Groups." *Int. J. Group Psychother.*, 1963, 16, 344–362.

Rabin, H. M. "How Does Co-therapy Compare with Regular Group Psychotherapy?" *Am. J. Psychother.*, 1967, 21 (2), 244–255.

Reeve, G. H. "Trends in Therapy: V. A Method of Coordinated Treatment." *Amer. J. Orthopsychiat.*, 1939, 9, 743–747.

Rockberger, H. "The Role of an Eclectic Affect Theory in Multiple Therapy." *Psychoanalytic Review*, 1966, 53, 283–292.

Rosenberg, L. M.; Rubin, S. S.; and Finzi, H. "Participant-Supervision in the Teaching of Psychotherapy." *Amer. J. Psychother.*, 1968, 22, 280–295.

Rubinstein, D. "Family Therapy." *Int. Psychiat. Clinics*, 1964, 1, 431–442.

Rubinstein, D., and Weiner, O. R. "Co-therapy Teamwork Relationships." In *Family Therapy and Disturbed Families*, edited by G. H. Zuk and I. Boszormenyi-Nagy, pp. 206–220. Palo Alto: Science and Behavior Books, 1967.

Rychlak, J. F. "The Similarity, Compatibility, or Incompatibility of Needs in Interpersonal Selection." *J. Pers. Soc. Psychol.*, 1965, 2, 334–340.

Sabath, G. "Intertransference: Transference Relationship Between Members of the Psychotherapy Team." *Int. J. Group Psychother.*, 1962, 12, 492–495.

Sager, C. J. "An Overview of Family Therapy." *Int. J. Group Psychother.*, 1968, 18, 302–312.

Salzberg, H. C.; Clarke, J. R.; Drennen, W. T.; Hamilton, J. W.; Heckel, R. V.; Long, T. E.; and Marr, M. J. "The Effects of Multiple Therapists in Relinquishing a Delusional System." *J. of Clin. Psychol.*, 1962, 18, 218–220.

Singer, M., and Fischer, R. "Group Psychotherapy of Male Homosexuals by a Male and Female Co-therapy Team." *Int. J. Group Psychother.*, 1967, 17, 44–52.

Slavson, S. R. *Analytic Group Psychotherapy.* New York: Columbia University Press, 1950.

—— "Common Sources of Error and Confusion in Group Psychotherapy." *Int. J. Group Psychother.*, 1953, 3, 3–28.

—— "Discussion." *Int. J. Group Psychother.*, 1960, 10, 225–226.

—— "Some Problems in Group Psychotherapy as Seen by Private Practitioners." *Int. J. Group Psychother.*, 1952, 2, 54–66.

Slipp, S., and Lewis, M. K. "Separation Problems in College Students." In *International Handbook of Group Psychotherapy*, edited by J. L. Moreno, pp. 619–625. New York: Philosophical Library, 1966.

Solomon, A.; Loeffler, F. J.; and Frank, G. H. "An Analysis of Co-therapist Interaction in Group Psychotherapy." *Int. J. Group Psychother.*, 1954, 3, 171–180.

Solomon, J. C., and Solomon, G. F. "Group Psychotherapy with Father and Son as Co-therapists." *Int. J. Group Psychother.*, 1963, 13, 133–140.

Sonne, J., et al. "The Absent-Member Maneuver as a Resistance in Family Therapy of Schizophrenia." *Family Process*, 1962, 1, 44–62.

Sonne, J. C., and Lincoln, G. "Heterosexual Co-therapy Relationship and Its Significance in Family Therapy." In *Psychotherapy for the Whole Family*, by A. S. Friedman et al., pp. 213–217. New York: Springer Publishing Co., 1965.

—— "Heterosexual Co-therapy Team Experiences During Family Therapy." *Family Process*, 1965, 4, 177.

—— "The Importance of Heterosexual Co-therapy Relationship in the Construction of a Family Image." *Psychiatric Res. Rep.*, 1966, 20, 196–205.

Spitz, H. H., and Kopp, S. B. "Multiple Psychotherapy." In *Group Psychotherapy and Group Function*, edited by M. Rosenbaum and M. Berger. New York: Basic Books, 1963.

Staples, E. J. "The Influence of the Sex of the Therapist and of the Co-therapist Technique in Group Psychotherapy with

Girls: An Investigation of the Effectiveness of Group Psychotherapy with Eighth-Grade, Behavior-Problem Girls, Comparing Results Achieved by a Male Therapist, by a Female Therapist, and by Two Therapists in Combination." *Dissert. Abstr.*, 1959, *19* (2), 2154.

Stein, M. H. "The Unconscious Meaning of the Marital Bond." In *Neurotic Interaction in Marriage*, edited by V. W. Eisenstein, pp. 65–80. New York: Basic Books, 1956.

Stranahan, M.; Schwartzman, C. C.; and Atkin, E. "Activity Group Therapy with Emotionally Disturbed and Delinquent Adolescents." *Int. J. Group Psychother.*, 1957, *7*, 425–436.

Tharp, R. G. "Psychological Patterning in Marriage." *Psychol. Bull.*, 1963, *60* (2), 97–117.

Treppa, J. A. "An Investigation of Some of the Dynamics of the Interpersonal Relationship Between Pairs of Multiple Therapists." Unpublished doctoral dissertation, Michigan State University, 1969.

Van Atta, R. E. "Effects of Co-therapy as a Supervisory Process." *Detroit Convention Abstracts.* Washington, D.C.: American Personnel and Guidance Association, 1968. P. 326.

Visher, J. S., and Brown D. T. "Procedures in Integrating Group Psychotherapy in a Mental Hygiene Clinic." *Int. J. Group Psychother.*, 1961, *11*, 175–179.

Waltuck, M. "Group Counseling of Marital Partners by Joint Therapists." *J. Jewish Communal Service*, 1960, *37*, 228–235.

Warkentin, J. "Partners in Psychotherapy." *Voices: The Art and Science of Psychotherapy*, 1967, *3*, 7–12.

Warkentin, J., Johnson, N. L., and Witaker, C. A. "A Comparison of Individual and Multiple Psychotherapy." *Psychiatry*, 1951, *14*, 415–418.

Warkentin, J., and Leland, T. "Partners in the Interview." *Voices: The Art and Science of Psychotherapy*, 1967, *3*, 43–52.

Warkentin, J., and Taylor, J. E. "Physical Contact in Multiple Therapy with a Schizophrenic Patient." *Voices: The Art and Science of Psychotherapy*, 1968, *4*, 58–60.

Westman, J. C. "Group Psychotherapy with Hospitalized Delinquent Adolescents." *Int. J. Group Psychother.*, 1961, *11*, 410–418.

Whitaker, C. A.; Felder, R. E.; and Warkentin, J. "Counter-Transference in the Family Treatment of Schizophrenia." In *Intensive Family Therapy*, edited by I. Boszormenyi-Nagy and J. L. Framo, pp. 323–341. New York: Harper & Row Publishers, 1965.

Whitaker, C. A.; Malone, T. P.; and Warkentin, J. "Multiple Therapy and Psychotherapy." In *Progress in Psychotherapy*, edited by F. Fromm-Reichmann and J. L. Moreno, vol. 1, pp. 210–216. New York: Grune & Stratton, 1956.

Whitaker, C. A.; Warkentin, J.; and Johnson, N. L. "A Philosophical Basis for Brief Psychotherapy." *Psychiat. Quart.*, 1949, *23*, 439–443.

——— "The Psychotherapeutic Impasse." *Amer. J. Orthopsychiat.*, 1950, *20*, 641–647.

Whitaker, C. A.; Warkentin, J.; and Malone, T. P. "The Involvement of the Professional Therapist." In *Case Studies in Counseling and Psychotherapy*, edited by A. Burton, pp. 218–257. New York: Prentice-Hall, 1959.

Winch, R. F. "Mate Selection: A Study of Complementary Needs." New York: Harper & Brothers, 1958.

Wolf, A. "The Psychoanalysis of Groups." *Amer. Psychother.*, 1949, *3*, 525–558.

Wright, W. T., Jr. "An Investigation of an Adjunctive Two-Therapist Group Psychotherapy Procedure Designed to Improve the Process of Consensual Validation in the Mother-Child Relationship: The Mother." Ph.D. thesis, Denver University, 1959. Cited by B. Lubin and A. W. Lubin, *Group Psychotherapy: A Bibliography of the Literature from 1956 Through 1964*. East Lansing, Michigan: Michigan State University Press, 1966. Reference No. 59229.

Yalom, I. D., and Handlon, J. H. "The Use of Multiple Therapists in the Teaching of Psychiatric Residents." *J. Nervous and Mental Disease*, 1965, *141*, 684–692.

Index

Abreaction
  avoided in therapy, 243
  example of, 241–242
  facilitated by multiple therapy, 242
  necessary limits on, 241–243
Accomplishment
  "added on" versus "incorporated," 65
  objective and subjective, 5–6
Acting out
  in cotherapist relationship, 261
  and nondifferentiation of feelings, 58
  and permissiveness of parents, 59
  in relation to anxiety, 59–60
Adults, and children's fantasy, 130–132
Affection
  and feeling states, 63–64
  as an interpersonal problem, 105–106
Ambivalence
  in clients, 34–36, 44–45, 69
  defined, 34
  resolution of, 42
  and seeking help, 69
  and timing, 34–35
  and unresolved feelings, 46, 58
Anger, as a substitute expression, 66
Anxiety
  and compulsivity, 101–104

and incomplete imagery, 141
as part of supervisory process, 184
and primary process, 81
in relation to acting out, 59–60
and secondary process, 81–82
in therapist, 76–77
transfer of, 101–104
Assessment
  during therapy, 155–156
  of insatiability by therapist, 160–161
  as part of interpersonal relationships, 153
  and process conceptions, 153
Authors, 3–9
  approach of, 5
  beliefs of, 3–4, 10–12, 15, 19–20
  needs of, 267–268
  set of, 11–12
  use of theory, 268
Autonomy, therapist need for, 222–223

Caring observer, role of in multiple therapy, 219
Case conference, as supervision method, 265
Castration
  of self, 74–75
  and sexual feelings in therapist, 74–75